Social Policy in the European Union

Second Edition

Linda Hantrais

First published in Great Britain 2000 by
MACMILLAN PRESS LTD
Houndmills, Basingstoke, Hampshire RG21 6XS and London
Companies and representatives throughout the world

A catalogue record for this book is available from the British Library.

ISBN 0–333–92007–4 hardcover
ISBN 0–333–92008–2 paperback

First published in the United States of America 2000 by
ST. MARTIN'S PRESS, LLC.,
Scholarly and Reference Division,
175 Fifth Avenue, New York, N.Y. 10010

ISBN 0–312–23733–2 (cloth)

Library of Congress Cataloging-in-Publication Data

Hantrais, Linda.
Social policy in the European Union/Linda Hantrais.--2nd ed.
p. cm
Includes bibliograhical references and index.
ISBN 0–312–23733–2
1. European Union countries--Social policy. 1. Title

HN380.5.A8 H36 2000
361.6'1'094--dc21 00-034492

First edition 1995
Reprinted three times
Second edition 2000

This book is printed on paper suitable for recycling and made from fully managed and sustained forest sources.

10 9 8 7 6 5 4 3 2
09 08 07 06 05 04 03

Printed in China

Contents

List of Figures and Boxes vii

Preface viii

1 The Social Dimension of the European Union **1**
Developing the social dimension 2
Reconceptualizing European social policy 17

2 Reconciling Diversity and Harmonization **21**
Harmonization of national social policies 23
Recognizing national diversity 29
Consolidating the European social model 37

3 Education, Training and Employment **41**
A growing commitment to education and training 42
Union initiatives on education and training 50
Trends in education and training in member states 57
The impact of European policy on national education and vocational training systems 62

4 Improving Living and Working Conditions **66**
Community policy on living and working conditions 67
Working conditions in member states 77
Living conditions in member states 83
From working to living conditions 87

5 Family Policies **91**
European family policy in embryo 92
Changing families and family policies 97
The family impact of European social policy 109

6 The Gender Dimension of Social Policy **113**
European legislation and women's social rights 115
The impact of European legislation on national policy and practice 125
The gender impact of equality policy 135

7 Policy for Older and Disabled People **140**
The development of European social policy for older and disabled people 141
The implications of population ageing for European social policy 147
National provisions for older and disabled people 153
The implications of European and national social policy for intergenerational solidarity 160

8 From Social Exclusion to Social Inclusion **165**
The development of European policy on poverty and social exclusion 166
Defining and measuring social exclusion 178
National responses to social exclusion 184
Concerted action for social inclusion 188

9 Social Policy and Mobility **191**
European legislation on freedom of movement 192
The impact of Union policy on mobility 196
Obstacles to intra-European migration 200
Union policy on non-European immigration 206
Freedom of movement in a multispeed Europe 212

10 Assessing European Social Policy **217**
The parameters of a European social policy 220
European social policy as a shared competence 230
The future shape of European social policy 241

Bibliography 244

Index 256

List of Figures and Boxes

FIGURES

2.1 Social protection expenditure in EU member states, as a % of GDP and *per capita* in PPS, 1997 33
2.2 The structure of social protection receipts in EU member states, as a % of total receipts, 1997 33

BOXES

1 Legislation and official publications relating to the social dimension of the European Union 19
2 Secondary legislation and official publications relating to the reconciliation of diversity and harmonization 40
3 Secondary legislation and official publications relating to education, training and employment 64
4 Secondary legislation and official publications relating to living and working conditions 89
5 Secondary legislation and official publications relating to family policies 112
6 Secondary legislation and official publications relating to gender and social policy 137
7 Secondary legislation and official publications relating to policy for older and disabled people 163
8 Secondary legislation and official publications relating to social exclusion and social inclusion 189
9 Secondary legislation and official publications relating to social policy and mobility 214
10 Secondary legislation and official publications relating to the assessment of European social policy 243

Preface

The challenges facing the European Union (EU) at the turn of the century confirmed the importance of social affairs for its policy agenda. In combination with technological, structural and political change, Economic and Monetary Union (EMU) and the prospects for further enlargement of the Union to the East, socio-demographic trends had intensified pressures on welfare systems, raising questions about the feasibility and desirability of achieving a common social policy and about the future shape of the 'European social model'. The continuing ambivalence of member states over the Community's responsibility for social affairs, in conjunction with these other concerns, contributes to the enduring interest shown in the social dimension of the EU by policy analysts, and justifies a wide-ranging review of developments in European social policy since the late 1950s.

As in the first edition, the primary aim of this book is to examine the interconnections between social policy development at EU level and national policy formation and implementation. By analysing European and national policy development and the possible impact of social policies formulated by the Union's institutions on measures adopted by member states, an attempt is made to unravel this complex interactive process, while also considering its theoretical underpinnings and implications. Rather than describing national welfare systems one by one, and subsequently comparing them across member states, the book is organized thematically. The main areas of social policy that the Union has addressed are examined, drawing on international comparisons to exemplify the measures introduced in different member states in response to similar social problems. Comparisons across countries enable conceptual variations to be identified in national systems of welfare. They also provide illustrations of the specificity of each country and the effects of cultural embedding.

This approach is based on the assumption that students and analysts of comparative social policy are concerned with identifying its socio-cultural determinants and are interested in examining different institutional arrangements, policy options and outcomes. The underlying hypothesis in the book is that national governments continue to differ in their policy responses to common social problems. All member states have had to tackle broadly similar issues over the period since the European Economic Community (EEC) was created in 1957: for example, how to prepare their workforce for rapidly changing labour markets in a context of widespread unemployment and social exclusion; or how to cope with the growing demand for ever higher standards of health and social care, particularly among older people during retirement, in the face of population ageing, changing intergenerational relations, the rising cost of providing services and the need to curb public spending to meet the criteria for EMU. The chapters show how the solutions adopted to common problems and their outcomes reflect not only varying socio-economic conditions but also differing political ideologies and conceptions of the legitimacy of state intervention.

The period since the first edition of the book was published in 1995 has seen a number of important changes within the Union that have implications for social policy. The signing and ratification of the 1997 Treaty of Amsterdam brought formal recognition of the centrality of employment as an issue at EU level. Monitoring progress in the social domain, including the demographic situation, which had been signalled in the Treaty on European Union, became a formal treaty obligation (article 143 in the consolidated EC Treaty). The Commission, and more especially Directorate-General V (Employment, Industrial Relations and Social Affairs, renamed Employment and Social Affairs, EMPL, in 2000), together with Eurostat in its capacity as the Statistical Office of the European Communities, consequently intensified their information gathering and dissemination efforts. Building on the ideas expressed in the 1994 white paper on social policy, the Commission implemented two new social action programmes. Following a change of government in 1997, the United Kingdom signed up to the Agreement and Protocol on Social Policy, enabling the social chapter to be incorporated into the body of the Treaty of Amsterdam. Directives in the social area that had long been on the table were finally unblocked. On 1 January 1999, EMU was launched by 11 of the 15 member states, rekindling the debate about the relationship between economic and social policy. Six of the applicant countries – the Czech Republic, Estonia, Hungary, Slovenia, Poland and Cyprus, and subsequently Malta – moved onto the fast track in preparation for membership of the Union early in the twenty-first century. They submitted proposals outlining their negotiating positions, and questions were raised about their ability to carry through the reforms required to bring them into line with EU social provisions. The entire Commission resigned in 1999. The elections to the European Parliament in the same year brought a shift to the Centre-Right and the possibility of a change in the approach towards social policy formation and implementation. This new edition takes account of these momentous changes by extending the coverage of policy developments up to the end of the century, and by attempting to assess their impact for EU social policy in the new millennium.

Academic and popular interest in the social dimension of the Union grew markedly over the same period, as testified by the abundant literature on the subject, addressing social policy developments from a variety of disciplinary perspectives. Lawyers (for example Burrows and Mair, 1996; Gormley, 1998; Hervey, 1998) have documented and analysed changing law and practice in selected areas of social policy. Political scientists (Leibfried and Pierson, 1995, 2000; Cram, 1997; Geyer, 1996, 2000) have focused on the process of European integration and examined how developments in social policy map onto different theoretical frameworks. Political economists (Buti *et al.*, 1999) have examined the conflicts between social and economic imperatives. Authors writing from an industrial relations perspective (Bosco and Hutsebaut, 1997; Rhodes and Mény, 1998; Teague, 1998) have paid attention to the impact of European integration and monetary union on social systems and employment regulations. Social security specialists have been interested in the process of harmonization of social protection systems across the Union (Pacolet, 1996; Pieters, 1998), while social policy analysts (George and Taylor-Gooby, 1996; Mullard and Lee, 1997; Sykes and Alcock, 1998) have examined the interplay between economic and political forces, as well as the debate over convergence and divergence of social protection systems.

Coverage of specific themes has concentrated primarily on analysis of policy at EU level. For example, equality issues have been examined with reference to education, training and labour market policies (Rees, 1998). A number of the (edited) thematic books on specific aspects of EU social policy, however, combine overview chapters with national case studies: for instance on gender and equality policy (Gardiner, 1997; Hantrais, 2000), lone parenthood (Lewis, 1997), ageing (Walker and Maltby, 1997) and social care (Lewis, 1998). Studies within the field of comparative social policy have usually not been confined to the European dimension, although it often serves as a strong focus (Hantrais and Mangen, 1996; Clasen, 1999). Since social policy draws on the methods and insights of other disciplines and can be said to operate as an 'interdisciplinary field' (Alcock, 1998, p. 7), analysis of social policy lends itself to a multidisciplinary approach, particularly when future developments, such as the social quality of Europe, are under discussion (Beck *et al.*, 1997).

Like the first edition, the ambition of this book is to draw on different disciplinary and methodological approaches to social policy analysis, while remaining as comprehensive as possible in the country coverage. The task has been made more difficult by past and prospective enlargement of the Union, and by developments in its social policy remit. When the first edition went to press, Austria, Finland and Sweden were not yet member states, and the other changes listed above were not all foreseeable. The present edition has therefore been extended to incorporate new material on membership, legislation and policy development. The references have been revised, and readers are directed to web sites to enable them to continue the updating process.

The first chapter provides an insight into the factors shaping European social policy by charting the Union's social remit over time, up to the end of the twentieth century. A major obstacle to effective social policy making at EU level has been the lack of a common understanding of central concepts and the societal contexts within which social policy is formulated and implemented. Both the first and second chapters therefore raise a number of questions about the status of social policy in the Union and the desirability of harmonization and co-ordination of national social protection systems: Why did the Union develop a social policy? How have its aims and objectives changed over time? How has EMU affected the social dimension? How does the social policy-making process operate? These questions lead on to the debate about citizenship versus workers' rights, equalization, competition, economic and social cohesion, including discussion of the notions of social dumping, welfare tourism, social devaluation, social inclusion and the emerging concept of a European social model.

The social protection systems of the six original EEC member states can be considered as variants of what has come to be known as the continental model of welfare. The new members that joined the Community in the 1970s, 1980s and 1990s did not share the same welfare models. The first wave of applicant states preparing for membership after the turn of the century also displayed different welfare profiles. While the goal of harmonizing social protection seemed to have become more pressing with the move towards the Single European Market (SEM) in 1993, and with the launching of EMU in 1999, doubts were increasingly expressed about the feasibility and desirability of harmonizing very different welfare systems. In the second chapter, the main obstacles to social union and to a common social policy are examined. The shift away from the original policy aims is charted through co-ordination, co-operation, cohesion, mutual recognition and convergence, leading to an analysis of national welfare systems, organized in relation to the different waves of membership, with a view to documenting the extent to which diversity has been reconciled with harmonization.

Education and training provide a good example of the shift towards a more pragmatic approach to convergence. After many years of work comparing the content and level of qualifications across the Community in an attempt to reach agreement over transferability from one member state to another, general directives were issued on the mutual recognition of the equivalence of diplomas. Measures of output suggest, however, that recognition does not mean vocational and educational training has been standardized. In the third chapter, after a review of the lengthy process leading to the mutual recognition directive and a survey of initiatives at Community level to encourage mobility among students and young workers, comparisons are made of developments in the educational and training systems of individual member states.

Several articles in the EEC Treaty were devoted to the improvement of living and working conditions as a means of equalizing opportunities and promoting mobility. Despite the early interest shown by the Community, comparisons of working conditions and health and safety at work, as governed by national labour law, demonstrate that member states are far from sharing common standards. In the fourth chapter, attention is given to the relationship between European law and national policies for health and safety at work, work-time arrangements and public health, which was incorporated into the revised EC Treaty.

Since family policy is only indirectly affected by employment rights, it is an area where member states have been reluctant to seek agreement on a common policy, and where the Commission, like many national governments, has preferred to monitor the situation rather than prescribing family policy measures. Although some convergence in family patterns may be occurring spontaneously, due to common demographic trends, member states have continued to hold differing views on what constitutes the 'benefit' family and on the aims and objectives of family policy. In the fifth chapter, changing family structures and the responses of national governments are examined with reference to the growing interest at EU level in socio-demographic issues.

The employment model of welfare that has been dominant in the Union put women at a disadvantage in access to social protection. The directives on equal pay for work of equal value, equal treatment and employment-related social insurance rights sought to redress the balance for women who are economically active for the greater part of their working lives. The 1990s saw the development of measures to assist both women and men in combining paid and unpaid work, and also the incorporation of the concept of mainstreaming into the European agenda. In the sixth chapter, changing gender relations are analysed at both EU and national level with reference to the situation of women as policy actors and as recipients of social policies.

In a context where greater life expectancy has been accompanied by heavy demands on health and care services, member states have become increasingly concerned, individually and collectively, about the effects of population ageing on social protection systems. The seventh chapter focuses on different forms of provision for older and disabled people, including maintenance and caring arrangements, and the overall impact of policy on living standards.

The effects of the emphasis placed on employment rights by most member states in a context of economic recession, rising unemployment and demographic ageing may have been offset to some extent by the structural funds. In the 1970s, the core–periphery debate intensified as the problem of poverty moved onto the policy agenda. The Commission responded by developing a series of action programmes to combat poverty and social exclusion. The eighth chapter examines these issues with reference to the attempts to define and measure poverty, and the initiatives taken at EU level to combat social exclusion and promote social inclusion through employment and economic integration.

Co-ordination of social protection systems, mutual recognition of qualifications, the general improvement of living and working conditions, the monitoring of family policy, directives on equality of access to social benefits and measures at EU level to reduce poverty were all justified, at least in part, as a means of breaking down barriers to the free movement of workers within the Union. Information about intra-European mobility suggests that, despite changes in the pattern of labour flows, net mobility has remained at a relatively low level. Even if the Union's policies on the recognition of qualifications or the co-ordination of social protection systems may have had some impact on the formal obstacles to mobility, other difficulties associated with linguistic and cultural traditions may be more resistant to EU social policy initiatives. In the ninth chapter, these issues are considered with regard to both intra-European and non-European mobility.

The final chapter tracks the progress of the social dimension of the Union across the topics that are identified in the introductory chapters and recur throughout the book in the discussion of different areas of social policy. It examines the changing parameters of European social policy as mediated by the relationship between the economic and social dimensions of the Community and Union, and by the centrality of workers' as compared to citizenship rights. An attempt is made to assess the extent to which the Union has developed its own social policy competence, despite the constraints arising from strong national interests, the threat posed to national sovereignty and the persistence of diversity in welfare systems and practices. In conclusion, the prospects are examined for a more broadly based European social policy in the twenty-first century as the Union enlarges its membership eastwards.

Although the chapters in the book are linked by common themes and approaches so as to provide a cumulative and wide-ranging overview of social policy in the Union and its member states, each of Chapters 3 to 9 can be studied independently by readers wishing to explore any one policy area in isolation. To supplement the Bibliography, which covers works cited throughout the book, separate lists have been compiled of legislation and the key policy documents relevant to each chapter. References in square brackets in the text indicate the EU documents cited in the boxes at the end of chapters. They include materials produced by the Commission as COM documents or published in the *Official Journal of the European Communities* (abbreviated to *OJ*), and publications by the Office for Official Publications of the European Communities in Luxembourg (abbreviated to OOPEC). The boxes also contain web site addresses for internet sources.

My thanks are due to all those who have given generously of their time to provide feedback on the two editions of this book and, in particular, to Jo Campling for her valuable advice and support. I am grateful to Eurostat and the European Commission for responding to requests for data and materials, and to the staff in the European Documentation Centre in the Pilkington Library at Loughborough University, especially Laurie McGarry, for their help in accessing information. Steen Mangen is to be thanked for commenting on drafts of the text, and Liz Monaghan and Liz Such for their technical assistance in preparing this new edition.

LINDA HANTRAIS

1 The Social Dimension of the European Union

When the Treaty establishing the European Economic Community (EEC) was signed in Rome in 1957 [1.2], the dominant political philosophy was market driven. The six original EEC member states – Belgium, France, the Federal Republic of Germany, Italy, Luxembourg and the Netherlands – believed that, if enterprises were allowed to compete on equal terms, the distribution of resources would be optimized, enabling untrammelled economic growth which would automatically result in social development. Social harmonization was seen as an end product of economic integration rather than a prerequisite. For these reasons, the social provisions contained in the treaty did not define precise social policy objectives; they limited EEC responsibility to promoting co-operation (Collins, 1975; Shanks, 1977). Member states did recognize the need to establish a social fund to help declining areas of the economy, but it was to operate on a very small scale.

As the optimistic assumptions of the founder members proved to be ill conceived, and as Denmark, Ireland and the United Kingdom joined the European Community (EC) in 1973, a more active approach to social reform was advocated on the grounds that the unevenness created by giving free rein to market forces was unacceptable and not in the long-term interests of member states. The next 20 years therefore saw a growing commitment, at least in principle, to the social dimension as a component of European integration and a necessary complement to economic policy, rather than simply a spillover from it.

This chapter provides a brief overview of the historical development of Europe's social dimension within the context of its treaties, charter and social action programmes. Several of the central concepts underlying European social policy are introduced, including social space, social dialogue, social plinth, subsidiarity, proportionality and social dumping. As well as exploring why and how the social dimension became a concern for member states, the chapter seeks to identify and track the changing aims, objectives and nature of the European social policy-making process.

DEVELOPING THE SOCIAL DIMENSION

In several respects the Treaty of Paris, which set up the European Coal and Steel Community (ECSC) in 1951 [1.1], and the Treaty establishing the European Atomic Energy Community (EAEC) in 1957 [1.3] were more interested in social policy than the EEC Treaty. The ECSC had to deal with the social impact of structural change in two major industries and was endowed with funds to cover the resettlement of displaced workers. It also conferred responsibility for looking into the living and working conditions of miners and steel workers. The EAEC laid down basic standards for the health and protection of workers and the general public, as well as procedures for monitoring and checking their implementation. The EEC Treaty had a limited, albeit specific, social remit, for example through its commitment to raising standards of living (article 2), the provision of a social fund (article 3 §i) and the task of promoting close co-operation in the social field (article 118). It did not set the framework for a fully developed European social policy, as was done in 1961 by the Council of Europe in its European Social Charter, which was later to serve as a source of inspiration for the Community Charter of the Fundamental Social Rights of Workers [1.10]. This section tracks the development of social provisions through European legislation and policy statements since the 1950s (for source materials see the documents and web sites listed in [1.21]).

The social dimension of the EEC Treaty

Twelve of the 248 articles of the EEC Treaty were devoted explicitly to social policy (articles 117–28). Since the aim of the treaty was to create an economic union, the relatively low priority given to social affairs was understandable. Justification for the inclusion of any reference to the social dimension can be found in the overriding principle that distortion of the rules of competition was to be avoided at all costs. In the negotiations leading up to the signing of the treaty, the French had argued that the high social charges imposed by the state in France on employers and employees in the best interests of the workforce, combined with the principle of equal pay for men and women, which was written into the French constitution, would put France at a competitive disadvantage. Consequently, they advocated harmonization of provision in these areas. The Germans countered the French case by arguing that social charges were a result of the operation of market forces and should not therefore be subject to regulation under EEC law.

A compromise solution was eventually reached whereby the treaty included a section on social policy (title III) but did not stipulate how most of the provisions should be implemented. Article 118, for example, specified that the Commission should promote close co-operation between member states in matters relating to training, employment, labour law and working conditions, social security and collective bargaining, but without specifying the form such co-operation should take (see Chapters 3 and 4). Article 119, which defined the equal pay principle in response to the demands of the French (see Chapter 6), and article 121, which was concerned with implementing common social security measures for migrant workers (see Chapter 9), were more explicit. Similarly, articles 123–8 set out specific arrangements for operating the European Social Fund. The ESF was intended to make the employment and re-employment of workers easier and to encourage geographical and occupational mobility within the EEC by providing assistance with the cost of vocational retraining and resettlement allowances (see Chapters 3, 8 and 9).

When discrepancies between the laws and practices of member states were considered to be distorting competition, article 101 of the treaty allowed for directives to eliminate any differences. The EEC was, however, premised on the principle that rules avoiding distortion of competition would make it unnecessary to interfere with redistributive benefits, which should remain a matter for individual states (Collins, 1975, p. 9). Provision was made for equal pay, the improvement of standards of living and social harmonization only insofar as they supported the goal of economic integration (see Chapter 2).

A second justification for the 'social' concerns of the original member states was free movement of labour, which had been a fundamental aim of the EEC Treaty. In addition to the establishment of the ESF, provision was made in the two chapters of the treaty on the free movement of persons, services and capital for issuing directives or adopting other measures to facilitate the mobility of workers (articles 48–51) and the right of establishment (articles 52–8), covering information on job availability in other countries, arrangements for mobile workers to retain social security entitlements and the recognition of professional qualifications (see Chapters 3 and 9).

Although the signatories to the treaty had flagged their interest in the social dimension of the EEC, the compromise that resulted from their failure to agree about objectives, and to set up mechanisms for achieving them, led to what could be described as a modest, cautious and narrowly focused social policy. The treaty which merged the

ECSC, EEC and EAEC in 1965 [1.4] to constitute a single Council and a single Commission of the European Communities did not bring any formal changes in the social policy field, although the clear social protection remit of the two other treaties may have had some impact on the subsequent development of European social policy, particularly in the area of health and safety at work (see Chapter 4).

The 1974 Community social action programme

While the EEC's approach to social policy was cautious, the Council of Europe was much more explicit and affirmative in the social charter it adopted in 1961, described as the economic and social counterpart of the Convention on Human Rights. The charter guaranteed a number of fundamental rights for workers and citizens, making explicit reference to the rights of the family, mothers and children to social, legal and economic protection. Although it did not have the same legally binding status as the convention, the Council of Europe's social charter established a comprehensive and coherent set of policy objectives.

Signs of a growing political commitment to social legislation and to a more positive and interventionist social policy within the EEC can be found more than a decade after the Council of Europe's social charter in the Commission's social action programme. In 1974, a resolution from the Council of Ministers (subsequently referred to as the Council) 'concerning a social action programme' [1.9] noted that economic expansion was not to be seen as an end in itself but should result in an improvement of the quality of life. The programme provided for action in three areas, primarily concerned with the working environment. It set out to achieve several broadly based objectives: the attainment of full and better employment; the improvement of living and working conditions; the increased involvement of management and labour in economic and social decisions, and of workers in the life of undertakings. The Council's view of Community competence in the area of social policy at that time was presented in cautious terms, foreshadowing the concept of subsidiarity, which was to remain prominent in statements on social policy through to the end of the century:

> [The Council c]onsiders that the Community social policy has an individual role to play and should make an essential contribution to achieving the aforementioned objectives by means of Community measures or the definition by the Community of objectives for national social policies, without however seeking a standard solution to all social problems or attempting to transfer to Community level any responsibilities which are assumed more effectively at other levels. [1.9, p. 2]

Since the EEC Treaty did not require a social programme, and the Community did not have direct powers of intervention, its responsibility being confined to promoting co-operation between member states, action had to be justified on political rather than legal grounds. The resolution expressed the 'political will' [1.9, p. 2] to adopt the measures required. In keeping with the priorities of the treaty, the principles of free movement of labour and equalization of competitive conditions between enterprises were stressed, and the importance of the ESF was reiterated as a means of palliating the uneven effects of economic growth on weaker sectors of the population.

The social action programme thus set the scene for the development of the Community's social policy over the next decade. The 1970s saw a spate of action in the areas of education and training, health and safety at work, workers' and women's rights and poverty, leading to the establishment of a number of European networks and observatories to stimulate action and monitor progress in the social field.

The social dimension and the Single European Act

By the mid-1980s, pressure was building up for a more regulatory social policy. The idea of creating a social space (*espace social*), put forward by the French President, François Mitterrand, in 1981, was taken up by Jacques Delors when he became President of the Commission in 1985. The social space was first mooted during the French Presidency of the Community at a time when the revitalization of social policy was still very much associated with economic performance (Beretta, 1989, p. 5). In line with the policy-making stance adopted by France's own left-wing government, employment was placed at the heart of proposals for European social policy, the dialogue between management and labour was intensified, and co-operation and consultation on social protection were strongly advocated. Social policy was promoted as the means of strengthening economic cohesion and was therefore to be developed on the same basis as economic, monetary and industrial policy. According to this neo-functionalist logic, 'social policy grows as a functional prerequisite of economic integration' (Room, 1994, p. 21).

Delors made clear his own commitment to the social dimension of the Community, stating that: 'The European social dimension is what allows competition to flourish between undertakings and individuals on a reasonable and fair basis.... Any attempt to give new depth to the Common Market which neglected this social dimension would be doomed to failure' (Delors, 1985, p. xviii). For Delors the social space was a natural complement to the completion of the internal market and a means of resolving the stalemate that had arisen over endeavours to establish the social dimension of the Community through legislation. Some member states opposed the legislative route on the grounds that it would go against national provision, but without legislation European social policy was not binding. By referring to a social space, Delors appeared to be seeking to introduce an equivalence of standards, which would be agreed by both sides of industry through social dialogue, a concept central to his thinking. The social dialogue was intended to make trade unions and employers act as the initiators of social policy, on the understanding that, in return, the Commission would refrain from developing new initiatives itself. The social partners would thus be concerned with principles and objectives, leaving member states to implement them within existing industrial relations frameworks, thereby achieving 'convergence in the employment and labour policy goals of the member states, rather than the standardisation of industrial relations institutions and processes' (Teague, 1989, pp. 69–70).

A series of discussions on socio-economic issues was organized at Val Duchesse (a castle in Belgium) in 1985 to secure the involvement of the social partners. Major participants were the European Trade Union Confederation (ETUC), the Union of Industries of the European Communities (UNICE) and the European Centre of Public Enterprises (CEEP). Although the talks fulfilled the objective of encouraging social dialogue between management and workers' representatives, the employers refused to sign the final texts unless Delors gave an undertaking that the Commission would not use the joint opinions as a basis for legislation, thereby preventing the outcome which he had been seeking to engineer. A more positive result was the renewed emphasis on social cohesion, involving closer co-ordination of the activities of the ESF to direct aid towards the poorer member states.

When the Single European Act (SEA) was signed in 1986 [1.5] by the then 12 member states, relatively little progress had been made towards building social policy into the legislative framework of the Community, although significant changes were introduced to speed up and facilitate the social policy-making process. A new article 118a, a supplement to article 118 of the EEC Treaty, stressed the importance of the working environment and the health and safety of workers, and provided for decisions to be taken in this area by qualified majority voting (see Chapter 4). By extending the use of this form of voting to health and safety at work, and by introducing a new co-operation procedure, which imposed time limits for the passage of legislation and strengthened the role of the European Parliament, the SEA gave the Council an opportunity to tackle more controversial issues in areas of social policy where agreement had previously been difficult to reach.

Another new 118 article (118b) placed emphasis on the idea of a social dialogue at EC level, as initiated in the Val Duchesse talks in 1985. Article 100 on the approximation of laws was modified by 100a to enable decisions to be taken by qualified majority voting for the approximation of provisions aimed at the establishment and functioning of the internal market. Fiscal provisions, free movement of people and workers' rights continued to be governed by the unanimity rule. Under subsection IV, a new title V was added on economic and social cohesion (articles 130a–e). Article 130b aimed to strengthen economic and social cohesion, particularly through closer co-ordination of the structural funds, namely the European Social Fund (ESF), the European Regional Development Fund (ERDF) and the European Agricultural Guidance and Guarantee Fund (EAGGF) (see Chapter 8).

Despite these changes, the SEA left the issue of the social space largely unresolved. Interest in the proposal was, however, revived by the Belgian government during their presidency in the second half of 1987, when the idea was developed of a social policy based on a 'plinth' (*socle social*) of social rights that would not undermine established statutory guarantees for workers (Teague, 1989, p. 76). The Belgian Minister for Labour spoke of the need 'to establish a platform [*socle* in the French version] of basic rights which would give the two sides of industry a stable, common basis from which they could negotiate to guarantee that the internal market has a real social dimension' (Soisson, 1990, p. 10). In 1988, before the ETUC, Jacques Delors had stressed the need for a 'revival' of social policy, advocating a 'minimum platform of guaranteed social rights with a view to the implementation of the single European market of 1992'. Echoing the words of the Belgian Minister for Labour, he explained that: 'This mandatory platform could be negotiated between the two sides of industry and then incorporated into Community legislation. It would serve as a basis for the social dialogue and for strengthening European cohesion.' (Soisson, 1990, p. 10)

The Community Charter of the Fundamental Social Rights of Workers

While the SEA did not provide a blueprint for European social policy, the preamble offered a statement of principle in which the signatories agreed to work together to promote fundamental rights as laid down in the Convention for the Protection of Human Rights and Fundamental Freedoms and the European Social Charter. Meeting in Strasbourg on 8–9 December 1989, the heads of all member states, with the exception of the United Kingdom, adopted the Community Charter of the Fundamental Social Rights of Workers [1.10], heralded as the social dimension of the SEA. The preamble to the charter stated resolutely that 'the same importance must be attached to the social aspects as to the economic aspects and..., therefore, they must be developed in a balanced manner'. Although preliminary drafts of the charter had referred to 'citizens' rather than 'workers', the final version did not define rights in terms of citizenship. Most clauses in the charter referred implicitly or explicitly to workers, a focus which was clearly identified in the title and in the section devoted to employment and remuneration, whereas the Council of Europe's social charter had included the right to social and medical assistance and social services without linking them to employment.

Like the Council of Europe's social charter, the Community charter did not have force of law and was not therefore binding on its signatories. As 'soft' law (Hervey, 1998, pp. 49–50), it took the form of a solemn declaration, leaving decisions on implementation procedures to individual member states. The social plinth had been an attempt to ensure that the areas to be covered by social protection would be accepted throughout the Community. Much of the debate about the charter focused on a related issue: whether the Community and its member states were aiming for a maximum or minimum level of social provision. Should equalization be based on an average, the highest or lowest level in the Community? Some states intent on defending what they considered as a higher level of social protection feared that the internal market would result in a downward alignment of social security allowances and benefits towards the lowest common denominator.

The nebulous terms 'adequate', 'sufficient', 'appropriate' and 'satisfactory', used in the charter to refer to the levels to be achieved, are indicative of the problems in reaching agreement over the definition of targets. They reflect the Council's reluctance to impose standards by regulation, the most binding form of legislation (Gormley, 1998, pp. 324–6). This lack of precision left open the possibility that some states would seek competitive advantage by not offering the same level of social protection to their workers, resulting in what has come to be known as 'social dumping', whereby companies may decide to move to countries, such as Greece and Portugal, with lower labour and social costs. The term 'dumping' was used in article 91 of the EEC Treaty, in the economic context, to describe the practice of differential pricing of goods with no economic justification. An example of what is meant by social dumping is the case of the firm Hoover, which decided in 1993 to move from Dijon to Glasgow where labour costs were lower. Since the United Kingdom had not accepted the stipulations of the Community charter, the French accused it of unfair competition. The term 'social dumping' was used (and disputed) to describe the advantage that the United Kingdom was gaining from not having to observe the same standards and conditions of employment as countries that had signed the charter. The reverse of the coin is that disparities in social protection between member states may also serve as an obstacle to mobility of labour and capital. It has been argued that firms will not invest in low social wage countries unless other factors, for example infrastructure and productivity, justify such investments, and that economic integration may lead rather 'to a more gradual and indirect process of social policy erosion' (Leibfried and Pierson, 1992, p. 350).

Another metaphor frequently found in this context is the 'level playing field' of competition, implying that everybody should be playing by the same rules and with equal chances of success in the market place. Accordingly, a higher level of social spending should be sought across member states to avoid putting national governments that do want to introduce more generous provisions at a competitive disadvantage.

These concepts were not invented with the SEA and the Community charter. Fears of social dumping and the creation of an unlevel playing field were, however, exacerbated when Greece joined the Community in 1981, and Portugal and Spain in 1986, since they were all countries with less developed social protection systems than in both the original EEC member states or those which became members in the 1970s (see Chapter 2). Although the charter may not have produced any innovations in the area of social protection, the surrounding debate did serve the purpose of focusing attention on a number of important issues concerning the social dimension of the Single European Market (SEM), or internal market, which came into operation on 1 January 1993. The different bodies of opinion that emerged over the interventionist role of the Community in social policy and the basis on which it should be founded were symptomatic of the diverging principles underlying systems of social protection in the 12 member states. They also signalled the concern felt in some countries about the possibility of losing national sovereignty and being forced to take action in areas where national governments have, at times, been reluctant to intervene.

In the absence of any direct legal means of enforcement, provision was made in the Community charter for an action programme. Under §28, the Council invited the Commission to prepare initiatives with a view to the adoption of legal instruments for the effective implementation of rights that fall within the Community's area of competence. The Commission responded with an action programme containing 47 initiatives for developing the social dimension of the SEM [1.11].

The Commission's description of its goals in the first annual report [1.12] is indicative of the status of the social dimension and the economic constraints within which policy makers were operating. The aim was 'to establish a sound base of minimum provisions, having regard on the one hand to the need to avoid any distortion of competition, and on the other to support moves to strengthen economic and social cohesion and contribute to the creation of jobs, which is the prime concern of completion of the internal market' [1.12, p. 5]. The measures proposed by the Commission were wide ranging, covering all the topics dealt with in the charter and also adding a chapter on the labour market. The methods to be used for implementing the action programme relied heavily on the consultation process, mediated by advisory committees and the social dialogue.

The report reiterated the point raised at the Luxembourg Council meeting in June 1991 that the achievements made in implementing the SEM programme had not been accompanied by comparable progress in the field of social policy [1.12, p. 22]. This and subsequent annual reports stressed the importance of maintaining a balance between the three fundamental principles underlying the Commission's initiatives: subsidiarity, diversity of national systems, cultures and practices, and the preservation of the competitiveness of undertakings, thereby confirming the secondary status of the social dimension.

It has been argued that the SEA had added nothing new in the field of social welfare, which remained no more than an area of indirect and limited competence for the Community (Berghman, 1990, p. 9). Some co-ordination of national systems of social security was needed to ensure free movement of workers, but these contingencies had already been covered in the early 1970s by relatively uncontroversial legislation on the application of social security schemes to employed persons and to members of their families moving within the Community (see Chapter 9). In all the policy areas encompassed by the charter, action had been initiated before 1989. The charter and action programme can, however, be credited with providing an impetus for a more concerted and coherent approach to social affairs.

The social chapter in the Maastricht Treaty

The principles set out in the Community charter were taken up in the Agreement on Social Policy annexed to the Treaty on European Union signed in Maastricht on 7 February 1992 [1.6]. The Maastricht summit again illustrated the difficulty of reaching agreement over the social chapter, which, on the insistence of the United Kingdom, was removed from the body of the treaty. By including a separate Protocol on Social Policy, the other 11 member states could proceed with the Community charter and make decisions without taking account of the views of the United Kingdom.

Article 1 of the Agreement on Social Policy amended article 117 of the Treaty of Rome by removing the references to harmonization of social systems, and to the belief that improvements would naturally ensue from the functioning of the common market and the approximation of provisions. Instead, it identified specific objectives: 'the promotion of employment, improved living and working conditions, proper social protection, dialogue between management and labour, the development of human resources with a view to lasting high employment and the combating of exclusion'. Significantly, these objectives were to be achieved through measures that 'take account of the diverse forms of national practices, in particular in the field of contractual relations, and the need to maintain the competitiveness of the Community economy'.

Article 2 of the agreement assigned a complementary role to the Community in the areas of health and safety at work, working conditions, information and consultation of workers, equality between women and men, and the integration of persons excluded from the labour market. It empowered the Council to act in the area of social affairs to adopt, 'by means of directives, minimum requirements for gradual implementation, having regard to the conditions and technical rules obtaining in each of the Member States'. It added that any constraints that might impede the creation and development of small and medium-sized enterprises should be avoided. Issues still requiring unanimous voting by the 11 signatories to the protocol were noted: social security and social protection of workers, protection of workers made redundant, representation and collective defence of workers and employers, conditions of employment for third-country nationals, and financial contributions for job promotion. The distinction between the areas subject to qualified majority and unanimous voting was important, since it tended subsequently to dictate the social agenda, limiting it to topics where some degree of consensus already existed.

As in article 118 of the EEC Treaty, the agreement stressed that the Commission's role was to monitor the social situation (article 7), consult, encourage co-operation and facilitate policy co-ordination (article 5). Member states were not to be prevented from introducing their own measures over and above those required at EU level (article 2 §5, article 6 §3). Action was, in any case, constrained by subsidiarity (article 3b of the treaty), one of the three principles regarded as 'cardinal' by the Commission. The principle of subsidiarity was set out in a communication of 27 October 1992 [1.13], and later in Protocol N° 30 of the consolidated EC Treaty [1.8]. Three related issues were emphasized: greater democratic control, more transparency in European legislation and respect of the principle of subsidiarity. While the treaty stipulated the competencies attributed to the Union, the principle of subsidiarity remained important in determining how those competencies should be exercised. By virtue of the principle, the Union is empowered to act when its aims can be more effectively achieved at EU rather than national level; for example in establishing minimum standards that member states should introduce, or in allowing them to maintain higher standards if this is not incompatible with the treaty. The burden of proof is on the Union's institutions to demonstrate a need to legislate at EU level and at the intensity proposed, with recourse to the most binding instruments as a last resort. Accordingly, wherever possible, preference should be given to support measures and framework directives rather than to detailed rules and regulations. The Union should only intervene if, and insofar as, the objectives of the proposed action cannot be satisfactorily achieved by member states themselves, judged by evaluating comparative efficiency and value added. Where the benefits being sought are, however, to be universally applied, EU-level intervention may be justified (Spicker, 1991, pp. 3–8).

The choice of the most appropriate policy instrument is made on the basis of the principle of both subsidiarity and proportionality. According to the principle of proportionality, the means employed should be commensurate with the objectives pursued. Decisions should be taken as closely as possible to the citizens themselves, without endangering the advantages to be gained from common action at the level of the Union as a whole, and without changing the institutional balance.

These constraints on action at EU level were to some extent offset by the new powers that the Agreement on Social Policy gave to management and labour. Article 3 required that the Commission should 'consult management and labour on the possible direction of Community action' (§2) and the content of proposals (§3), as well as enabling them to forward an opinion or recommendation to the Commission and to initiate agreements with the Community (§4), thereby confirming the commitment to the social dialogue.

The green and white papers on European social policy

While the Community charter of 1989, the action programmes and the Agreement on Social Policy in the Maastricht Treaty together provided a clearer statement of thinking on social policy at EU level than was present in the EEC Treaty drawn up in the 1950s, they did not signal a strong commitment to social affairs as an objective in its own right, or on a par with economic union. Nor did they put in place the administrative structures needed for producing a common European social policy. By incorporating the principle of subsidiarity in the Maastricht Treaty, member states seemed to be confirming their continued reluctance to develop an overarching social policy that might impinge on national sovereignty. In 1993, however, the Commission published a consultative document, which demonstrated that the issue of a European social policy remained firmly on the agenda. The green paper on European social policy [1.14] announced a wide-ranging review of social policy in the Union, the *acquis communautaire* (legal attainments) and the areas where further action was needed. Government departments, social partners, the European Parliament, the Economic and Social Committee and other organizations and individuals were invited to assist the Commission in preparing the next phase of the Union's social policy. The green paper sought views on the objectives, targets and measures that would be acceptable to member states and social partners in the areas of the labour market, social protection and exclusion, equal opportunities and training, thereby reaffirming the wide range of issues that fell within the Union's competence. It also demonstrated that the Commission wanted to be seen to take account of the opinions expressed by other social actors. The green paper was intended as a stocktaking exercise rather than a prescription for future action.

The white paper on European social policy [1.15], published eight months later in 1994, went on to set the scene for European social policy through to the end of the decade by providing a comprehensive statement of policy directions and goals. The document described the 'vital part' social policy had to play 'in underpinning the process of change' [1.15, p. 7], by building on the achievements of the past and putting forward new proposals for the future. The aim was to ensure that the people of Europe benefit from 'the unique blend of economic well-being, social cohesiveness and high overall quality of life which was achieved in the post-war period' [1.15, p. 7]. Future policy was to be broadly based, meaning that, although jobs would remain at the top of the agenda, categories of people who were not in work should also be taken into account, with a view to establishing 'the fundamental social rights of citizens as a constitutional element of the European Union' [1.15, p. 69], a goal that the Community charter had not espoused. Like previous policy statements, however, the white paper affirmed that the Union should not 'seek to supplant the responsibilities at national, regional and local level' [1.15, p. 7].

The social action programmes for 1995–2000

The white paper offered a long-awaited framework for the management of change and for action through to the end of the century. The Commission was quick to take advantage of the momentum by launching a medium-term social action programme for 1995–97 [1.16]. The first progress report on the programme opened with the statement that it was based on the concept of social policy as 'a productive factor facilitating change and progress, rather than a burden on the economy or an obstacle to growth' [1.17, p. 1], reflecting the Commission's increasingly proactive approach. The report also stressed how important the dialogue had been between political (member states), social (employers and unions) and civil (non-governmental organizations, NGOs) actors in enabling successful implementation of the programme.

The 1998–2000 social action programme maintained the pressure for recognizing the importance of the social dimension in responding to the major social challenges the Union was facing at the turn of the century [1.19]. Firstly, Economic and Monetary Union (EMU) was creating the economic conditions needed to underpin social progress. Secondly, population ageing and, more particularly, the ageing of the workforce were raising concerns about the implications of demographic trends for employment and social protection systems in Europe. Thirdly, the prospect of enlargement was fuelling debates about the role that social policy could play in the transition to a market economy in applicant states, raising questions about how they would bring their social legislation into line with other member states and develop adequate systems of social protection [1.19, pp. 2–3]. Echoing article 2 of the Treaty on European Union, the programme took as its starting point that 'economic and social progress go hand in hand' [1.19, p. 3]. The objectives set out confirmed a more proactive role for social policy at the close of the century and beyond: 'social policy should promote a decent quality of life and standard of living for all in an active, inclusive and healthy society that encourages access to employment, good working conditions, and equality of opportunity' [1.19, p. 3].

The social dimension and the amended treaties

The Treaty of Amsterdam [1.7], signed on 2 October 1997, amended the Treaty on European Union and the Treaties establishing the European Communities. A consolidated version renumbering the articles in the original EEC Treaty was published in the same year [1.8]. Following the British opt-in, the Agreement on Social Policy was incorporated into the main body of the consolidated treaty under title XI on social policy, education, vocational training and youth, thereby endorsing the commitment of member states to the development of the social dimension as an important component in the process of European integration. Reflecting public concern about unemployment across the Union, the reference to 'a high level of employment and of social protection', which had been introduced into the Treaty on European Union in article 2 of the Principles in part I, moved into second place in the list of priority areas at the beginning of the amended EC Treaty. In line with the Union's policy on mainstreaming, 'equality between men and women' was inserted in third position before 'sustainable and non-inflationary growth'. On the insistence of the Germans, Dutch and British, the reference to 'convergence of economic performance' was amended to include 'competitiveness'. The reference to the environment was expanded to cover 'a high level of protection and improvement of the quality of the environment'. A new article 13 enabled action to be taken 'to combat discrimination based on sex, racial or ethnic origin, religion or belief, disability, age or sexual orientation'.

Under the new title XI, the original EEC Treaty articles 117–28 on social provisions and the European Social Fund were replaced by renumbered articles 136–50, incorporating the text of the Agreement on Social Policy. The first article (136) in the chapter on social provisions opens with a reference to both the Council of Europe's and the Community's charters. In other respects, it is an amalgam of article 117 in the EEC Treaty and article 1 of the Agreement on Social Policy. Articles 137–9 reproduce articles 2–4 in the agreement, while article 140 conflates EEC article 118 and article 5 in the agreement. A new paragraph was added to article 141 (EEC article 119) on equal pay, endowing the Council with the authority to act to ensure the application of measures on equal opportunities, treatment and pay, thereby giving this policy area a specific legal base. The reference in article 6 §3 of the agreement to member states not being prevented from taking specific measures to assist women was amended to read 'the under-represented sex' in article 141. Article 7 of the agreement became article 143, and EEC Treaty articles 120–2, unchanged except for the reference to the European Parliament, became articles 142 and 144–5.

A shortened chapter on the European Social Fund (renumbered articles 146–8) retained an amendment, added in the Maastricht Treaty, referring to the role of vocational training and retraining as a means of helping workers to adapt to industrial and technological change. A third chapter from Maastricht, replacing EEC 126–8, on education, vocational training and youth became articles 149–50.

Title XIII introduced article 152 on public health. Here, a number of insertions reinforced the complementary role attributed to the Union at the same time as the need to respect the responsibilities of member states in the organization and delivery of health services and medical care. Paragraphs were added stressing the importance of high standards of quality and safety, and can be seen as a response to the major public health scares of the 1990s.

While the new title XVII on economic and social cohesion and title XIX on the environment focus largely on economic aspects, reference is made, in both cases, to the role of the Cohesion Fund in contributing to projects in the environmental field. The link with the concern about public health is confirmed in article 174. The status of the environment as an area for attention was also written into a new article 6 in the first part of the treaty, requiring that environmental protection must be integrated into the definition and implementation of all Community policies and activities.

Few alterations were made to the chapters on the free movement of workers (articles 39–48), but a new and much disputed title IV (articles 61–9) was inserted covering visas, asylum, immigration and other policies related to free movement of persons across the Union's external borders. As many of the provisions concern issues of security and administrative procedures, they are not developed here. They are, however, relevant to the social dimension insofar as they impact on the living conditions of residents in member states and on questions of racial equality (see Chapter 9).

Arguably, the most significant change to the treaty, at least at the symbolic level, was the addition of title VIII on employment (articles 125–30), which set out the objectives and responsibilities of member states and the Union, calling for co-operation and co-ordinated action. Despite the efforts by the French to try and persuade the other heads of government to attribute a more interventionist role to the Union and to commit additional funds (Duff, 1997, p. 64), as in other areas of social policy, the treaty reaffirms that Community action will be confined to a supportive and complementary role (article 127). In article 128, the Council and Commission are assigned the tasks of reporting on the employment situation, drawing up guidelines and examining the measures taken by national governments as well as their implementation. Article 130 empowers the Council to set up an Employment Committee, with advisory status, to monitor the employment situation and formulate opinions, in consultation with management and labour.

The priority given to employment in the treaty dominated the social scene in the period immediately following its signing. The Luxembourg European Council meeting on employment in November 1997 and the Council resolution of 15 December 1997, adopting the first employment guidelines [1.18], went much further than the treaty in agreeing an overall strategy and a common approach with regard to objectives, targets and means. Four main lines of action were identified, and retained in the 1999 guidelines [1.20], as the four pillars to be incorporated in the national action plans: improving employability, developing entrepreneurship, encouraging adaptability of businesses and their employees to enable the labour market to react to economic changes, and strengthening policies for equal opportunities. The guidelines confirmed the shift towards more active employability measures, with emphasis on training, but they also set out the means for encouraging job creation, including by making taxation systems more employment friendly. The social partners were invited to modernize work organization by negotiating over flexibility and removing barriers to employment. In accordance with the Union's commitment to mainstreaming gender, the guidelines contained recommendations on equal opportunities policies. The success of the plans was to be judged by their ability to improve the employment situation.

RECONCEPTUALIZING EUROPEAN SOCIAL POLICY

The preceding sections go some way towards answering the questions as to why and how the Union progressively, but cautiously, extended its intervention in social affairs. They provide an indication of the philosophy underlying its social policy and the possible interconnections between EU and national levels. This relationship is explored more fully in subsequent chapters with reference to specific policy areas. In conclusion to the present chapter, an assessment is attempted of the way in which European social policy has been reconceptualized over the years since the founding of the Community.

Many of the early policy statements cited in this chapter were based on a conception of social policy as a handmaiden to economic objectives, and as a spillover from economic policies. By the 1990s, due in no small part to the efforts of the Commission, under the leadership of Jacques Delors, the social dimension had moved up the agenda. Since, by definition, economic policy was the justification for the EEC, Maastricht and Amsterdam Treaties, social policy was cast in a supporting role. If social affairs have become a more central concern of the Union and its member states, nowhere is the economic justification difficult to find. Just as the French had insisted on provision for equal pay between men and women in the EEC Treaty to prevent the distortion of competition, the principle of guaranteed access to adequate social protection in the 1989 Community charter was also justified on economic grounds. The development of a large European internal market based on free trade and economic progress dictated the priority given to economic objectives. Application of the principles of subsidiarity and proportionality meant that areas of Union competence in the social field were not easy to identify or demarcate. Neither the charter nor the Agreement on Social Policy gave clear guidance on how to define and legitimate minimum levels of provision across member states.

In the absence of a treaty commitment to a well-defined interventionist role, it could be argued that European social policy did not develop further because, apart from the case of migrant workers, the Union did not really need its own common social policy. Mark Kleinman and David Piachaud (1993, p. 18) have suggested that, if in the future the life chances of Europeans are going to be determined increasingly by economic integration and political union, the emergence of some form of European social policy becomes inevitable. Such a policy can be justified on grounds of efficiency, equity and solidarity, but it does not have to imply uniformity of social protection systems.

A common approach to social policy became a topical issue in the 1990s, when the Union was facing major social problems as a result of slow economic growth and persisting long-term unemployment, population ageing, the increasing cost of providing social protection, the pressures to meet the targets for EMU and the prospect of further enlargement. The decision to write employment into the Treaty of

Amsterdam, in response to public concern about unemployment, may have marked another turning point for the social dimension. The Union affirmed its commitment to achieving a high level of employment, and to adopting a more proactive and concerted approach. The 1998 employment guidelines [1.18] began the task of setting quantifiable targets. Policy statements produced by the Commission from the mid-1990s had been preparing the way for an upgrading of the social dimension. Addressing the European Forum on Social Policy in 1996, the then President of the European Commission, Jacques Santer, had stated: 'There can be no social progress without economic progress; but conversely, economic wealth cannot be built in a social desert.' He added that 'the social dimension is not a cost or a burden, but rather a source of dynamism that will enable us to take on the challenges of the future, including that of international competition'. These points were reiterated in the social action programme for 1998–2000 [1.19]. High social standards were presented as a key element in the competitive formula and a factor contributing to the efficiency of European society. The Commission had attempted to seize the initiative, at least insofar as the rhetoric was concerned, arguing for the productive and creative role that social policy could play as a more equal partner, although no plans were on the table for social union.

Box 1 Legislation and official publications relating to the social dimension of the European Union

PRIMARY LEGISLATION

1.1 Treaty establishing the European Coal and Steel Community (ECSC), signed in Paris on 18 April 1951.
1.2 Treaty establishing the European Economic Community (EEC), signed in Rome on 25 March 1957.
1.3 Treaty establishing the European Atomic Energy Community (EAEC), signed in Rome on 25 March 1957.
1.4 Treaty of 8 April 1965 establishing a Single Council and a Single Commission of the European Communities (the Merger Treaty).
1.5 Single European Act (SEA), signed in Luxembourg on 17 February 1986 and at The Hague on 28 February 1986.
1.6 Treaty on European Union, signed in Maastricht on 7 February 1992; Protocol and Agreement on Social Policy, concluded between the member states of the European Community, with the exception of the United Kingdom.
1.7 Treaty of Amsterdam amending the Treaty on European Union, the Treaties establishing the European Communities and certain

related acts, signed in Amsterdam on 2 October 1997.

1.8 European Union Consolidated versions of the EU Treaty and the EC Treaty, incorporating the changes made by the Treaty of Amsterdam.

SECONDARY LEGISLATION AND OFFICIAL PUBLICATIONS

1.9 Council Resolution of 21 January 1974 concerning a social action programme (*OJ*, C 13/1 12.2.74).

1.10 Community Charter of the Fundamental Social Rights of Workers, adopted in Strasbourg on 9 December 1989 by the member states, with the exception of the United Kingdom.

1.11 Communication from the Commission concerning its action programme relating to the implementation of the Community Charter of Basic Social Rights for Workers (COM(89) 568 final, 29 November 1989).

1.12 Commission of the European Communities, First report on the application of the Community Charter of the Fundamental Social Rights of Workers (COM(91) 511 final, 5 December 1991).

1.13 Communication of the Commission to the Council and the European Parliament, The principle of subsidiarity (SEC(92) 1990 final, 27 October 1992).

1.14 Commission of the European Communities, *Green Paper – European Social Policy. Options for the Union*, OOPEC, 1993 (COM(93) 551, 17 November 1993).

1.15 European Commission, *A White Paper – European Social Policy. A way forward for the Union*, OOPEC, 1994 (COM(94) 333 final, 27 July 1994).

1.16 European Commission, Medium-term social action programme 1995–97, *Social Europe*, 1/95.

1.17 European Commission, Progress report on the implementation of the medium-term social action programme 1995–97, *Social Europe Supplement*, 4/96.

1.18 Council Resolution of 15 December 1997 on the 1998 employment guidelines (*OJ* C30/1 28.1.98).

1.19 European Commission, *Social Action Programme 1998–2000*, OOPEC, 1998 (COM(1998) 259 final, 29 April 1998).

1.20 Council Resolution of 22 February 1999 on the 1999 employment guidelines (SEC(1998) 2175 final, *OJ* C 69/2 12.3.99).

1.21 European treaties, legislation and social policy documents:
http://europa.eu.int/abc/obj/treaties/en/entoc.htm
http://europa.eu.int/scadplus/scad_en.htm
http://europa.eu.int/comm/dgs/employment_social/index_en.htm

2 Reconciling Diversity and Harmonization

The intention in the Treaty establishing the European Economic Community (EEC) [1.2] in 1957 was to remove barriers to mobility and ensure that no one nation would be at a competitive advantage or disadvantage because of its social provisions. Under the section on social policy, article 117 introduced the principle of harmonization of social systems across the six original member states, implying that they would ultimately converge. Although the first paragraph of article 117 was expanded, redrafted and renumbered following the signing of the Treaty of Amsterdam [1.7] in 1997, the original reference to the term 'harmonization' was neither removed nor amended. Article 136 of the consolidated EC Treaty [1.8] set out the objective of both the Community and member states to promote improved living and working conditions 'so as to make possible their harmonisation while the improvement is being maintained'. As in the original EEC Treaty, such a development was expected to 'ensue not only from the functioning of the common market, which will favour the harmonisation of social systems, but also from the procedures provided for in this Treaty and from the approximation of provisions laid down by law, regulation or administrative action'.

The founder members – Belgium, France, the Federal Republic of Germany, Italy, Luxembourg and the Netherlands – had developed social protection systems that can be considered as variants of a 'continental' model of welfare, based on corporatist rights and derived from income-related insurance contributions. This shared tradition did not mean that harmonization would be easy to achieve, since each country had its own particular brand of social protection in terms of both the principles underlying the system and the policy-making process itself. The new members that joined the Community in later years brought with them different welfare models, making harmonization more difficult. The social protection systems in the Nordic/Anglo-Saxon countries that became members in 1973 – Denmark, Ireland and the United Kingdom – had developed in line with the principle of universal coverage of risks funded from taxation. The southern or Mediterranean countries, sometimes described as the Latin rim, that joined the Community in the 1980s – Greece in 1981, and Portugal and Spain in 1986 – had much more limited welfare systems. They still relied heavily on family, community and religious support in dealing with social problems (Rhodes, 1997). Of the states that became members in 1995, Austria was closer to the continental model, while Finland and more especially Sweden belonged to the universalist tax-based welfare variant, previously exemplified by Denmark.

The goal of harmonizing social protection was made more pressing, but also more complex, by the preparations for Economic and Monetary Union (EMU), and by the need to maintain the principle of freedom of movement within an enlarged Community. In addition, over the years doubts were expressed increasingly about the feasibility, or even desirability, of harmonization. Although the Community Charter of the Fundamental Social Rights of Workers used the term in three contexts [1.10, §3, §8 and §9], the Agreement on Social Policy, concluded by 11 of the 12 member states and annexed to the Maastricht Treaty [1.6], made no reference to harmonizing social protection systems across the Union. Instead, it stated unambiguously that account should be taken of the 'diverse forms of national practices, in particular in the field of contractual relations' (article 1), laying stress on the need to maintain the competitiveness of the Community's economy. While reinstating the reference to harmonization cited above, the second paragraph of article 136 in the consolidated EC Treaty retained the amendment in the agreement, thereby somewhat incongruously juxtaposing harmonization and diversity of systems.

This chapter examines the shifting focus between these two seemingly irreconcilable objectives: how to harmonize social protection systems while, at the same time, respecting national diversity and specificity. Firstly, the concepts of approximation, harmonization, co-ordination, co-operation, cohesion and convergence are introduced and located in relation to the development of the Union's social dimension. Differences in national welfare systems, which are deeply embedded in national cultural traditions, are then explored with reference to the concept of welfare models or regimes. Finally, in the absence of a harmonized European social protection system that can be applied to all citizens of the Union, an attempt is made to identify the components of what is frequently described as the European social model, and to assess the extent to which it would seem to be capable of accommodating diversity.

HARMONIZATION OF NATIONAL SOCIAL POLICIES

The EEC Treaty [1.2] carried conflicting messages about harmonization of social policy. The establishment and functioning of the common market were founded on the principle that provisions should be approximated (article 100). Approximation as laid down by law, regulation or administrative action was intended to affect the establishment and functioning of the common market, thereby favouring 'the harmonisation of social systems', as advocated in article 117. From the outset social policy was, however, primarily a matter for individual member states to determine, except in the case of migrant workers (articles 51 and 121). The Commission was required in article 118 to 'act in close contact with Member States by making studies, delivering opinions and arranging consultations both on problems arising at national level and on those of concern to international organisations', but it was under no compulsion to propose legislation. It has been argued that article 117 did no more 'than direct attention to the need to consider the removal of artificial restrictions which have grown up over the years as part of national policies', and that the close collaboration referred to in article 118 'did not imply the necessity for subsequent action' (Collins, 1975, pp. 22–3). Rather, the EEC Treaty could be seen as 'broadly educational and promotional' (Collins, 1975, p. 31), leaving member states to define their own approaches to social policy.

The co-ordination of national systems, with the intention of safeguarding social security arrangements for migrant workers and their dependants, figured among the very first regulations adopted by the Council of Ministers in 1958 (see Chapter 9). Elsewhere the treaty was less prescriptive about how harmonization, or approximation, of social systems was to be achieved. Article 122 required the Commission to report annually on social developments within the Community and gave it the ill-defined brief of drawing up reports on 'any particular problems concerning social conditions'. This section examines more closely the goal of achieving harmonization of social protection systems by charting the progressive shift towards the concepts of convergence of objectives while pursuing subsidiarity in implementation.

From harmonization . . .

Harmonization of social protection, as written into the EEC Treaty, implied that member states should work together and adapt their own social security systems to bring them into line with one another through a change in the substance of national laws. It goes further than co-ordination, which involves a linkage of separate legal systems at supranational level and an acceptance of certain common principles and standards without changing the content, the aim being to minimize loss of rights by migrant workers (Holloway, 1981, pp. 11–12). It falls short, however, of unification (as applied in Germany), which requires a fundamental reshaping of existing systems.

Controversy over the desirability and feasibility of harmonization continued almost unabated over the years, with individual member states taking up entrenched positions in defence of national sovereignty. The debate was reactivated each time new treaty amendments were being negotiated. At the outset, the French government had argued that, if the overriding aim of the Community was to avoid distortion of competition by evening out labour costs, harmonization of social protection, particularly in terms of funding, was a desirable objective and even a precondition for fair competition. Other countries used the economic argument against harmonization. For the Germans, indirect labour costs were seen as only one of a number of factors determining competitiveness. Others, such as the taxation system, geographical location, labour productivity, the climate of labour relations, had to be taken into account and needed to be kept roughly in balance. According to this line of reasoning, any attempts to harmonize national social security arrangements at Community level might even upset the balance, thereby obstructing competition. British governments also argued strongly against any approximation of welfare systems on economic grounds. They vehemently opposed European legislation that might encroach on national social space and present a threat to competitiveness in a global economy. For the Mediterranean states, harmonization of provisions implied a heavy cost they could ill afford, whereas the Swedes were concerned that approximation would mean a levelling down of their high standards once they joined the Union.

The early member states feared not only that social dumping (see Chapter 1) would become a widespread practice but also that 'welfare' or 'social tourism' might develop if some countries offered more attractive living and working conditions than others (see Chapter 9). Summarizing thc obstacles to closer integration at the end of the 1980s, Abram De Swaan (1990, p. 9) argued that the welfare state is essentially exclusive and anti-international, and that national welfare systems are kept apart by two contradictory concerns: firstly, the fear that the national arrangements of individual member states might have to be extended or reduced; secondly, the likelihood of differences in provisions provoking welfare tourism, as labour becomes mobile in order to take advantage of higher social benefits in another member state. Welfare tourism describes the process whereby older, unemployed and poor people may be induced to seek refuge in the countries and regions within the Union affording the most generous systems of social protection. According to this line of reasoning, measures to encourage harmonization can serve to prevent welfare systems from becoming a bargaining counter between member states.

Jos Berghman (1990, pp. 11–12) has suggested that the German argument against the need for close harmonization of social protection systems may have been valid when the EEC Treaty was signed but was less applicable by the 1990s. Trends towards harmonization of monetary and fiscal policies and the greater diversity between the 12 member states, as compared with the original six, according to the same author, created a new set of conditions where harmonization of social security systems could in fact help restore the overall balance. This view was supported by Danny Pieters (1991, p. 182) on the grounds that marked differences in the funding of social security, as well as direct or indirect subsidies, can distort competition. As other elements of labour costs and other factors determining competitiveness converge following the completion of the Single European Market (SEM), for example through approximation in the area of fiscal and employment law, improvement in infrastructures and standards of education and training, Pieters argued that it would become imperative for national social security systems to be harmonized. By 1992, however, the Commission's view was that harmonization of social protection systems was no longer on the agenda. Rather, it recognized their diversity, and 'the fact that they are firmly anchored to specific cultures, traditions and models' (Quintin, 1992, p. 9).

. . . through social cohesion and convergence to diversity

When Jacques Delors became President of the Commission in 1985 in the period leading up to the signing of the Single European Act (SEA), he was faced with a dilemma over the best way of introducing a social dimension. He was aware that legislation requiring harmonization would be opposed by member states unwilling to adapt national systems but, without legislative controls, states would not be bound to respond. Delors' plan represented a compromise. He rejected the idea that the social dimension implied uniformity or unification and, instead, advocated 'coherence' (Delors, 1985, p. xviii). His plan involved a social dialogue, whereby unions and employers would become the initiators of policy in the social field, rather than the Commission (see Chapter 1).

The SEA confirmed the shift away from harmonization towards respect for national systems. While still referring to the 'harmonisation of conditions', the new article 118a stressed that directives should be adopted setting out 'minimum requirements for gradual implementation, having regard to the conditions and technical rules obtaining in each of the Member States'. The SEA (title V) also introduced the concept of 'cohesion', subsequently incorporated into the consolidated EC Treaty (articles 158–62). Member states were encouraged to co-operate and co-ordinate their efforts in order to bring about greater economic and social cohesion between the regions. The structural funds were identified as the main instrument available to compensate for possible losses arising as a result of economic integration, and to enhance social cohesion (Hannequart, 1992).

A more pragmatic and less legalistic approach was pursued during the preparatory phase of the Community Charter of the Fundamental Social Rights of Workers [1.10] in the late 1980s. In an analysis of the climate of opinion at that time, the European Institute of Social Security (1988, p. 9) argued that, after more than 30 years of operation, the Community was no longer seeking to modify systems. Instead, it was directing its efforts towards encouraging national policies to converge over a number of precisely defined common objectives without encroaching on systems that have developed from different traditions.

The Community charter took some account of this change in approach. The term 'harmonization' was used in the context of freedom of movement with the object of harmonizing the conditions of residence in all member states (§3); the duration of paid leave was to be harmonized (§8); and measures were to be taken to achieve further harmonization of conditions for safety at the workplace (§19). Member states undertook, however, to recognize national differences in social protection systems. Reference was made, for example, to the need to act in accordance with national practices (§8) and with the arrangements applying in each country (§9). The action programme for the implementation of the Community charter [1.11] stated that the diversity of national practices was to be retained as a positive input. At the same time, a balance was to be sought between economic and social measures with a view to protecting the competitiveness of business. Member states were given responsibility for guaranteeing the social rights embodied in the charter and implementing the necessary social measures to ensure the smooth operation of the internal market, but the Commission invited them to submit initiatives with a view to the adoption of appropriate legal instruments. These conflicting objectives were to be reconciled by observing the principle of subsidiarity, whereby the most appropriate minimum level of involvement by the Union's institutions is applied, whether it be harmonization, co-ordination, convergence or co-operation (see Chapter 1). In other words, the Community should intervene only where necessary, and where measures cannot be better put into effect at national level, so that the rules established do not prevent member states from acting in accordance with their own circumstances.

The Agreement on Social Policy, annexed to the Maastricht Treaty [1.6], mentioned neither harmonization nor approximation. Instead, it reaffirmed the intention to respect national specificity, recommending that its terms should not prevent member states from either maintaining or introducing their own more extensive measures (articles 2, 6). The Commission's role was to be limited to encouraging co-operation between member states and facilitating the co-ordination of their action in all the social policy fields covered by the agreement (article 5). In line with the Delors approach, social dialogue and consultation were to be essential components in the process.

The term 'convergence' was introduced into article 2 of title II in the Maastricht Treaty, but in the context of economic performance. At the time when the treaty was signed, a Council recommendation was being prepared 'on the convergence of social protection objectives and policies' [2.1]. On the grounds that differences in social security cover might act as a serious brake to the free movement of workers and exacerbate regional imbalances, particularly between the north and south of the Community, the Council proposed that 'a strategy be promoted for the convergence of Member States' policies in this field, underpinned by objectives established in common, making it possible to overcome such disadvantages' [2.1, p. 49]. The Community's strategy was to be flexible in nature, progressive and non-binding [2.2, p. 7]. The *de facto* convergence that was said to be occurring as the result of common trends leading to common problems was to be further promoted by establishing common objectives, based on the principles of equal treatment and fairness, to guide national policies and avoid all forms of discrimination and disadvantage. The recommendation did not clarify how these principles were to be operationalized, stating only that social protection systems were to be adapted and developed as necessary, and administered with maximum efficiency and effectiveness.

The consolidated version of the EC Treaty retained the reference to convergence of economic performance in article 2 but did not extend it to the social area. Title VIII on employment referred to a 'coordinated strategy for employment' (article 125), described as a topic of 'common concern' (article 126 §2). Member states were, however, left to formulate their own employment policies 'in a way consistent with the broad guidelines…of the Member States and of the Community' (article 126 §1), respectful of national competences (article 127 §1). The Council is empowered to make recommendations to member states, but only within well-defined circumstances (article 128 §4). Article 129 allows for incentive measures to be adopted to encourage co-operation, but the harmonization of national laws and regulations is explicitly excluded.

The same exclusion is found in the chapters on education, vocational training and youth (article 150 §4), culture (article 151 §5), and public health (article 152 §4c), while co-operation and complementarity become key concepts. Even though article 136 in the chapter on social provisions retained a reference to harmonization, the force of the term is modified by the fact that it is presented as a possibility rather than an obligation. The most forceful use can be found in title XIX on the environment but, even here, a safeguard clause allows member states to take provisional measures for non-economic environmental reasons, subject to Community inspection procedures (article 174 §2).

As in other social policy areas, the social chapter in the consolidated version of the EC Treaty observed the conciliatory tone already present in the Agreement on Social Policy, stressing the subsidiarity principle and the supportive role of the Union. It confirmed the failure to achieve a treaty commitment to a strongly interventionist European social policy, aimed at harmonizing social protection systems.

However, as indicated in the previous chapter, while national governments appeared to be vacillating, the Commission was actively cultivating a consensual approach in shaping the social policy agenda. It had prepared and implemented a series of action programmes [1.11; 1.16; 1.19]. It was confidently promoting the convergence of employment policies 'towards jointly set, verifiable, regularly updated targets' [1.18, p. 1], requiring proactive strategies, as a complement to the convergence required by EMU. In addition, it was looking for ways of modernizing and improving social protection, while taking care to observe the subsidiarity principle and acknowledging that each member state remained responsible for framing, organizing and financing its own social protection system [2.1, p. 50; 2.3, p. i].

RECOGNIZING NATIONAL DIVERSITY

The amended version of the treaties thus left the way open for co-operation and co-ordination based on recognition and tolerance of diversity. If the result of policies happens to be convergence of national social protection systems, at least as far as the treaties are concerned, such an outcome is incidental rather than being actively and explicitly sought. Many of the problems associated with adopting a common approach to social provisions, as well as the resistance to harmonization in the social area and the reluctance to develop quantifiable targets for social convergence, except with regard to employment [1.18], can be attributed to the different starting points of member states. As Catherine Jones Finer (1999, p. 17) has argued, postwar welfare statism may have contained the same ingredients across countries, but the mix was very different. National governments have remained alert to what they stood to lose if a uniform system, guaranteeing a minimum level of provision, was universally applied. In this section, different models of welfare, as represented by EU member states and applicant countries, are explored with a view to identifying areas of common concern, similarities and differences in approaches to social issues and the characteristics of an emerging European social model.

Models of welfare

In the 1960s and 1970s, proponents of convergence theory were arguing that welfare states in industrial societies were a logical outcome of industrialization, and that attitudes towards social problems were converging as similar conclusions were being reached about how to resolve them. The convergence thesis was countered by other writers who criticized it for being too deterministic and for oversimplifying patterns of development in social policy. Critics such as Ramesh Mishra (1977, pp. 33–42) stressed the persistence of diversity in welfare patterns in advanced industrial societies, where the influence of technology was only one among a number of factors shaping social policy, as exemplified by the mix between state and occupational welfare provision. In the early 1980s, Peter Flora and Jens Alber (1984, pp. 60–3) reviewed the argument that diffusion of welfare systems had occurred as some countries imitated and adopted innovative pioneering institutions from elsewhere. They found that internal socio-economic problems and political mobilization also had to be considered. Although none of these commentators was referring specifically to the EEC or the possible influence of policy formulated in Brussels on the convergence of different welfare systems, the arguments about economic forces driving social policy have a strong resonance in the context of EMU.

Concurrently with the debate over convergence, several attempts were made to identify typologies that might help to describe and explain the diffusion of different patterns of welfare and their diversity. In the 1960s, again without reference to the EEC, Richard Titmuss (1974, pp. 30–1) had developed a conceptual approach to the analysis of welfare which distinguished between three models. In the residual model, social welfare institutions came into play when the private market and the family broke down, thereby limiting state intervention to marginal and deserving groups. According to the industrial achievement–performance model, social welfare institutions were adjuncts of the economy, and social needs were met on the basis of merit, work performance and productivity. Under the third, institutional redistributive, model, social welfare was seen as a major integrated institution in society, operating to provide universalist services outside the market.

Residual, industrial and institutional interpretations thus represented very different conceptions of welfare: minimum, targeted provision, performance-related and optimum universal provision. The residual concept of social policy has also been extended to describe welfare as a 'residual luxury' supported by economic surpluses (Heclo, 1984, p. 403). When, in the 1970s, an economic surplus could no longer be assured, welfare states were criticized as a drain on resources. Governments adopted crisis containment measures. The postwar welfare capitalist consensus was challenged, and fundamental questions were raised about the relationship between economic and social policy (Pierson, 1992, p. 222), an issue that assumed greater salience as member states moved towards EMU and further enlargement (Pieters, 1998).

The reactions to the challenges of the 1980s highlighted both quantitative and qualitative differences between welfare states in terms of ends and means (Jones Finer, 1999, p. 23). In the early 1990s, renewed interest in analysing models of welfare as an alternative to convergence theory had led to several proposals for typologies based on the different ways in which welfare is organized in relation to social structures, political interests and market forces. The three welfare regimes proposed by Gøsta Esping-Andersen (1990) for the capitalist nations were widely discussed and provoked a number of alternative suggestions. Liberal welfare states, according to Esping-Andersen, could be exemplified by the Anglo-Saxon countries. As in the Titmuss residual model, in the absence of a class alliance, selective welfare was targeted at the poor, a dual system of private and occupational services provision was available for the middle classes, and an attempt was made to minimize direct intervention by the state to give free rein to market forces. As in the Titmuss industrial achievement–performance model, Esping-Andersen's conservative corporatist regime applied to countries, such as Germany, where conservative central government had developed systems of occupational social insurance welfare, shaped in no small measure by the influence of the Church, and predicated on the subsidiarity principle, in an effort to ensure support from the working and middle classes. His social democratic regimes corresponded to the Titmuss institutional redistributive model, as represented by Scandinavian countries, especially Sweden, where the welfare state, responding to the solidarity of the working and middle classes, provided universalist services, premised on equal opportunities and full employment.

In Esping-Andersen's (1990, p. 74) classification, among EU member states, Austria, Belgium, France, Germany and Italy were rated high on conservative attributes, with Ireland and the Netherlands obtaining a medium score. Denmark, Finland, the Netherlands and Sweden were rated high on social democratic criteria, with Belgium, Germany and the United Kingdom in the medium band. None of the member states was found to record a high degree of liberalism. If the United Kingdom was awarded a medium rating in this category, so too were Denmark, France, Germany, Italy and the Netherlands.

The southern European member states and the applicant countries of Central and Eastern Europe were not included in Esping-Andersen's analysis. Proponents of the logic of industrialism thesis might have argued that Greece, Portugal and Spain would in time develop the same level of welfare provision as their more advanced, wealthier Mediterranean neighbours. Since they already relied heavily on social insurance, mainly funded by employers' contributions well above the European average, as illustrated below, a strong case could be made for expecting their systems to develop in line with the continental model.

The applicant states in Central and Eastern Europe, set to join the Union in the first wave of membership after the year 2000, had been forced to revise their approach to welfare provision following the collapse of state socialism in 1989. Their welfare systems had in common their bureaucratic state collectivist origins. They were, according to Esping-Andersen's terminology, highly decommodified in that care was essentially provided by the state, but they were also openly redistributive, like the social democratic regimes. Since they reserved special treatment for the party state apparatus, they contained elements of corporatist conservative arrangements. In the early 1990s, they were expected to react to the perceived failures of the previous system by becoming highly commodified, by generating inequalities and by placing greater reliance on the market place. It seemed likely that their postsocialist welfare systems would be determined by variables such as differences in their institutional legacies, the nature and character of the 1989 revolutions, their economic transformation in the 1990s, the political impact of transnational agencies and, not least, the criteria laid down for membership of the Union (Deacon, 1993, pp. 190–7; Nielsen, 1996, pp. 206–11).

Characterizing welfare states in the European Union

It has been argued in this chapter that the different waves of membership of the European Community and Union made harmonization of social protection systems a more distant goal. Each wave of membership was accompanied by a fall in *per capita* gross domestic product (GDP). The enlargement to the East early in the twenty-first century was set to produce an unprecedented reduction in *per capita* GDP, greater than that resulting from all previous enlargements [2.4, vol. 2, p. 22], thereby contributing to the severe strains already placed on social protection by the drive towards EMU. In taking stock of developments in social protection systems across the Union, the intention here is to test the argument that, at the very least, the expansion of the Community complicated the harmonization process and made the prospects for achieving convergence more distant, while EMU may have made it more likely, if not more necessary.

Financing social protection

During the 1980s and through to 1995 when Austria, Finland and Sweden became members of the Union, *per capita* spending on social protection increased by more than 40 per cent across the Union, largely due to slow economic growth and high unemployment. As a proportion of GDP, between 1990–93 expenditure rose from 25.4 to 29 per cent before stabilizing in the mid-1990s. Over the same period, initially *per capita* spending also grew rapidly, with Portugal displaying a particularly high rate of growth, having started from a very low base (Eurostat, 2000, tables 1 and 2). Figure 2.1 shows the classification of countries by wave of membership in terms of social protection expenditure, both in relation to GDP and *per capita* in 1997.

Figure 2.1 Social protection expenditure in EU member states, as a % of GDP and *per capita* in PPS, 1997

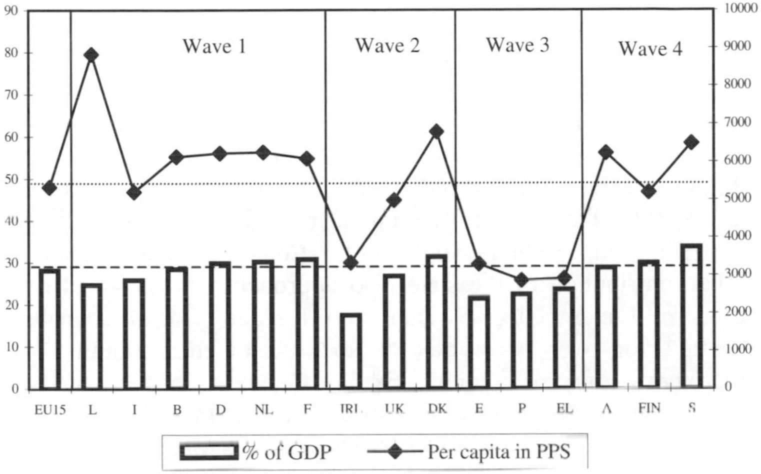

Source: Data from Eurostat (2000), table 1 and figure 2.

Figure 2.2 The structure of social protection receipts in EU member states, as a % of total receipts, 1997

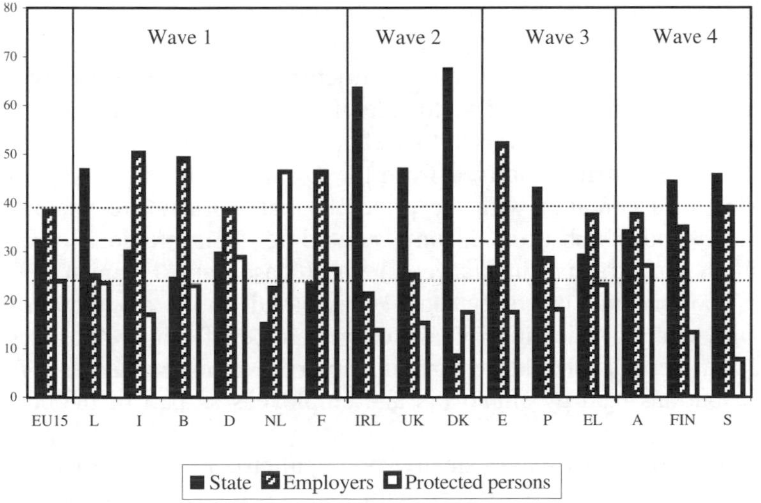

Source: Data from Eurostat (2000), table 7.

The figure brings out clearly the contrast, for the percentage of GDP, between the Nordic states, which are above the EU average, and the Mediterranean states and Ireland, which fall well below the average. The difference between the high and the low spenders is even more marked for *per capita* expenditure, measured in purchasing power standards (PPS), with Luxembourg spending 3.1 times more than Portugal. Although the same countries still belong to the low-spending group, Luxembourg moves up the rank order into the highest position.

Figure 2.2 shows how social protection was financed across member states in 1997. The second wave countries – Denmark, Ireland and the United Kingdom – relied heavily on tax-funded government subsidies, but the contribution of the state also approached 50 per cent of total receipts in Luxembourg, Sweden and Finland. Social contributions accounted for over two-thirds of social protection funding in the Netherlands, France, Belgium, Spain, Greece, Germany and Italy. Employers made the largest contribution in Spain, followed by Italy, Belgium and France. Protected persons were responsible for nearly 50 per cent of total receipts in the Netherlands. Analysis of the combined impact of tax receipts and social contributions indicates that, in the mid-1990s, Denmark and Sweden both levied taxes and social contributions amounting to over 50 per cent of GDP, whereas the level in Greece, Ireland, Portugal, Spain and the United Kingdom was closer to one third of GDP (Eurostat, 1997e, table 2).

Administration and structure of welfare systems

The legal basis and administrative structures of national systems vary across the Union [2.7]. The founder members of the EEC shared a certain similarity of approach to welfare in that their social protection systems were mainly derived from the Bismarckian statist corporatist model, in accordance with the principle that workers are guaranteed benefits and a substitute income related to their previous earnings through a contractual insurance scheme (Clasen and Freeman, 1994). This 'continental' insurance model was based on the assumption that employment qualified individuals for welfare benefits as well as wages, and that benefits should be funded primarily, if not exclusively, from contributions paid by employers and employees as part of the cost of labour.

The model was intrinsically non-egalitarian in that access to employment is known to vary with age, gender, ethnic origins and qualifications, among other factors (see Chapters 3, 6, 7, 8 and 9). Over the postwar period, schemes were perpetuated that offered different arrangements to different categories of workers, ensuring distribution of income over the lifetime of individuals. They were less concerned with redistribution from one sector to another across society. The original schemes in Bismarckian Germany, such as that instituted in 1889 for old age pensions, were targeted at industrial workers and provided compensation for loss of income, calculated on the basis of earnings, rather than a minimum income. They thereby reproduced in retirement the inequalities of income earned from employment. Provision for public sector workers was particularly generous and constituted an additional source of inequality.

Belgium, France, Italy, Luxembourg and the Netherlands followed a similar principle to Germany in creating employment-related social insurance schemes. In most member states, social protection was first introduced in the areas of industrial injuries and occupational diseases at the end of the nineteenth century, followed by invalidity, sickness and maternity benefits, unemployment, then old age, survivors' and family benefits [2.7, 1998]. The provision of health care was also based on insurance contributions, although Italy established a national health service in 1978. In addition, all six EEC founder members developed some form of non-contributory minimum social assistance as a safety net, subsidized by the state from general taxation (see Chapter 8). These six countries not only display commonality in the underlying principles and organizational structures of their social protection systems, but they also have in common that, with the exception of Italy, their *per capita* spending on social welfare, particularly in Luxembourg, is above the EU average, as shown in Figure 2.1.

Although they all share several of the broad characteristics of the continental welfare model, the social protection systems in the founder member states are far from being uniform, either structurally or in terms of their funding arrangements. The social costs of labour are, for example, likely to be much higher in France and Italy where contributions fall heavily on employers, as indicated by Figure 2.2. While the Italian national health service shifts some of the burden to the state, reforms in the 1990s were moving in the direction of a partial withdrawal of the state in favour of quasi-markets to improve quality and efficiency [2.5, 1997, pp. 138–9]. Where social assistance is organized at regional or local level, considerable variations in coverage are likely to arise, not only between but also within countries, as illustrated in particular by the case of Italy, where major disparities occur between north and south, or between the old and new *Länder* in Germany.

By contrast, the three states that joined the Community in 1973 – Denmark, Ireland and the United Kingdom – shared a general conception of social protection closer to what can be described as the citizenship or welfare model. According to the Beveridge scheme for social welfare in Britain and to the Scandinavian, or social democratic, model (Esping-Andersen, 1990), which developed in Denmark, the right to a pension, health care and family allowances was granted on the basis of social citizenship. The assumption was that employment provided a living wage, whereas welfare benefits were distributed through taxation to all citizens on equal terms, whatever their employment status.

The social security systems in these three countries continue to be distinguished from the 'continental' model by their preference for fiscal resources and the universal provision of health care, rather than insurance contributions and income-related benefits. In Denmark, however, emphasis was placed on income maintenance, whereas in Ireland and the United Kingdom the aim was to ensure subsistence by providing low flat-rate payments or means-tested benefits, which may help to explain the difference in the overall level of spending on social protection in relation to GDP and to *per capita* income.

Greece, Portugal and Spain, which joined the Community in the 1980s, were characterized by less advanced and less coherent social security systems compared to most of the earlier members. Apart from the core labour market, they continue to rely heavily on traditional forms of support through family and kinship networks and the Church, with discretionary provision at local level. Social protection is broadly based on corporatism, as in the continental model, with employers carrying the major burden of the cost of providing benefits in Spain, although in both Portugal and Spain health care is covered by a national health service, largely funded from taxation. In the late 1990s, Greece still did not have a general social assistance scheme. Its spending on social protection increased at a relatively slow rate in the early 1990s, and it also failed subsequently to meet EMU criteria for membership in the first phase.

While the EU membership of Austria in 1995 further reinforced the dominant continental model of welfare, Finland and Sweden strengthened the tax-based, social democratic model (Esping-Andersen, 1990), hitherto represented by Denmark. Here, the right to a pension, health care and family allowances is granted on the basis of social citizenship, with the state providing the largest share of the funding (Figure 2.2). The percentages of GDP and of *per capita* spending on social protection were in both cases above the EU average in 1996 (Figure 2.1).

Given their low levels of *per capita* GDP, and the economic problems facing them, the fifth wave of Eastern rim membership might be expected to follow the more residual pattern of welfare provision of the Mediterranean states. Despite their shared tradition of state socialism, in the 1990s the applicant states from Central and Eastern Europe did not constitute a homogeneous grouping, corresponding to one of the three welfare regime types outlined above. The preference in most countries seemed to be to shift away from state financing in favour of social insurance contributions, oriented towards the needs of workers. Most governments were introducing earnings-related rather than flat-rate benefits, though at a relatively low level of support due to fiscal restraints. Private and semi-private solutions were being adopted, with a minimal safety net subject to local discretion. Universalism had been largely replaced by means-testing, and workfare was being promoted in preference to welfare. Towards the end of the 1990s, Hungary, Slovenia and the Czech Republic seemed to have moved furthest towards the conservative corporatist regime, while Poland and Estonia appeared to be developing in line with the liberal welfare model (Ferge, 1992, 1997; Deacon, 1993; Nielsen, 1996).

CONSOLIDATING THE EUROPEAN SOCIAL MODEL

The social protection systems examined in this chapter share a common core, both in terms of the risks they cover and the general administrative arrangements set up to deal with contingencies. However, closer scrutiny reveals numerous differences within and between groupings with regard to the legal status of social protection, funding mechanisms, the distribution of responsibilities and the population groups covered by contributory and non-contributory schemes [2.6; 2.7]. Each country has developed its own peculiar brand of social protection as a result of a long process reflecting idiosyncratic socio-economic, political and cultural traditions, which would seem to give the lie to the thesis of the logic of industrialism, at least as far as administrative and financial structures are concerned.

In line with convergence theory, it could be argued that disparities in systems might be due to the stage of socio-economic development reached by each country. Accordingly, the Mediterranean and Eastern European countries might be expected to learn from, and imitate, their more advanced neighbours. While there is some evidence to suggest that innovatory schemes may be used as models, as was the case with the Bismarckian and Beveridgian social security schemes, the economic and political conditions in which these two groupings of countries were developing their social protection systems when they joined the Community, or applied for membership in the case of the East Europeans, were very different from those of the 1960s and 1970s, even if the structural funds did contribute to some upwards levelling.

Over the second half of the twentieth century, all welfare regimes had to adapt in response to changing socio-economic and political circumstances. In the 1990s, most governments were engaging in welfare retrenchment. The result was a mixed economy of welfare, or welfare pluralism, but in which the employment-insurance model had become predominant. The corporate welfare systems, based on employers' and workers' contributions and income-related benefits, did not entirely replace existing occupational schemes, which continued to provide supplementary cover for contingencies such as old age for some groups of workers. Although it might be expected to serve the economic interests of the Union, such a model of welfare has been criticized at the social level for moving member states away from a more redistributive conception of welfare citizenship and for reinforcing differentiation, segregation and polarization (Abrahamson, 1992, pp. 10–11). While the market can be expected to take care of workers in regular employment, those unable to enter or re-enter the labour force run the risk of being marginalized. The underlying principle that rights are derived from employment and that paid work is the only means of achieving social integration was in evidence in schemes like the *revenu minimum d'insertion* (RMI) in France, where benefits were made to depend upon claimants undertaking some form of employment or social training to prepare them for re-entry to the formal labour market.

Evidence can also be found for the development of a welfare mix in member states, like the United Kingdom, which had initially based their social protection systems on universal state provision of health care and flat-rate benefits for other contingencies. Schemes for earnings-related payments and occupationally-based pensions and private health care had progressively been extended to other sectors of the working population. By the late 1990s, emphasis had shifted towards more active labour market policies designed to move the unemployed off benefits and into work. Universality still depended on a high degree of involvement of public sector institutions in Denmark and Sweden, but here too pressure was increasingly being exerted by public opinion and government to turn to market and civil society solutions as a means of reducing the tax burden.

A certain amount of involuntary or spontaneous, rather than intended or planned, convergence may thus have taken place under the influence of market forces and economic imperatives that have been driving social policy. The actual welfare mix continues, however, to depend on the political context in which it occurs and the human and social processes involved in policy development at national level. Just as industrial technology and state intervention in social affairs were not considered sufficiently powerful to bring about convergence of social policy in the past (Mishra, 1977, p. 40), the economic factors that seem to be a major force behind welfare pluralism may not necessarily suffice to overcome differences in national welfare state ideologies.

If, by the late 1990s, diversity appeared to have been accepted in the treaties, the explanation may lie, at least partly, in the fact that member states were broadly in agreement about the overriding objectives of social policy. Highly developed social protection systems have been described by the Commission as a 'fundamental component and a distinguishing feature of the European social model' [2.3, p. 1]. In the absence of harmonization of the administrative and financial structures delivering welfare, a more powerful unifying force for EU member states, which has been developing outside the regulatory framework, is that they share the core values of such a model and the desire to preserve them. These values include 'democracy and individual rights, free collective bargaining, the market economy, equality of opportunity for all and social welfare and solidarity' [1.15, p. 9].

Social progress has been identified as a key element in the model, aimed at high levels of employment and of social protection, raising the standard of living and quality of life, and promoting economic and social cohesion, while striking a balance between social justice and economic efficiency. The fear being expressed within the Union in the late 1990s was that the applicant states would be unable to conform to the European social model, leading it to become unsustainable in the context of enlargement [2.4, vol. 2, p. 38].

Another possible reason for the apparent lull in the debate over diversity and harmonization could be that member states had realized collectively that the erosion of national sovereignty through economic integration had gone far enough. In the face of further enlargement, allowing national welfare states to retain what was left of their autonomy in the social area therefore seemed to offer an effective way of preserving the European social model.

Box 2 Secondary legislation and official publications relating to the reconciliation of diversity and harmonization

2.1 Council Recommendation of 27 July 1992 on the convergence of social protection objectives and policies (92/442/EEC) (*OJ* L 245/49 26.8.92).

2.2 Commission of the European Communities, The convergence of social protection objectives and policies, *Social Europe Supplement*, 5/92.

2.3 Communication from the Commission, Modernising and improving social protection in the European Union (COM(97) 102 final, 12 March 1997).

2.4 Commission of the European Communities, Agenda 2000, vol. 1, For a stronger and wider Union; vol. 2, The challenge of enlargement (COM(97) 2000 final, 15 July 1997).

2.5 European Commission, *Social Protection in Europe*, OOPEC (published every two years to 2000, then annually).

2.6 Eurostat-ESSPROS, *Social Protection Expenditure and Receipts* OOPEC (yearbook).

2.7 MISSOC, *Social Protection in the Member States of the European Union* (annual publication), OOPEC, available on-line at: http://europa.eu.int/comm/employment_social/soc-prot/missoc98/english/f_main.htm

3 Education, Training and Employment

In the Community's and Union's treaties and charter, most legislative provision refers to the social protection of workers under labour law and in social security systems. The basis for entitlements is derived primarily from employment. When the Treaty establishing the European Economic Community (EEC) [1.2] was signed in 1957, member states were concerned with social provisions only insofar as differences in national systems might impede freedom of movement for workers within the Community or distort competition. For the EEC founder members, education and training were therefore of only indirect interest.

If social policy is defined in a broad sense as the collective provision of particular services, or as government interventions with the aim of shaping society in some way (Kleinman and Piachaud, 1993, p. 3), covering both non-economic and economic objectives (Titmuss, 1974, p. 29), education and training can be considered legitimate areas for intervention by European institutions. As its social remit was gradually extended, and as the promotion of high levels of employment moved onto the agenda (see Chapter 1), both education and training developed as a recognized policy area for the Union. An agreed set of objectives was formulated, and administrative measures were organized for their implementation, albeit with due regard to the principles of subsidiarity, respect for diversity and the relevance of education and training to employability.

In this chapter, education and training are first located within the wider context of European social policy development, including a review of the concepts of educational space and mutual recognition of qualifications. The relationship between education, training and employment is then examined, followed by an appraisal of Community initiatives in this field, before going on to compare the arrangements for education and training across member states. In conclusion, consideration is given to the possible impact on national systems of the Union's actions in this area of policy.

A GROWING COMMITMENT TO EDUCATION AND TRAINING

The interests of the Union have been bound up primarily with economic concerns, as shown in previous chapters. The issue of competition for labour was relevant when the Community was established, since employers were expected to seek to poach well-qualified workers and to compete in offering the most favourable terms of employment in an effort to attract appropriate skills in areas of labour shortage (see Chapter 9). Since the 1970s, another labour market-related reason for interest in vocational training has been the growing problem of unemployment, particularly among young people. Improvement in the quality and skills of the labour force has been promoted to further the goal of economic cohesion (see Chapter 8). In the 1994 white paper on growth, competitiveness and employment, attention turned towards the adaptation of education and training systems with the aim of 'stimulating growth and restoring competitiveness and a socially acceptable level of employment in the Community' [3.8, p. 133]. In this section, the development of the Union's remit in the area of education and training is considered with reference to vocational training, mobility and the mutual recognition of qualifications, and also as a component in active labour market policies.

Towards an 'educational space'

Although article 118 of the EEC Treaty gave the Commission the task of 'promoting close cooperation between Member States' in the area of basic and advanced vocational training, among others, the subject of education was not explicitly addressed. Article 128 provided for the establishment of a 'common vocational policy capable of contributing to the harmonious development both of the national economies and of the common market'. The first phase of a programme for the exchange of young workers was launched in 1964, setting a pattern for a series of initiatives designed to encourage mobility during training. Under the section on the right of establishment, article 57 §1 empowered the Council to 'issue directives for the mutual recognition of diplomas, certificates and other evidence of formal qualifications', the purpose being to make it easier for the self-employed to take up and pursue activities in another member state.

When, ten years later, in 1974 the Commission signalled an interest in the social dimension of Europe through its social action programme [1.9], education moved onto the agenda. A resolution of the Council in

1976 'comprising an action programme in the field of education' [3.1] identified a number of priorities, including improved facilities for education and training, closer relations between educational systems, improved statistics on education, greater co-operation between member states in the field of higher education, covering recognition of qualifications and periods of study abroad, the promotion of foreign language teaching and of equal opportunities in access to education. The programme addressed the questions of unemployment among young people, the educational needs of the children of migrants, the preparation of young people for work and the smooth transition from education to working life. European Social Fund rules were later recast to give priority to the under-25s, and a range of measures were introduced that had implications for employment. The programme thus prepared the ground for subsequent action.

While the final stages of the Community Charter of the Fundamental Social Rights of Workers [1.10] were being negotiated, the Commission issued a communication 'on education and training in the European Community', setting out medium-term perspectives for education over the period 1989–92 [3.3]. It provided a clear statement of the Community's objectives and initiatives in this area. The introduction spoke of the need to create an 'educational space for mobility and interchange', analogous to Jacques Delors' 'social space' (see Chapter 1). The same document stressed the broad consensus reached over the pivotal role that education and training would be called upon to play in the overall development strategy of the Community, spearheading its commitment to invest in people. The communication suggested, moreover, that human resources could provide 'an essential bridge between economic and social policies' [3.3, p. 1].

The Commission's views on the subject were to some extent incorporated into the Community charter. Under the heading for the protection of children and adolescents, the rights of young people included a minimum working age, which 'must not be lower than the minimum school-leaving age and, in any case, not lower than 15 years' (§20). Vocational training was mentioned in five of the 12 sections of the charter, indicating the priority being given to this area of social policy insofar as it had immediate relevance for workers. As in the EEC Treaty with regard to vocational training, it reiterated the need to eliminate obstacles arising from the non-recognition of qualifications (§3). Emphasis was placed on the right of workers to vocational training and retraining throughout their working lives, without discrimination on grounds of nationality. The aim was to help workers improve or extend their skills, 'particularly in the light of technical developments' (§15). Young people were to be entitled to receive 'initial vocational training of a sufficient duration to enable them to adapt to the requirements of their future working life', and such training was to take place during working hours (§23). The right of men and women to equal treatment was to extend beyond access to employment, remuneration, working conditions and social protection to equality in access to education, training and career development (§16). The section on health protection and safety at the workplace included measures to cover the need for training (§19), and disabled persons were to be entitled to vocational training, 'aimed at improving their social and professional integration' (§26).

Following on from the Community charter, a series of Council conclusions, recommendations and resolutions was issued in the early 1990s setting out policy for education and training. While the economic motivation of encouraging freedom of movement of workers continued to dictate policy, the concept of an educational space was gaining acceptance. Emphasis was gradually shifting towards more qualitative objectives, with mobility being presented as a source of mutual enrichment and cultural interchange, rather than an end in itself. In 1991, a memorandum from the Commission on higher education clearly set out the Community's policy objectives for post-compulsory education and training. It referred to the 'wider responsibilities of higher education institutions for maintaining, developing and transmitting the cultural heritage of Europe and its Member States and for mobilising the creativity of people to advance the boundaries of knowledge, in the humanities as well as in science and technology' [3.4, pp. 1–2]. A number of factors were identified in the same document as influencing higher education in the Community: the increasing pace of European integration and labour mobility following the completion of the internal market and the advance towards monetary and political union; the impact of scientific and technological advances for economic and daily life; the enlargement of the Community and increasing opportunities for co-operation, partnership and mutual support both within Europe and on the world scene. These changes were expected to have an impact on the level and mix of skills required by the workforce, and thus on the form that education and training took, if skill shortages were to be avoided, and competitiveness was to be maintained. The conclusions of a meeting of the Council and of the Ministers for Education in 1993 'on furthering an open European space for cooperation within higher education' [3.6] stressed the demands that the greater mobility due to result from European union would place on educational policy. Access, quality and relevance of studies were identified as areas requiring particular attention.

Documents such as these make it possible to identify two major dimensions of the Union's policy objectives in the 1990s. From the economic point of view, the aim was to promote quality education, vocational training and retraining, designed to ensure the supply of multiskilled, polyvalent and mobile workers, capable of operating on a European scale and of adapting to meet changing labour market needs. From the social perspective, the Union was seeking to 'secure equality of opportunity for young people to develop their talents and skills without regard to their financial means, social class, gender, ethnic origin, or geographical location of residence' [3.4, p. 8].

Mutual recognition of qualifications

As in other areas of social policy, over the years the focus of interest in education and training shifted progressively from harmonization to co-operation and exchange of information and experience, but not before much effort had been expended comparing the content and level of qualifications across the Community, in an attempt to reach agreement over transferability between member states. The overall shift in education and training policy did not mean that the original aim of achieving mutual recognition of qualifications had been forgotten. Although the charter specified that the intention was not to harmonize the content and duration of education and training systems across member states, it reiterated the initial objective of the EEC Treaty by proposing that obstacles to mobility arising from the non-recognition of diplomas or equivalent occupational qualifications should be eliminated [1.10, §3]. A likely practical effect of actions, such as the mutual recognition of qualifications, would be 'to stimulate movements towards convergence in the training for particular professions' [3.4, p. 6].

Whereas the completion of the internal market was heralded as marking the advent of a new era of enhanced mobility of human capital and labour, harmonization and convergence within the Community, most of the measures resulting from the Single European Act (SEA) of 1986 [1.5] with reference to recognition of qualifications had already been initiated before that date. A large number of directives relevant to the harmonization of the professions had become statutory before 1986. Since 1964, about 60 sectoral directives had been adopted, ensuring the mutual recognition of conditions for access to particular occupations. In many cases, the directives sought to enable recognition of work experience acquired in another member state. Between 1964 and 1982, directives were issued covering industry and crafts, the retail trade, personal services, such as restaurants, bars and hotels, food industries and drinks production, wholesale trade in coal, trade in toxic products, itinerant activities, insurance agents and brokers, transport agents and hairdressers. Occupations involving the transport of goods or passengers by road were granted freedom of establishment and freedom to provide services, as stipulated in the EEC Treaty.

For other occupations, such as the health professions, a more complex set of measures was needed to cover the conditions under which the relevant occupation could be exercised. Two directives were required for each occupation: the first to co-ordinate and harmonize training, covering both quality (content) and quantity (number of years and hours of study); the second to establish the automatic recognition of diplomas conforming to Community norms. Minimum standards were imposed, leaving each country to determine additional expectations, but without requiring that they should be met. The directives were binding but, in order to leave room for flexibility, they did not go into the details of education and training provision.

Co-ordination and mutual recognition directives were issued between 1976 and 1985, covering doctors, nurses, dentists, veterinary surgeons, midwives, accountants, architects and pharmacists. Seventeen years of negotiations were needed before architects with specified diplomas were granted the right to establishment and to exercise their profession in another member state in 1985. Where important differences existed between the types of education concerned, compensatory requirements could be imposed. Professionals in regulated activities were given the right to establish themselves in another member state, subject to fulfilling the requirements of the host country by undertaking a period of adaptation or undergoing aptitude tests. For lawyers, recognition concerned not the diploma but the status of lawyer as recognized in the country of origin. The directive laid down conditions for the provision of services and the rules to be observed (Séché, 1994).

These lengthy and abortive attempts at harmonization for individual professions progressively gave way to a more global approach, as exemplified by Council Directive 89/48/EEC 'on a general system for the recognition of higher-education diplomas awarded on completion of professional education and training of at least three years' duration' [3.2], which came into force in 1991. The directive applied to all diplomas not covered by sectoral directives involving higher education and training of at least three years. The same principle was adopted in Directive 92/51/EEC issued in 1992, which extended recognition to other post-secondary qualifications and training courses previously excluded, and was later supplemented by Directive 95/43/EC [3.5].

Whereas equivalence is generally understood to refer to a detailed comparison of the individual elements constituting a programme of study, recognition involves a more global evaluation of the whole of a student's education, taking account of the function and overall level of academic study for the purposes of admission to further study or employment. The directives were intended to operate on a case-by-case basis, relying on mutual confidence between member states and assuming comparability between levels of education and training. By the early 1990s, the necessary steps had thus been taken at the legislative level to comply with formal provisions for the mutual recognition of qualifications, as stipulated in the EEC Treaty and the Community charter.

Adapting education and training in a changing society

Unlike many other areas of social affairs, the Treaty on European Union [1.6] addressed the issue of education and training directly rather than relegating it to the Protocol and Agreement on Social Policy (see Chapter 1). Chapter 3 of title VIII in the main body of the treaty was devoted to education, vocational training and youth, and became title XI in the revised version of the EC Treaty [1.8]. Article 128 in the original EEC Treaty was replaced by two new articles (149 and 150) in the consolidated EC Treaty. They set out the Community's commitment to encouraging quality education through co-operation between member states, and reaffirmed that individual member states were to retain responsibility for the content of programmes and the organization of their educational and vocational systems. Cultural and linguistic diversity were to be respected, and even promoted according to article 151 under a new title XII on culture. The aims expressed were wide ranging: to develop the European dimension in education through language teaching and dissemination; to encourage the mobility of students and teachers, including the recognition of qualifications and periods of study in another country; to promote co-operation between educational institutions; to develop the exchange of information and experience on common issues, of young people and socio-educational instructors, and of distance learning (article 149). Vocational training policy was intended, in addition, to ease the process of adaptation to industrial change, and to improve initial and continuing training, with a view to assisting entry and re-entry into the labour market and access to vocational training, as well as stimulating co-operation among training establishments, or between them and firms (article 150). Both articles allowed for the Council to act to shape policy content, in the case of article 149 by adopting incentive measures and recommendations, and in the case of article 150 by adopting measures to contribute to the achievement of its objectives. The wording of article 123 of the original EEC Treaty on the European Social Fund was also revised (article 146 in the consolidated EC Treaty), by adding a reference to vocational training and retraining as the means of helping workers to adapt to industrial change. The treaty revisions in these three articles thus provided a legal framework for proposing co-operative actions in the area of education and training, supported by financial incentives.

A green paper on the European dimension of education [3.7], issued in 1993 shortly before the treaty came into force, seized the opportunity to stimulate discussion about future action. It identifed areas where the Union could complement the efforts of member states and bring added value to the development of quality in education. The 1994 white paper on European social policy further demonstrated the Commission's commitment to investing in education and training as 'one of the essential requirements for the competitiveness of the Union as well as for the cohesion of our societies' [1.15, p. 15].

The white paper on growth, competitiveness and employment, published in the same year, recognized that education and training alone could not provide the answer to the immediate challenges facing the Union, but they were presented as a significant element in the emergence of a new development model in the longer term [3.8, p. 133]. The member states were of the opinion that training, both initial and continuing, was an instrument of active labour market policy, and that investment in human resources through lifelong learning was necessary to increase competitiveness. The white paper recommended that member states should develop training policies involving public authorities, business and the social partners, and that fiscal incentives should be used to reallocate resources from unemployment compensation to training. Action was to be promoted at Community level to extend existing programmes and regulations, with a view to developing further the European dimension of education. Emphasis was placed on the need for innovation, exchange of experience and information on good practice, mutual recognition of qualifications and skills, and also the process of lifelong learning [3.8, pp. 135–8].

The momentum was maintained and reinforced by the 1995 white paper on education and training [3.9], which stressed their value to both individuals and society. It argued strongly for a European approach to education in the context of globalization, the spread of new technologies and enlargement, as a means of preserving diversity and providing a focal point for co-operation between the Union and member states. The white paper set out guidelines for building a learning society on the basis that education and training are vital not only for the Union's competitiveness but also to preserve its social model and avoid social divisiveness between those with and without knowledge [3.9, p. 40]. Special emphasis was placed on the need to promote the European dimension in education and training 'to avoid the risk of a watered-down European society' [3.9, p. 29]. To this end, the white paper identified five main objectives, and presented proposals for achieving them: to encourage the acquisition of new knowledge; to bring school and the business sector closer together; to combat exclusion; to develop proficiency in three European languages; and to treat capital investment and investment in training on an equal basis.

The white paper opened with a statement that education and training have 'emerged as the latest means for tackling the employment problem' [3.9, p. 1], but it also commented that they cannot solve the problem alone. While article 125 under title VIII on employment in the consolidated version of the EC Treaty [1.8] referred simply to the importance of promoting a 'skilled and trained and adaptable workforce', the Council's employment guidelines [1.18] made training a central plank in the strategy for improving employability, and for easing both the transition from school to work and the return to work.

The position at the end of the 1990s, confirmed in a Commission communication, entitled 'Towards a Europe of knowledge' [3.10], was that education and training were strongly anchored in treaty commitments underpinning the economic goals of European union. When the terms of the Community charter are read in conjunction with the revised and renumbered articles 149 and 150 of the consolidated version of the EC Treaty, it is clear, nonetheless, that education and training policies, while firmly on the agenda, were being handled with the usual caution characteristic of the Council's approach to social affairs. The Union continued to be concerned primarily with promoting co-operation between member states through programmes aimed at encouraging mobility and the exchange of information. According to the treaty, the intention was not to interfere with national education systems, nor to use the legislative channel to bring pressure to bear on member states to persuade them to harmonize systems. Provision was, however, made for incentives to encourage member states to achieve the Union's objective of building a dynamic European education area.

UNION INITIATIVES ON EDUCATION AND TRAINING

Statements from the Council and the Commission on education and training have constantly emphasized the importance of the European dimension and of broadening the understanding of other cultures. A number of programmes have been established since the mid-1980s to encourage mobility of students and researchers in Europe, with a view to providing opportunities for exposure to different languages and cultures as part of the learning experience.

Mobility of scholars within Europe is not a new idea. Of all institutions, universities have one of the longest traditions of co-operation dating back to the Middle Ages, when they shared a *lingua franca* (Latin) and the itinerant scholar was a common phenomenon. Yet, over the centuries, national higher education systems have tended to diverge, with the effect that they display quite marked differences in their aims and objectives, structures, programmes and qualifications. Having formally recognized that 'Blanket harmonisation or standardization of the educational system is entirely undesirable' [3.3, p. 4], the Union has taken as its objective 'to improve the overall quality of educational provision by bringing the different systems into a long-term process of contact, cooperation and concertation and by avoiding unnecessary divergences which would otherwise impede the free movement of persons and ideas' [3.3, pp. 4–5]. More specifically, co-operation is seen as essential in developing a commitment to lifelong learning based on quality and solidarity. One means of achieving closer co-operation has been by devising arrangements whereby educational reforms and restructuring within member states are carried out in full awareness of the wealth of experience accumulated across the Community.

The aim of improving opportunities for vocational training has resulted in a number of programmes to encourage the mobility of students, with the explicit objectives of promoting shared democratic values, increasing the understanding of the multicultural dimension of the Community and preparing young people for European citizenship [3.3, p. 5]. As Director of the Task Force for Human Resources, Education, Training and Youth, Hywel Jones (1990, p. 9) presented education as the 'binding force for cooperation and partnership in all other sectors', stressing the importance of 'mutual understanding' and the 'capacity to work together', which these programmes were intended to stimulate. Patrick Venturini (1989, pp. 29, 38), when a member of the Lacroix Group of advisers to the Commission in the late 1980s, went so far as to describe a students' Europe as one of the 'Beacons for a European Social Area'.

The programmes launched over the years can be divided into four main overlapping categories, outlined below, that broadly cover the objectives contained in the amended EC Treaty: programmes for collecting and disseminating information about education and training arrangements across the Union designed to provide a better understanding of other national systems; programmes designed to encourage mobility of students and young people, and promote co-operation between educational institutions in different member states, with a view to extending knowledge of Europe and its languages, and adding a European dimension to education and training; programmes providing work experience and vocational training in another national setting in order to enhance social and economic integration and promote co-operation between educational institutions and industry; programmes concerned with the need to adapt to new technologies and extend opportunities for collaboration in research and development. Together, these programmes have established wide-ranging opportunities for cross-border participation.

Information on education and training

In 1975, the Council set up a special agency, the European Centre for the Development of Vocational Training (Cedefop), as an information network to increase and improve the circulation of information on education policy. The agency was originally located in Berlin. Then, following a decision by national governments in 1993, it was moved to Thessaloniki. The Eurydice education information network was set up a few years later and came into operation in 1981, with responsibility for developing a data bank on education and training. While recognizing the diversity of education systems in member states, the Council wanted to ensure that it would not become an obstacle to the free movement of people. Cedefop was charged with providing information in all the Community languages, involving a process that was both costly and laborious. The decision in the 1980s to pursue the recognition of vocational qualifications for occupations through a more general directive, similar to that for professional occupations, can be seen as a means of avoiding the problems associated with trying to standardize different national practices with regard to qualifications and training.

Despite the efforts of Cedefop and Eurydice to underpin the programme of educational co-operation within the Community, in its 1989 communication on education and training [3.3, p. 15], the Commission noted that national governments were continuing to implement major educational reforms without systematic reference to practices in other member states and without adequate consideration of the implications for different systems. Therefore, it recommended that arrangements should be made to ensure a regular flow of information on experience across the Community and that a forum should be provided for co-ordinating discussion of policy issues, with technical assistance from Eurydice. To meet this commitment, Cedefop and Eurydice were given the task of compiling information on the structure of education and initial training systems for young people across EU member states [3.11], and Eurostat, the Union's statistical agency, publishes regular updates of statistical indicators on education [3.12].

Mobility and co-operation between institutions

The Exchange of Young Workers Programme was one of the earliest Community actions, dating back to 1964, in compliance with article 50 of the EEC Treaty, which invited member states to encourage the exchange of young workers within the framework of a joint programme. The Community's programme for the Vocational Training of Young People and their Preparation for Adult and Working Life (Petra), set up in 1988, was another response to this particular need. It involved placements or exchanges for young people undergoing training and a network of transnational partnerships and initiatives for young people.

In the late 1980s, several programmes, such as the European Community Action Scheme for the Mobility of University Students, named after the sixteenth-century humanist scholar and priest Desiderius Erasmus, were designed to foster co-operation without requiring harmonization. Awarding bodies were called upon to recognize formally the period of training in another member state, but each country remained free to decide on the content and organization of its own programmes in respect of the principle of subsidiarity, as reaffirmed in the treaties. In 1984, a network of National Academic Recognition Information Centres (Naric) was established, subsequently co-ordinated by the Erasmus bureau, to provide information on the recognition of qualifications across member states and of periods of study in other member states or countries in the European Free Trade Association (EFTA). The European Community Course Credit Transfer System (Ects) was set up in 1989/90 to enable students to undertake all or part of their higher education in another member state.

The aim of the Youth for Europe programme was to extend opportunities provided by Erasmus to countries or categories of young people that were under-represented in student exchanges or whose language was less widely spoken. The Lingua programme was introduced by the Commission as a response to the realization that foreign languages should be an essential part of European education and training and that inadequate knowledge of languages was a major obstacle to mobility as well as a handicap in international trade. The Trans-European Mobility Scheme for University Studies (Tempus) extended exchanges to Central and Eastern Europe from 1991.

The Socrates programme was launched in 1995 to build on the previous generation of programmes. The first phase ran from 1995 to 1999, and a second phase was planned for 2000–04. The aim of Socrates was to strengthen the European dimension of education at all levels, in particular through the development of language learning, the promotion of co-operation by encouraging exchanges, the removal of obstacles to mobility by recognizing diplomas and periods of study abroad, and the encouragement of innovation, particularly in the field of new technologies. Within the programme, a variety of elements was identified, each targeting a specific activity or level of education. For example, in phase II, Comenius was aimed at the European dimension of school education, covering transnational partnerships between schools, the education of the children of migrant workers and teacher training activities. Erasmus continued to deal with exchanges in higher education. Grundtvig focused on European co-operation in relation to educational pathways for young people without formal educational qualifications. Lingua continued to contribute to the goal of maintaining linguistic diversity. Atlas covered open and distance learning and the use of new technologies in language learning. Provision was made for accompanying measures such as information campaigns and dissemination activities. From 1997, the programme was extended to associated countries in Central and Eastern Europe.

Phase III of Youth for Europe for the period 1995–99 covered young people aged between 15 and 25. It extended the scope of earlier measures, while at the same time providing positive action for disadvantaged young people. Five main areas of action were identified: intra-

Community activities directly involving young people; youth workers; co-operation between member states over the exchange of experience; exchanges with non-member countries; and information for young people and youth research.

New technologies, training and co-operation between education and industry

Several action programmes were created in response to the need of the workforce to master technological change through a partnership between education and industry. A programme in the Field of Vocational Training and Technological Change (Eurotecnet) was set up in 1985 and formalized in 1990. The programme on Cooperation between Universities and Enterprises regarding Training in the Field of Technology (Comett), another of the Community's flagship programmes, was launched in 1986. Both programmes recognized the blurring of the boundaries between jobs under the pressures of technological change, as well as the need to introduce young people to new technologies, not only while they are in full-time compulsory education but also once they begin initial training.

The 1991 action programme for the Development of Continuing Vocational Training in the European Community (Force) was designed to encourage information exchange and good practices. In recognition of the problems that women have in gaining access to training, the European Network of Vocational Training Projects for Women (Iris) was established in 1988 to meet the specific needs of women. The aim was to develop both a methodology on women's vocational training and evaluation tools. A further impetus was given to equal opportunities for women in education and training under the provisions of the Community charter. The New Opportunities for Women (Now) initiative, which was included in the third medium-term Community action programme on equal opportunities for women and men [6.11] in 1991, was intended to offer member states opportunities for cofunding actions. All the action programmes implemented in the 1990s contained an equal opportunities statement. However, as Teresa Rees (1998, pp. 132–3) points out, most of the applicants' guidelines did not.

Drawing on the experience gained from implementing earlier programmes, in 1994 the Commission launched phase I of a new initiative on vocational training, called Leonardo da Vinci. Phase II covered the period 2000–04. The programme combined Force, Petra, Eurotecnet and Lingua. It had been developed in conjunction with the Union's structural funds, and was designed to rationalize and streamline existing actions and improve their effectiveness on the basis of a common vocational training policy. The aim was to improve the social and occupational integration of young people by enhancing their employability, while expanding and developing access to high quality continuing training and lifelong skills.

In keeping with the principle of subsidiarity and in recognition of the diversity of systems, the action programme took account of the need to ensure that, within a common framework of objectives, member states would be free to choose means appropriate to their situation. The measures proposed were intended to support national systems, arrangements and policies, innovative actions for the training market and the development of a European dimension in vocational training, while also encouraging the dissemination of best practice.

Together, these training programmes represented a substantial input of resources: 850 million euros for the first phase of Socrates, 126 million for Youth for Europe III and 620 million for Leonardo. Most of the schemes have proved to be administratively onerous to operate, and their success is difficult to evaluate, particularly in cases where the intention has been to heighten awareness of other cultures. In quantitative terms, the total number of beneficiaries is probably small in relation to the number of potential clients and the target figures. When they were introduced, Erasmus, Lingua and Youth for Europe were promoted as the Community's 'flagship' programmes [3.3, p. 3]. The target set for student mobility was that 10 per cent of all students should experience a period of training abroad. An estimated 127 000 students in the Union (representing about 1 per cent of the student population in higher education) and EFTA countries and over 10 000 teachers participate every year in mobility programmes. Another 40 000 young people take part in young people's exchange schemes under the Youth for Europe programme. Phase I of the Leonardo programme was expected to support about 17 600 young people undergoing initial training or in employment.

While the number of students undertaking part of their studies in another member state has been increasing over the years, so too has the total student population in the Union. By the mid-1990s, approximately 5.5 per cent of all students in EU member states were from another country, but only 1.9 per cent from elsewhere in the Union. Austria, Belgium and the United Kingdom recorded the largest proportion of nationals from another member state, with about 5 per cent. Finland and Portugal had the smallest proportion with 0.4 per cent [3.12, 1998, table

E1]. Despite the Commission's best efforts, during the 1990s the main obstacles to intra-European mobility were still identified as admission restrictions, language, recognition problems, practical, administrative and financial problems and inadequate information [3.4, pp. 25–7; 9.15] (see Chapter 9).

Research, development, training and mobility of researchers

EU-funded research and technological development are an important area of co-operation and mobility between member states. Since 1984, the Commission has managed a series of framework programmes, designed to strengthen the scientific and technological base of European industry, and improve the competitiveness of the European economy in the world market, by co-ordinating transnational research partnerships, and by disseminating and utilizing research findings. The budget devoted to the programmes increased almost six-fold between 1984 and 1998, when Framework Programme 4 came to an end. Framework Programme 5 (FP5) for the period 1998–2002 was allocated almost 15 billion euros, an amount much greater than for the other programmes discussed above, but it represented less than 4 per cent of all research and development expenditure in the Union.

Built into the general objectives of FP5 was a specifically social dimension aimed at 'improving the human research potential and the socio-economic knowledge base' [3.13]. This horizontal programme was responsible for supporting the training and mobility of researchers through Research Training Networks and Marie Curie Fellowships (allocated 858 million euros). It also incorporated a key action concerned with improving understanding of the structural changes taking place in European society, identifying ways of managing change and involving European citizens in shaping their own futures.

The implications of societal change for education and training were introduced as a research task and also as a cross-cutting theme in FP5. They provide a further insight into the Commission's thinking on the subject. Firstly, interest focused on ways of developing tolerance and understanding between different cultures, supporting the sociability of learners, developing a more active involvement of learners as citizens, and strengthening self-esteem. Secondly, ways were sought of preventing and addressing social inequality, marginalization and exclusion in education and training, and improving access to, and successful participation in, learning processes. Thirdly, the focus was the acquisition of new competencies, designed to enhance employability [3.13].

TRENDS IN EDUCATION AND TRAINING IN MEMBER STATES

Although directives on the mutual recognition of vocational and professional qualifications involved examining their content, European policy on education and training has not sought to influence national education systems, except indirectly by exposing educators and trainers to different approaches through the exchange and mobility programmes described in the previous section. The consolidated version of the EC Treaty [1.8, articles 149–50] explicitly ruled out all attempts to harmonize national legislation or to interfere with national practices in this area. The non-interventionist stance may be attributed to two factors in particular. Firstly, member states have resisted supranational legislation in areas where they consider national sovereignty to be paramount. Secondly, the experience of seeking to harmonize qualifications showed how difficult and counterproductive it would be to attempt to standardize education systems. In this section, some of the main trends in education and training arrangements across member states are examined with a view to determining whether national policies in this area are showing any signs of convergence in a context of increasing economic integration.

Participation in national education and training systems

In keeping with the spirit of European policy, all member states have invested heavily in the education and training of their young people. During the 1990s, at any one time, some 72 million pupils were in preprimary, primary and secondary education, and about 12 million were in higher education across the Union. Despite the fall in the proportion of younger people in the population due to lower birthrates (see Chapter 5), the percentage of 5–23-year-olds in education rose steadily during the 1980s and 1990s, reaching almost 80 per cent of the relevant generation by 1995/96 across member states [3.12, 1998, tables C1-1, C1-15–19].

Differences remain, however, between member states with regard to the length of compulsory schooling and the levels of participation at the end of the compulsory period. In the late 1990s, schooling began at the age of four in Luxembourg (two years' compulsory preschool education), at five in the Netherlands and the United Kingdom, and at six in all other member states, except Denmark, Finland and Sweden, where children started school at seven. In Belgium and France, preschool education was standard practice from the age of three. In Denmark,

Germany, Spain and Sweden, over 50 per cent of three-year-olds were at school. By the age of five, across the Union over 75 per cent of children were in schooling, with the exception of Finland, Portugal and Sweden. The minimum age for leaving full-time education also varied: from 15 in Austria, Greece, Ireland, Luxembourg and Portugal, to 16 in all other countries, except Italy where it was 14. Following a decree issued in 1999, school-leaving age in Italy was due to be raised (initially to 15), to satisfy the requirements of the Community charter [1.10, §20]. In Belgium and Germany, full-time education was compulsory up to the age of 15, and part-time up to 18, as was also the case in the Netherlands. In Austria, vocational training was standard practice from the age of 15 under the dual system or apprenticeship arrangements [3.12, 1998, tables A2, C1-1].

Lynne Chisholm (1992, pp. 131–8) has suggested a classification of education systems according to the stage at which pupils select or are selected for important transition routes which determine later participation rates. Among the countries in northern Europe, in the early 1990s, the British education system was characterized by relatively early selection and low participation rates in further and higher education, whereas Belgium and the Federal Republic of Germany exemplified early selection and high participation systems. France and the Netherlands selected later and retained slightly lower proportions of each age group in education and training. Denmark provided an example of late selection and high participation.

Towards the end of the decade, the extension of schooling and vocational training meant that, across the Union, almost 85 per cent of all 16–18-year-olds were remaining in education and training after completing compulsory schooling. The proportion ranged from over 90 per cent in Belgium, Denmark, Finland, France, Germany, Luxembourg and Sweden to less than 80 per cent in Italy, Portugal, Spain and the United Kingdom. The proportion of the 19–22 and 23–24 age groups in education and training had reached 51 and 28 per cent, respectively, across the Union by the late 1990s, due mainly to the lengthening of the period of study in response to labour market conditions (job shortages and the growing demand for qualifications). Again the situation was subject to national variations: the rate in Belgium, Denmark, France and the Netherlands reached 60 per cent, or more, for 19–22-year-olds, compared to 32 per cent in the United Kingdom. Over 40 per cent of 23–24-year-olds were still in education in Denmark and Finland, but less than 20 per cent in Greece, Ireland and the United Kingdom [3.14, 1999, table 024].

The proportion of 19–22-year-olds in education has, moreover, been increasing at a faster rate for women than for men, with the result that over 52 per cent of women in this age group were continuing their education in the late 1990s, compared to 49 per cent of men. Overall, more women than men in the 23–24 age group were also remaining in the educational system [3.14, 1999, table 024]. With longer schooling and higher education and training, the gender balance had therefore shifted. Whereas at primary level boys outnumbered girls in all member states (except Sweden where the number was the same), mainly because more boys are born than girls, by the upper secondary level, girls outnumbered boys in Finland, France, Ireland, Portugal, Spain, Sweden and the United Kingdom [3.12, 1998, tables C1-15, C1-18]. Only in Austria, the Netherlands and the United Kingdom did men classified as being in education outnumber women in the 19–22 age group. The disparity in favour of women was particularly marked in Finland, Spain and Sweden [3.14, 1999, table 024].

Despite efforts at EU level to promote the study of technical subjects, particularly among women, in the 1990s in most member states, and especially in Greece, women were more often undergoing general rather than vocational training at upper secondary level. In higher education, they were more likely to study subjects in the humanities, applied arts and medical science. Business studies and law were more evenly divided between the sexes, while mathematics and computer science were more popular with men. The disparity was greater still for engineering and architecture, especially in Finland (Eurostat, 1997c, tables 2–3).

Although a Council Directive recognizes qualifications based on three years of higher education after the school-leaving certificate as being equivalent throughout the Community, differences in the arrangements for upper secondary level education and training, in combination with disparities in the nature, structure and content of university higher education, make it difficult for employers to interpret qualifications obtained in another member state. While British students, for example, routinely graduate after three years, and leave higher education by the age of 21 or 22 with a qualification which is recognized in the United Kingdom as an indication of general intellectual and academic ability, it is far from unusual for students in Austria, France, Germany, Greece, Italy, Portugal or Spain to complete study for very specialized higher education qualifications at, or after, the age of 24, particularly if a period of compulsory national service has to be intercalated. However, data on age at entry to tertiary education show that as many as 25 per cent of all new entrants to this level of education in the United Kingdom are aged 30 or over, whereas in France, Greece and Ireland, very few new entrants are aged over 21, indicating differences in lifelong learning opportunities from one member state to another [3.15, 1998, table 6].

Vocational training and national labour markets

Many attempts have been made to construct typologies portraying the relationship between the labour market and education. The linkage that has developed between schools, firms and labour markets has been shown to take a number of different forms. It may be market led and industry based as in Italy and the United Kingdom. It may be training led and school based as in Belgium, Denmark, France, the Netherlands and Sweden. Or it may be training led and industry based as in Austria and Germany. These interlinkages have arisen as the result of elaborate historical trade-offs between social partners, central and regional government, different pressure groups, taxpayers and workers themselves, each with their own objectives and time horizons (Drake, 1994). The outcome is that the effectiveness of initial vocational and educational training may be influenced by culturally determined conditions, and job opportunities for young people can consequently differ significantly according to the social and economic environment of the country or region in which they live.

Despite these underlying differences in approach, by the late 1990s, all member states made provision through the school system for vocational training, and they were progressively incorporating practical work experience and 'second chance' and 'alternance' schemes to help smooth the transition from school to work. Across the Union, entirely school-based initial vocational training remained the most common arrangement. Efforts were being made to involve enterprises in the organization of vocational education and training programmes, resulting in more than half of vocational training being delivered, at least partly, at the workplace. In Austria, a significant proportion of training was at the workplace, whereas in the Netherlands, France and particularly Sweden, it took place essentially in an education or training institution. In Finland, training was carried out exclusively in institutions designated for that purpose. By contrast, Denmark and Germany were characterized by an arrangement whereby training was primarily 'on-and-off the job'. In the United Kingdom, where rates for training carried out in education or training institutions were at a level close to the EU average, a relatively large proportion of vocational training was also on-and-off the job [3.15, 1998, figure 7].

Data for the late 1990s across the Union show that the development of training provision for 15–19 year-olds was associated with a marked decline in employment rates for this age group. By 1997, the EU average was under 21 per cent. In Belgium, the level had fallen to below 5 per cent, and was under 10 per cent in France, Greece, Luxembourg and Spain. Notable exceptions were recorded in Denmark where the rate remained over 60 per cent and in the Netherlands and the United Kingdom where it was over 40 per cent. Employment rates for the 20–24 age group had fallen to almost 50 per cent across the Union, but with rates above 70 per cent in Denmark and the Netherlands, compared to less than 40 per cent in Italy and Spain [3.14, 1999, table 003].

Much of the comparative research undertaken in the 1980s on vocational education and training seemed to lead to the conclusion that Britain was trailing behind countries such as France and Germany in terms of the effectiveness of its training when measured by economic performance indicators. Britain, in particular, was criticized for its poor record on intermediate skills (Ryan, 1991, pp. 2–3). As more emphasis was placed on qualifications, the implication was that it would become increasingly difficult to find a job without a recognized qualification, and workers from the United Kingdom would be at a particular disadvantage in the European market place. Approaching the topic from a different angle, Robert Lindley (1991, p. 193) used Dutch evidence to question the assumption that skill shortages were developing as a result of inadequate training. In the Netherlands, the output of qualifications appeared to have increased more rapidly than the skill requirements of jobs, leading to the possible threat of over-qualification and what he described as 'educational crowding-out'. Lindley thus gave the lie to exaggerated claims about the 'burgeoning job content of the economy as a whole and the need for educational levels to rise to keep pace with the increasing sophistication of the modern world of work' (Lindley, 1991, p. 194). Similarly, the phenomenon of 'diploma inflation' has been identified in several member states. The tendency in most countries is to overproduce graduates and underproduce technicians, resulting in the 'downward filtering' (Lindley, 1991, p. 203) of able people and the placing of graduates in what were previously non-graduate jobs. Another effect of higher participation rates in education and training and rising occupational skills levels is that young people without academic and vocational qualifications tend to be stigmatized and marginalized (Kirsch, 1998, p. 4).

Labour Force Survey data for the late 1990s do not give a precise indication of the fit between qualifications and jobs, but they do suggest a close correlation between employment and educational level. Across the Union, employment rates for the 25–59 age group were more than 25 percentage points higher for tertiary-level education than for lower secondary-level qualifications. The disparity rose to more than 30 points in Belgium, Germany and Ireland. Overall, the impact of higher education on employment is greater for men than for women. At the lower level of attainment, women are also much less likely than men to be employed. The disparity in employment between the two levels is twice as large for women, reaching over 40 points in Belgium, Ireland and Italy [3.14, 1999, table 031]. Women may thus be affected more than men both by educational crowding out and by downward filtering.

THE IMPACT OF EUROPEAN POLICY ON NATIONAL EDUCATION AND VOCATIONAL TRAINING SYSTEMS

Since the signing of the EEC Treaty in 1957, the Community has progressively broadened its social remit. In the area of education and training, policy objectives have been extended to take account of the changing needs of the economy and of society at large. The demands of the labour market for more workers with a high level of knowledge and skills, as well as the ability to adapt to technological change, have stimulated action programmes designed to ensure that national education systems are equipped to respond not only to initial training requirements but also to the need for constant upgrading and updating of qualifications throughout working life. The growing emphasis on the importance of being able to operate across national and cultural boundaries has given a new impetus to the European dimension of education 'perceived as a practical economic necessity apart from its desirability on cultural and political grounds' [3.4, p. 40]. Within this context, the recognition of qualifications for academic and professional purposes can be interpreted as a necessary support for freedom of movement, which was a primary aim of the original treaty.

As in other areas of social policy at EU level, it is difficult to evaluate the success of policies for education and training or to assess their impact on national policy making. The Commission has clearly defined its role in this area: it sees itself essentially as a 'catalyst and facilitator of cooperative and common action' [3.4, p. 41], working in accordance with the principle of subsidiarity and respecting diversity of provision.

Although tangible results have been achieved at regulatory level in terms of the mutual recognition of qualifications and the increase in the number of students and young people who have had the opportunity to spend periods of study or gain work experience in other member states, and who might not otherwise have done so, the evidence is that the mobility of workers has not expanded commensurably, suggesting that acceptance of qualifications may not be the key factor in relocation of labour as originally believed (see Chapter 9).

The impact of European policy on the harmonization of education and training systems may also be much less than anticipated. It has been argued that, because the process of mutual recognition of qualifications involved close scrutiny of the structuring of occupations, it provoked a certain amount of convergence of concepts (Merle and Bertrand, 1993, p. 42). Some procedures have been called into question, for example the *numerus clausus* imposed in higher education subjects such as medicine in different member states, the professional qualifications required for practice or the mix of qualifications and work experience. As in other areas of European social policy, the growing importance of the principle of subsidiarity and the reluctance of the Union to legislate have encouraged a shift towards the idea of identifying common European standards, which can serve as reference points, irrespective of differences in national educational systems.

Awareness of educational and training practices in other member states has undoubtedly been enhanced, but here too it is not possible to demonstrate that greater cross-cultural knowledge and mutual recognition have necessarily resulted in the convergence of education and training systems. The very different national training traditions, as exemplified by the corporatist German dual system, or the British neo-liberal on-the-job system, would seem to reflect irreconcilable conceptions of training policy, demonstrating the extent to which national systems remain 'highly societally specific' (Milner, 1998, p. 175). The proportion of the population participating in post-compulsory secondary and higher education has been growing throughout the Union, and educational opportunities for women, in particular, have improved, but there is no convincing evidence to show that these changes can be attributed to the Union's legislation and action programmes, or that they have resulted in upwards convergence in terms of the quality of the labour force.

During the 1990s, a consensus did seem to be emerging among member states over the need for better co-ordination between education and vocational training systems and for closer association of the social partners in the design and delivery of training. By bridging the gap between economic and social policy, investment in human resources through quality education and training was being projected as an important component in the European social model and in a European identity, where 'the three essential requirements of social integration, the enhancement of employability and personal fulfilment, are not incompatible' [3.9, p. 4].

Box 3 Secondary legislation and official publications relating to education, training and employment

3.1 Resolution of the Council and of the Ministers of Education, meeting within the Council of 9 February 1976 comprising an action programme in the field of education (*OJ* C 38/1 19.2.76).

3.2 Council Directive 89/48/EEC of 21 December 1988 on a general system for the recognition of higher-education diplomas awarded on completion of professional education and training of at least three years' duration (*OJ* L19/16 24.1.89).

3.3 Communication from the Commission to the Council, Education and training in the European Community. Guidelines for the medium term: 1989–92 (COM(89) 236 final, 2 June 1989).

3.4 Memorandum from the Commission on higher education in the European Community (COM(91) 349 final, 5 November 1991).

3.5 Council Directive 92/51/EEC of 18 June 1992 on a second general system for the recognition of professional education and training to supplement Directive 89/48/EEC (*OJ* L 209/25 24.7.92); supplemented by Council Directive 95/43/EC of 25 July 1995 (*OJ* L 184/21 3.8.95).

3.6 Conclusions of the Council and of the Ministers for Education, meeting within the Council of 11 June 1993 on furthering an open European space for cooperation within higher education (*OJ* C 186/1 8.7.93).

3.7 Commission of the European Communities, Green paper on the European dimension of education (COM(93) 457 final, 29 September 1993).

3.8 European Commission, *White Paper. Growth, Competitiveness, Employment – the challenges and ways forward into the 21st century*, OOPEC, 1994.

3.9 Commission of the European Communities, White paper on education and training. Teaching and learning. Towards a learning society (COM(95) 590 final, 29 November 1995), OOPEC, 1994.

3.10 Commission Communication, Towards a Europe of knowledge (COM(97) 563 final, 12 November 1997).

3.11 Eurydice/Cedefop, *Structures of the Education and Initial Training Systems in the European Community*, OOPEC, 1995.
Available on-line at:
http://europa.eu.int/comm/dgs/education_culture/index_en.htm
http://europa.eu.int/comm/education/cedefop.html
http://www.eurydice.org
3.12 Eurostat, *Education across the European Union: statistics and indicators*, OOPEC (annual).
3.13 Framework Programme 5, horizontal programme 3:
http://www.cordis.lu/improving
3.14 Eurostat, *Labour Force Survey*, OOPEC (annual publication).
3.15 Eurostat, *A Social Portrait of Europe*, OOPEC (annual publication).

4 Improving Living and Working Conditions

The emphasis in the Community's and Union's treaties and charter on workers' rights and on the need to create conditions that would facilitate freedom of movement of labour between member states explains why issues concerned with the equalization of living and working conditions have always been high on the policy agenda. As with social security and educational qualifications, disparities between member states in the treatment of workers could be seen not only as a factor inhibiting mobility but also as a source of unfair competition. Therefore, the objective of achieving harmonization at the same time as the improvement of living and working conditions featured in the Treaty establishing the European Economic Community (EEC) [1.2]. It was retained in subsequent treaties and in the Community charter of the Fundamental Social Rights of Workers in 1989 [1.10], albeit with the accent on working, rather than living, conditions.

In the EEC founder member states, industrial accidents and occupational diseases were among the first contingencies to be covered by national employment insurance. Since industrial health problems had long been a concern of the original member states, the Community's role in industrial welfare was primarily to try and stimulate interest in co-ordinating action to protect workers and thereby remove barriers to the mobility of goods, services and labour. The rights of workers to a decent standard of living and a high level of protection at the workplace have continued to be given priority. Progressively, the areas encompassed under the general heading of living and working conditions have been clarified and widened to include health and safety at work, working hours, employment contracts, conditions governing collective redundancies and bankruptcies, information, consultation and participation of workers, the environment and public health.

As the Union's remit was extended (see Chapter 1), the improvement of living and working conditions remained firmly on the policy agenda. Although the approach has tended to be cautious for reasons that will become more apparent in this chapter, living and working conditions provide another example of the way in which policy can be moved forward at European level through the legislative process, action programmes and information campaigns.

The first part of the chapter looks at the development of Community policy, with particular reference to health and safety at work, work-time arrangements and public health. Practices in individual member states are then compared, with a view to assessing the extent to which the Union's action may have encouraged member states to adopt common standards in line with the developing European social model.

COMMUNITY POLICY ON LIVING AND WORKING CONDITIONS

The 1951 Treaty establishing the European Coal and Steel Community (ECSC) [1.1] set a number of precedents for the six original member states. Article 3(e) stated the aim of promoting improved working conditions and an improved standard of living for workers in the coal and steel industries while also seeking harmonization. The 1957 Treaty establishing the European Atomic Energy Community (EAEC) [1.3] devoted ten of its 225 articles to health and safety. Articles 30–9 set out the basic standards to be observed for the protection of the health of workers and the general public against the dangers of ionizing radiations, and stipulated the legal procedures for ensuring they were harmonized and respected. This section examines how the themes of living and working conditions have developed in Community law, policy statements and action programmes since the 1950s.

Living and working conditions in the EEC Treaty

Several references were made in the EEC Treaty to the need to improve living and working conditions, although no clear guidance was given about how equalization between member states should be defined and achieved. Extending article 3(e) of the ECSC Treaty, article 117 affirmed 'the need to promote improved working conditions and an improved standard of living for workers, so as to make possible their harmonisation while the improvement is being maintained'. Such improvements were expected to ensue automatically from the functioning of the common market, both through harmonization of social systems and from procedures for approximation of provisions as laid down by law, regulation or administrative action (see Chapter 2).

Among the tasks assigned to the Community, article 2 of the EEC Treaty referred to 'an accelerated raising of the standard of living'. Article 36 included an oblique reference to 'the protection of health and life of humans' in the context of the customs union. In addition, one of the objectives set for the European Social Fund was to improve employment opportunities for workers, thereby contributing to the raising of their standard of living (article 123).

The areas identified in article 118 of the treaty for close co-operation covered employment, labour law and working conditions, basic and advanced vocational training, prevention of occupational accidents and diseases, social security, occupational hygiene, the right of association and collective bargaining. Article 120 dealt with the equivalence of paid holiday schemes. The key aspects of working conditions were thus recognized as social policy issues.

The treaty did not specify the standards to be achieved, nor did it set a timetable for implementation. Notwithstanding these limitations, in the field of industrial welfare, economic interests provided a powerful incentive for Community action in the early years of the EEC. Common standards of protection against industrial hazards were needed to prevent any one country from gaining a competitive edge and to avoid a situation where migrant workers might be treated differently from one member state to another. In the 1960s, studies were commissioned on topics such as occupational diseases, industrial safety, the influence of human factors in the prevention of accidents, and the health and protection of women and young people. Programmes were organized to enable senior management to visit other member states with the intention of alerting them to practices elsewhere, and safety consciousness raising exercises were initiated. A series of directives and recommendations was drafted in an attempt to standardize practices and to protect and compensate workers in the areas of industrial medical services and diseases, paying special attention to young workers and working mothers in industry. Substantial progress was made during the 1960s in reaching agreement over safety standards, thus creating a sound basis for future legislation.

Action programmes to improve living and working conditions

Industrial health and safety were already under consideration in 1974 when the Commission presented its social action programme (see Chapter 1). In the same year, the Council set up an Advisory Committee on Safety, Hygiene and Health Protection at Work. Its brief included issues such as training, research, data collection, provision in sectors subject to special hazards and groups of workers at risk, as well as the harmonization of regulations for products and processes. The Commission extended its interest to medical research and common action on emerging health problems, such as bad environmental conditions and stress. An environmental protection programme was prepared at the same time as the social action programme in response to growing public concern about pollution from noxious materials, and also in recognition of the fact that pollutants do not respect national borders.

In 1975, the Commission signalled its commitment to this rapidly developing policy area by establishing the European Foundation for the Improvement of Living and Working Conditions in Dublin. The Foundation was assigned the task of monitoring progress, undertaking analyses, studies and research. It was also made responsible for disseminating knowledge on a systematic and scientific basis concerning the consequences of economic development, diminishing natural resources and environmental quality, as well as persistent social and regional disparities in living and working conditions. Its brief included advising Community institutions and other policy-making bodies in member states on objectives and guidelines for action.

Living and working conditions in the Single European Act

The next landmark in policy for the improvement of living and working conditions was the Single European Act (SEA) of 1986 [1.5]. A new article 118a advised member states to 'pay particular attention to encouraging improvements, especially in the working environment, as regards the health and safety of workers'. It reiterated the aim of harmonizing conditions, but introduced the important principle of qualified majority voting for decisions on legislative action in this area (see Chapter 1). Article 100a confirmed that health, safety, environmental and consumer protection were to be governed by qualified majority voting and added that 'a high level of protection' should be taken as a base. While facilitating the legislative process, article 118a limited the scope for Community intervention to avoid imposing administrative, financial and legal constraints that might adversely affect small and medium-sized undertakings. Nor were member states to be prevented from maintaining or introducing more stringent measures to protect working conditions. Article 118b referred to the need to develop the dialogue between management and labour at European level, one of the planks of Jacques Delors' negotiating platform (see Chapter 1).

The SEA coincided with a spate of action in the area of public health, even though the Community had no authority in this field. In 1987, for example, the Commission launched the 'Europe against Cancer' programme aimed at reducing mortality from cancer. The main thrust of policy was the promotion of co-operation in the area of research and dissemination of information about the most effective national practices. The programme contained actions for prevention, information, education and training, leading to proposals for a ban on smoking in public places, rules on the maximum tar content of cigarettes, and the labelling and advertising of tobacco products [4.3].

Living and working conditions in the Community charter

Despite the action programmes of the 1970s, the Community had been reluctant to intervene in the industrial bargaining process. Delors' attempt to launch the social dialogue was slow to gather momentum, but labour relations progressively came to the fore, even if the input of the social partners to Community policy tended to lack 'purpose and rigour' (Teague and McClelland, 1991, p. 20).

By the late 1980s, worker participation and consultation over changes in working conditions and work organization were high on the collective bargaining agenda, as illustrated by the Community charter of the Fundamental Social Rights of Workers of 1989. Several articles in the charter focused on the improvement of living and working conditions, presented as an important element in policies for equalizing opportunities and promoting mobility. The charter provided a firm statement of the Community's objectives in this area:

> The completion of the internal market must lead to an improvement in the living and working conditions of workers in the European Community. This process must result from an approximation of these conditions while the improvement is being maintained, as regards in particular the duration and organisation of working time and forms of employment other than open-ended contracts, such as fixed term contracts, part-time working, temporary work and seasonal work. [1.10, §7]

In addition, the reference in the EEC Treaty to maintaining 'the existing equivalence between paid holiday schemes' (article 120) was made more specific. The charter laid down the right of workers to a weekly rest period and to annual paid leave, stipulating that the duration 'must be harmonised in accordance with national practices while the improvement is being maintained' (§8).

In accordance with the general aim of improving living and working conditions, Community policy on health protection and safety at the workplace was also set out in §19 of the charter, which stated that: 'Every worker must enjoy satisfactory health and safety conditions in his [*sic*] working environment. Appropriate measures must be taken in order to achieve further harmonization of conditions in this area while maintaining the improvements made.' The same paragraph required that account should be taken of 'the need for the training, information, consultation and balanced participation of workers as regards the risks incurred and the steps taken to eliminate or reduce them'. The terms used to define levels of provision ('satisfactory' and 'appropriate') were unspecific, like those referring to social protection. As in §3, which covered freedom of movement and conditions of residence, and §8 on rest periods and annual leave, the objective of achieving harmonization was, however, made explicit (see Chapter 2).

Under a section on the protection of children and adolescents, the charter set out restrictions on working hours for young people and the prohibition of night work under the age of 18 (§22). In recognition of the different practices adopted across the Community, and in accordance with the subsidiarity principle, exceptions could be made to conform to the stipulations in national legislation.

The Community charter thus confirmed and reinforced the general aims set out more than 30 years previously in the EEC Treaty. Work organization and the employment contract were presented as major components in the improvement of living and working conditions and as areas where the Community was competent to act.

Implementation of the Community charter's provisions

Although the charter did not have binding force, it did empower the Commission to submit proposals for initiatives under the terms of the treaties, with a view to adopting the legal instruments needed for effective implementation within the context of the completion of the Single European Market (SEM).

The programme for implementing the charter [1.11] demonstrated the capacity of the Commission to work within the constraints of national and sectoral interests in taking forward action in this area. It included a series of quite specific proposals for binding instruments in fields where safety is a cause of concern. Council Directive 89/391/EEC 'on the introduction of measures to encourage improvements in the safety and health of workers at work' [4.1], issued in 1989, laid down the main principles to be applied in other directives on the subject. It covered all sectors of activity and all workers except the self-employed and domestic servants. Employers were to take a much more proactive stance. Their obligations were clearly set out. Not only were they required to ensure health and safety of workers in every aspect of work, and to develop a health and safety policy, but they also had the duty of assessing and recording risks, informing and consulting workers, providing training and taking preventive measures. Workers were given the right to make proposals relating to health and safety and to appeal to stop work if in danger. In return, they had the duty to follow instructions from employers regarding health and safety and to report on potential dangers.

Following on from this framework directive, ten proposals were made to improve conditions for specific categories of workers. Council recommendations on occupational diseases were updated, and a regulation was proposed on the establishment of a European Agency for Health and Safety at Work. After receiving approval from the Council in 1994, the agency was set up in Bilbao. It was given the task of collecting and disseminating technical, scientific and economic information on health and safety at work, promoting the exchange of information and co-operation between member states, and contributing to the development of protective action programmes.

The year March 1992 to March 1993 was designated 'European year of safety, hygiene and health protection at the workplace'. It was a response to the realization that, despite the efforts made in this area and the problem of collecting reliable data, of approximately 120 million workers in the Community about 10 million suffered an industrial accident or occupational injury every year [1.14, p. 65]. The aim was to alert member states to the importance of the social and economic aspects of problems concerning safety, hygiene and health at work and to make workers, employers and young people more aware of the risks at the workplace and the action needed to deal with them.

The Commission took advantage of the provisions of article 118a of the SEA to bring forward legislation that had made little progress during the 1980s, thereby demonstrating how qualified majority voting can be exploited within the context of health and safety at work to introduce contentious legislation. Despite continuing British opposition, a draft proposal was brought forward in 1990 covering the organization of working time. The aim was to protect workers against excessively long working hours and against an organization of working time that could be detrimental to their health and safety [4.2]. It raised the issue of the harmful effects of practices introduced under the banner of flexibility. Directive 93/104/EC 'concerning certain aspects of the organization of working time' [4.10], which was eventually adopted in November 1993, laid down a set of minimum provisions not only for daily and weekly rest periods, but also for conditions relating to shift work, night work, and health and safety protection for workers subject to changes of rhythm in their working hours. The minimum daily rest period was set at 11 consecutive hours for a 24-hour period, and minimum paid holidays at four weeks. The maximum working week was fixed at an average of 48 hours. The definition of night work was extended to cover workers who occasionally worked at night, and provisions were made for health assessments. The Commission's concern to avoid creating problems for individual firms or sectors of activity with special needs, for example because their activities are subject to seasonal fluctuations, meant that a number of possibilities were left open for derogation, and consultation procedures were strengthened. Employers and representatives of workers were not, however, to be prevented from concluding collective agreements on the organization of working time, provided equivalent compensatory rest periods were granted.

The Commission had also been trying since the early 1980s to have proposals adopted on a related topic, atypical work, in its efforts to resolve the problems created by the rapid growth in the number of workers not covered by a standard open-ended full-time employment contract. The interests of atypical workers were dealt with indirectly by two Council directives in 1991. In Directive 91/383/EEC [4.4], a proposal was put forward as a measure for health and safety at work aimed at improving the working conditions of workers with a fixed duration employment relationship or a temporary employment relationship. Directive 91/533/EEC [4.5] made provision for a form of proof of an employment relationship, as a means of improving the transparency of the labour market in a context where more flexible forms of employment, such as part-time, distance working, home or teleworking, had become widespread and were tending to marginalize large sectors of the labour force. The purpose of the directive was to make clear to all workers for whom they were working and the essential conditions of the employment relationship.

A proposal for a directive concerning the protection at work of pregnant women, or women who have recently given birth, was also brought forward under article 118a within the meaning of the framework directive as a health and safety measure. Directive 92/85/EEC [4.7] covered not only exposure to agents liable to damage health but also the contentious issue of leave arrangements, duration of work and employment rights, which would most probably have prevented the passage of the proposal had it been subjected to unanimous voting.

Since the focus was on workers, the charter did not refer to public health. In 1991, however, the Commission launched a programme for 'Europe against AIDS', aimed at containing and combating the spread of the disease throughout the Community. A resolution of the Council and the Ministers for Health in the same year drew attention to the importance of health policy choices [4.6]. Member states were urged to work together to identify common problems and, if appropriate, develop common solutions, thereby preparing the way for the higher profile that was to be given to public health in the Maastricht Treaty.

Living and working conditions in the amended treaties

The Agreement on Social Policy, signed in 1992 by all member states except the United Kingdom and annexed to the Treaty on European Union, set out further details of European policy in the area of living and working conditions [1.6]. The provisions made were subsequently incorporated into the Treaty of Amsterdam in 1997 [1.7]. The consolidated version of the EC Treaty [1.8, article 137] confirmed that measures could be taken by qualified majority voting to improve the working environment and working conditions, to protect workers' health and safety, to promote information and consultation and equality between men and women, and to integrate persons excluded from the labour market. Unanimous voting was still required for matters concerning social security of workers, protection of employment contracts, representation, collective defence and codetermination, the employment conditions of third-country nationals and financial support for employment promotion. The right of association, to strike or impose lock-outs was explicitly excluded from the treaty provisions.

Council Directive 94/45/EC [4.11] on the establishment of works councils was the first directive adopted after the signing of the Agreement on Social Policy. Due to the British government's opt-out, the directive's stipulations did not apply to the United Kingdom. They concerned Community-scale undertakings with more than 1000 employees and at least two establishments in different member states, each employing at least 150 people, with the purpose of improving the right of employees to information and consultation.

During the 1980s, an attempt by the Commission to formulate a directive requiring the extension to part-time workers of the rules governing full-time workers had been blocked by the British government. Council Directive 97/81/EC [4.14] on part-time work was also finally concluded under a framework agreement between the social partners. Its main objective was to eliminate discrimination against part-time workers, by ensuring their rights on a *pro rata temporis* basis, with a view to encouraging greater flexibility in work-time organization in the interests of employees and management. Although the directive was binding as far as the results were concerned, it left national authorities to choose the form and methods to be used, and to introduce more favourable provisions if they so wished.

The revised treaties reinforced the Union's remit with regard to health and safety at work and working conditions, but they also extended its powers into an area that had been only indirectly alluded to in the original treaty. The Union's activities listed in the consolidated EC Treaty [1.8] included 'a contribution to the attainment of a high level of health protection' (article 3 §p). Article 152 of the new title XIII on public health set out the aim of ensuring a 'high level of human health protection…in the definition and implementation of all Community policies and activities', as exemplified by article 174 under title XIX on the environment. This aim was to be achieved by encouraging co-operation between member states and, if necessary, by lending support to their action (article 152 §2). As in other social areas, member states were to retain responsibility for co-ordinating their own policies and programmes and for the delivery of health and medical care, but the Commission was authorized to take initiatives to promote such co-ordination.

In the Maastricht Treaty, action at EU level was to take the form of research, health information and education, covering major health scourges such as drug dependence, an example subsequently removed by the Amsterdam Treaty, although a European Monitoring Centre for Drugs and Drug Addiction was established in Lisbon in 1994. Instead, a later section of article 152 (§4 subsections a and b) in the consolidated EC Treaty was expanded and reinforced, laying down the measures the Council was empowered to take to achieve the objectives specified in the article. The changes introduced reflected growing public concern during the 1990s over the spread of AIDS, the BSE crisis and the possible dangers to public health from genetically modified foods. A third subsection specified that incentive measures would be adopted to protect and improve human health but, in this case, harmonization of national laws and regulations was explicitly ruled out. The final paragraph of the article (§5) stressed, once more, the importance of respecting the responsibilities of member states for the organization and delivery of health services and medical care.

In a communication 'on the framework for action in the field of public health' [4.9], published in the year following the signing of the Maastricht Treaty, the Commission reiterated the need for member states to identify common objectives and goals, and set out the legal bases for action at EU level. In 1996, the European Parliament and the Council adopted a programme of Community action on health promotion, information, education and training within the framework for action in the field of public health for the period 1996–2000 [4.12]. The programme included actions on health promotion strategies and structures, specific prevention and health promotion measures, health information, health education and vocational training in public health and health promotion. At the same time, a third action plan to combat cancer (646/96/EC) and a programme of Community action on the prevention of AIDS (647/96/EC) and drug dependence (97/102/EC) were also adopted [4.12; 4.13]. All these actions were aimed at encouraging member states to co-operate in exchanging information, policies and programmes, and to co-ordinate their actions. Thus, they can be seen as part of the Community's overall health promotion strategy.

With the completion of the SEM, the signing of the Community charter, the revisions to the EEC Treaty, the framework directive on health and safety at work, and the many action programmes proposed by the Commission, the Union's competence in the broad area of living and working conditions had become far reaching. The introduction of qualified majority voting in the SEA for issues concerning health and safety at work and the improvement of the working environment meant that member states would more easily be able to implement any measures thought necessary. It also implied that attempts could be made to use the revised voting and consultation procedures to push forward proposals in the social field that would most probably have been rejected had unanimous voting been applied. The treaty revisions gave some impetus to Community action in the field of public health, moving it on from the focus on health and safety at work. By requiring that a high level of health protection should be ensured in the definition and implementation of all Community policies and activities, article 152 highlighted the need for member states to co-operate in obviating all sources of danger to human health.

The Commission sought to maintain the momentum by presenting a communication in 1998 'on the development of public health policy' [4.15], setting out the case for a fundamental revision to the Community's public health strategy in the face of new health threats, increasing pressures on health systems, the enlargement of the Union and the new treaty provisions. Three main strands were identified for future Community policy: improving information for the development of public health; reacting rapidly to threats to health; and tackling health determinants through health promotion and disease prevention. In all three areas, the Commission clearly marked out the role it would play in collecting, analysing and disseminating information, in surveillance, and in promoting actions designed to improve public health, thus giving substance to the extension of its own remit.

WORKING CONDITIONS IN MEMBER STATES

The Union's treaty obligations, and the directives, resolutions and recommendations issued over the years, established high target standards for living and working conditions, for the provision of health and safety at work and for public health, that member states are required to meet. With the notable exception of article 152 on public health in the consolidated EC Treaty, legal and policy documents constantly emphasized the need to harmonize regulations and processes between member states. Yet, standards of health and safety at work, living and working conditions, public health and compliance with Community legislation continue to show marked variations between countries.

The slow progress made by proposals from the Commission for reorganizing working time and resolving anomalies in working conditions may be explained, in part, by the problems involved in trying to reach agreement between countries with different collective bargaining processes. In some member states, for example France and countries with a Latin tradition, decisions regulating employment contracts and working conditions are taken by central government and become an integral part of labour law. In others with a stronger contractual tradition, such as Denmark and the United Kingdom, negotiations are generally decentralized, either at branch or enterprise level. Germany and the Benelux countries probably lie between the two extremes. Other national traditions, particularly those associated with differences in welfare regimes, may also determine reactions to proposals aimed at avoiding distortion of competition by aligning working conditions. Some member states are, for instance, likely to be reluctant to support the institutionalization of new work-time patterns in the cause of international solidarity when the impact would be to raise labour costs.

A major difficulty facing the Union is how to ensure that member states with relatively poor provisions for health and safety at work are able to improve their standards, so that they approximate to those found in neighbouring countries, while avoiding any levelling down. Progressively, the obstacles to harmonization have been recognized. Article 137 of the consolidated EC Treaty (§2 and §5) stipulates that national conditions and rules must be respected, that administrative and financial constraints should not be imposed on small and medium-sized enterprises (SME), and that individual member states should not be prevented from introducing or maintaining their own more stringent measures in these areas of social policy. The let-out clause for SMEs meant that countries, such as those in southern Europe where commerce and industry continued to be largely dominated by small family firms, would be allowed to maintain lower levels of protection from industrial hazards. The Union has thus formally recognized, and accepted, the concept of a two-speed Europe, and also the distinction between core and periphery, which is likely to be reinforced as applicant countries from Central and Eastern Europe become member states.

In this section, the focus is on national policies for the improvement of working conditions. An attempt is made to assess the extent to which they are compatible with the Union's requirements, while also providing an explanation for some of the problems that have arisen in trying to reach agreement at EU level.

Health and safety at work

The momentum for policy on health and safety at work came largely from the member states in northern Europe, where insurance schemes to protect workers against the consequences of industrial accidents were established before the end of the nineteenth century. As the southern Mediterranean countries that joined the Community in the 1980s – Greece, Portugal and Spain – did not share the same long legislative tradition for the protection of workers from industrial hazards, they had difficulty in conforming to the high standards set. On similar grounds, health and safety at work was considered to be an area where the accessor states in Central and Eastern Europe would need considerable assistance if they were to adopt the *acquis communautaire* [2.4, vol. 2, p. 38].

Some member states, namely Greece, Italy, Luxembourg and Portugal, made provision for the control of health and safety at work in their national constitutions. Basic occupational health and safety principles were set out in national legal codes and labour law in Austria, Finland, France, Germany, the Netherlands, Spain and Sweden. In Belgium, the civil code provided protection for all individuals both at the workplace and outside work. In Denmark, Ireland and the United Kingdom, civil or common law established individual rights to agreed standards of health and safety at work.

In several member states, the scope of existing legislation already went beyond what was required by the 1989 framework directive: Ireland and the United Kingdom, for example, covered the self-employed, and legislation in Greece, the Netherlands and the United Kingdom offered protection for third parties. Most countries already had statutory provision for consultative procedures for health and safety at the workplace: elected worker's councils in Germany, Italy, Luxembourg and the Netherlands; health and safety committees in Belgium, France and Portugal; elected safety representatives in Denmark and the United Kingdom. Greece, Ireland and Spain were expected to have most difficulty in meeting the requirements of the framework directive [4.8, p. 114]. The new member states that joined the Union in the 1990s – Austria, Finland and Sweden – brought with them high health and safety standards and were able to comply with the 1989 directive. By the mid-1990s, all 15 EU member states had transposed the requirements of the directive into their national legislation, and their record on compliance in the area of health and safety at work looked very strong [4.18, 1998]. In the United Kingdom, questions were even being raised about the British government's tendency to over-implement Community directives and to be stricter over enforcement than other member states (Burrows and Mair, 1996, p. 273).

Work-time organization

Agreement among member states was more easily reached over technical standards than over the deployment of human resources. The growing problem of unemployment since the mid-1970s, the diversification of forms of work as a result of technological change, the declining number of workers in manufacturing and agriculture, and the growth in the service sector, combined with the increasing proportion of women in the workforce, gave a new impetus to policies designed to deal with the impact of more flexible practices on working conditions.

European legislation on employment contracts, the organization of working time, atypical and part-time work affords some interesting examples of the shifting emphasis in policy and the resistance to change associated with disparities in existing practices between member states. National legislation and statistics on various aspects of working conditions provide an indication of the reasons why some member states supported, or opposed, any harmonization of working arrangements designed to reduce competitive advantage.

In the early 1990s when Directive 91/533/EEC [4.5] was under discussion, temporary contracts were, for example, most common in Greece, Portugal and Spain, and least common in Belgium, Italy, the United Kingdom and especially Luxembourg. Women were, everywhere, more likely than men to be employed on temporary contracts [4.17, 1999, pp. 127–42]. Although all member states except the United Kingdom had transposed the directive by the deadline in 1993 [4.18, 1998, pp. 14–17], the use of fixed-term contracts was still not regulated in Denmark, Ireland and the United Kingdom by the late 1990s [4.19, 1997, 2.1.1.4]. At that time, the proportion of workers on temporary contracts had risen across the Union, and particularly in Spain, possibly due in part to the greater visibility the directive accorded to contractual obligations. In Finland, Greece, Portugal, Sweden and particularly Spain, the overwhelming reason given by workers for being employed on fixed-term contracts was that they had not been able to find a permanent job. In Austria and Germany, by contrast, the main reason given was that the temporary work contract was combined with a training arrangement [3.14, 1999, table 064].

The second survey of working conditions in the European Union, carried out in 1996 by the European Foundation for the Improvement of Living and Working Conditions, demonstrated that precarious (temporary or fixed-term) status still entailed poorer working conditions in terms of exposure to noise, repetitive movements and tasks, training opportunities and autonomy of time management. In addition, employees with precarious contracts were found to work both longer and shorter working hours (atypical) than those on permanent contracts (Letourneux, 1998, p. 24). The conditions of undeclared workers, who, by definition, fall outside labour law, were likely to be worse still. During the 1990s, the number of undeclared workers was thought to be growing, with estimates ranging from 7 to 19 per cent of total declared employment. At the lower end, with about 5 per cent, were the Scandinavian countries, Ireland, Austria and the Netherlands, and at the higher end Greece and Italy, with over 20 per cent of declared work, followed by Belgium and Spain [4.16, p. 5]. High levels of undeclared work were also a source of concern for governments because of the effect they could have on competitive conditions by lowering labour costs.

Another aspect of work-time organization subject to marked national variations in practices was working hours. Not only the United Kingdom, which had opposed legislation on working time, but also France, Greece, Italy, Luxembourg and Portugal, failed to meet the deadline for transposing Directive 93/104/EC on the organization of working time into national law [4.18, 1998, pp. 165–70]. Such was the opposition of the United Kingdom to the directive that the British government instituted proceedings before the European Court of Justice challenging the validity of the directive on the grounds that the wrong legal base had been used. They argued that the directive went beyond the concept of the working environment and constituted an abuse of the Council's powers (Burrows and Mair, 1996, pp. 279–83). The change of government in 1997, however, brought the ideological shift needed for the directive to be implemented: New Labour's opt-in to the social chapter enabled the directive to be transposed into British law in 1998.

With the notable exception of the United Kingdom, no clear relationship emerges between length of working hours and legislation on the duration of working time. By the late 1990s, most member states had set a statutory limit of 40 hours a week. Only Germany, Ireland, Italy and the United Kingdom (following the opt-in) operated a higher statutory limit of 48 hours [4.19, 1997, table 2.1.2.1]. In all cases, collective agreements or arrangements between employers and workers could be used to introduce lower limits. During the 1990s, average weekly working hours had fallen across the Union. France was progressively moving towards the 35-hour week as a policy instrument for reducing unemployment. By 1997, the Netherlands and Sweden were registering the highest proportion of workers overall with the shortest working week, while the proportion of men usually working more that 40 hours per week was still much greater in the United Kingdom and Portugal, with over 60 and 50 per cent respectively, than in all other member states [3.14, 1999, table 076].

Night work was another area covered by the working time directive. When it was adopted in 1990, two patterns could be identified. In Belgium and the Netherlands, night work was generally forbidden but with derogations for a number of activities. Elsewhere, night work was generally permitted, unless expressly prohibited [4.8, p. 41). In several cases, namely Belgium, France, Germany and Greece, restrictions on night work applied to women. In others, Italy, Luxembourg, the Netherlands and Portugal, the prohibition applied only to pregnant women. Elsewhere, the ban on night work had progressively been lifted for all adults. By the late 1990s, across the Union less than 6 per cent of the workforce usually carried out night work. The highest rates were recorded in Finland and Austria, while that in Portugal was negligible [3.14, 1999, table 061].

The other aspect of working time covered by the directive concerned weekly rest periods and annual paid leave, where practices again varied cross-nationally. In all member states, except the United Kingdom, weekly rest periods had been introduced into legislation or collective agreements by the time the directive was to be implemented. In most cases, employees who worked on a Sunday had the right to take a compensatory day of rest in the following week or could receive financial compensation [4.8, pp. 45–6]. Denmark and the United Kingdom again had no legal statutes governing public holidays; elsewhere the number of days ranged from six in the Netherlands to 14 in Spain. Paid annual leave was governed by legislation everywhere except in the United Kingdom. The number of days ranged from 15 in Ireland to 30 in Spain [4.8, p. 49]. By the late 1990s, all member states, except Ireland, made provision for at least 20 days paid leave either through national legislation or collective agreements. The number of public holidays ranged from eight in the United Kingdom (normal working days), Germany and the Netherlands to 16 in Finland (inclusive of Saturdays and Sundays) [4.19, 1997, table 2.1.2.1].

Part-time work affords another means of adapting the total volume of working time and of raising labour productivity. Although Directive 97/81/EC [4.14] on part-time work was not adopted until 1997, the proportion of women employed on a part-time basis had been growing rapidly during the 1990s across the Union. As with temporary contracts, the regulation of part-time work afforded a means of removing obstacles to competitiveness. When the directive was introduced, the overall distribution of part-time working hours showed important variations from one member state to another, ranging from under 5 per cent of total employment in Greece to almost 40 per cent in the Netherlands. Rates of over 20 per cent were also recorded in Denmark and the United Kingdom. Part-time work was predominantly a female working pattern, affecting almost 70 per cent of women in employment in the Netherlands, and over 40 per cent in Sweden and the United Kingdom [4.17, 1999, pp. 127–42]. The term 'part-time' may be something of a misnomer in that part-time hours can be close to full-time hours: in the Nordic states, over 40 per cent of women employed part-time were working 25 hours or more a week, whereas over 60 per cent of women part-timers in the Netherlands and the United Kingdom were working under 20 hours a week [3.14, 1999, table 078]. During the 1990s, progressively member states sought to align the rights of part-time and full-time workers, usually by providing *pro rata* entitlements. As for other aspects of working conditions, in Denmark arrangements were a matter for individual and collective agreements. In the United Kingdom, employers and employees were left to make their own contractual arrangements, although part-time workers were entitled to the same statutory rights as full-timers. In France, Germany and the United Kingdom, reductions or exemptions were granted from social security contributions to make part-time work attractive for employers.

These examples suggest that issues involving the organization of work time have been a concern of the Union for two main reasons. Firstly, working time is a factor in production capacity that can be used to create competitive advantage or disadvantage, as exemplified by the use of undeclared or temporary labour. Secondly, by adapting working time and making it more flexible, the Union has been seeking a solution to the problem of unemployment. EU data on the relationship between hours worked and gross domestic product (GDP) show that, across the Union during the 1990s, while average hours worked were declining, GDP per total hours worked had been rising. The increase was most marked in Ireland, while the change was relatively small in Belgium, Greece and the Netherlands [4.17, 1999, pp. 143–5]. The evidence for a causal linkage between flexible working arrangements and the reduction of unemployment was, however, specious, since most of the jobs being created were temporary and part-time [4.17, 1999, p. 40].

LIVING CONDITIONS IN MEMBER STATES

Directives aimed at improving living and working conditions have focused primarily on issues concerned with the workplace and, more generally, the working environment. Industrial health and disease, and health and safety at work were areas where the Union was able to move relatively quickly to adopt common policies, while public health and wider environmental concerns were less obvious targets for intervention at EU level. In this section, public health is considered as a component of policies for the improvement of living conditions in the context of the growing interest shown in this area during the 1990s.

National health-care systems

Whereas harmonization of social security systems was advocated in the EEC Treaty (see Chapter 2), but progressively abandoned in favour of the principle of co-operation, the alignment of public health provision was an area of little interest for the Community's founder members, compared to health and safety at work. Given the very marked differences in health-care systems between member states, it is not difficult to understand why, when reference is made to public health as in the revised treaties, the principle of subsidiarity has been strongly upheld.

Except for Italy, which had a mixed system and introduced a national health service in 1978, all the health-care schemes of the EEC founding members were based on employment-insurance contributions, which gave workers entitlement to income-related sickness benefits in cases where they were prevented by ill health or disability from pursuing their economic activity. Both workers and their dependants had the right to medical treatment. Provision of health care was also extended to pensioners, the unemployed and other categories without a regular income from employment. The member states that joined the Community in the 1970s – Denmark, Ireland and the United Kingdom – had state-run national health services, financed from taxation, to which all residents had access on the basis of need. Of the countries that became members of the Community in the 1980s, Greece and Spain operated a mixed system closer to that of the continental model but strongly subsidized by the state. Portugal provided health care through a national health service on the basis of residence. Spain introduced such a service in 1986. Of the new member states in the 1990s, Austria operated a social insurance system, while Finland and Sweden provided health care on the basis of residence, funded mainly from taxation but organized at local or regional level. During the 1990s, the provision of health care in the accessor states was undergoing the transition from a centralized publicly-funded universal system to a predominantly social insurance employment-related variant of the Bismarckian model.

By the 1990s, in all EU member states, virtually the whole population was covered for health care, be it through a nation-wide health service in return for insurance contributions, through private insurance or social assistance schemes, or through a combination of arrangements. Economic, political, social and demographic pressures for reform were, however, being exerted on health-care systems across the Union and beyond, encouraging greater diversification in funding and delivery mechanisms. Population ageing, rising expectations for health-care standards, combined with the need to contain public spending to meet the criteria for Economic and Monetary Union (EMU), triggered a wave of reforms in member states. Most countries were adopting strategies aimed at establishing 'a viable balance between various market-oriented mechanisms in allocating resources and managing institutions, on the one hand, and a complicated mix of public sector decentralization, sharpened state vigilance, and greater citizen empowerment, on the other' (Figueras *et al.*, 1998, p. 4). Thus, countries with national health services were introducing market incentives, involving contracting for services and competition between providers. In the continental healthcare systems, governments were increasing their powers of control and regulation to protect equity and solidarity. Everywhere, cost-sharing arrangements and global budgets were being applied to contain demand for services. More effective delivery mechanisms, in terms of both processes and outcomes, were being sought, often resulting in decentralized services and a reduction of the amount of in-patient hospital care.

Many examples can be found in the area of European health-care reform of cross-national transfer and evidence-based public policy learning (Saltman *et al.*, 1998). Although it would be premature to conclude that the sharing of objectives and experience may lead to a bottom-up harmonization of systems, the search for solutions to the common problems created by external economic and social forces may exert greater pressure for change than directives from Brussels.

Access to health care and patterns of provision

Equality of access to health care within the Union has served as a major justification for state intervention, not only in systems where services are provided on a universal basis but also increasingly in those with insurance-based systems. Access to health care can vary both within and between countries, depending on the conditions governing entitlements. In the late 1990s, three countries – Belgium, Greece and France – required a qualifying period before benefits could be claimed. Everywhere except Greece, patients had a free choice of medical practitioner, albeit relatively limited in Finland. Public sector hospital treatment was free of charge across the Union, but Austria, Belgium, Finland, France, Germany, Luxembourg and Sweden levied a *per diem* maintenance charge on hospital beds. All countries operated charges for medicines, usually on a variable scale according to the financial circumstances of the sick person and/or the nature of the illness. Doctors were salaried employees in Finland, Greece, Portugal and Sweden. They were paid on a capitation basis, often combined with a fee for service, in Denmark, Ireland, Italy, the Netherlands, Spain and the United Kingdom. Elsewhere, they received a fee for service, and patients were generally expected to bear at least part of the cost themselves, which was also the case in Finland and Sweden. In Belgium, France and Luxembourg, patients were generally required to pay for treatment in full and were then partially reimbursed [2.7, 1998, table III].

Patterns of provision can affect access to services. In all member states except Germany, the total number of hospital beds has been falling since the 1980s, particularly in Sweden, while the number of physicians has been growing. In 1996, the number of doctors per inhabitant varied from below 2 per 1000 in the United Kingdom to 5.5 in Italy, while in-care hospital beds ranged from less than 4 per 1000 in Ireland to over 11 in the Netherlands in the mid-1990s (OECD, 1999, table 2). Admission rates and the average length of stay were higher on average in Central and Eastern Europe than for EU member states, which may be explained by norm-based planning and a heavier reliance on hospital care (Edwards *et al.*, 1998, pp. 237–40).

Whatever the administrative arrangements and the sources of funding, all member states have in common the growing cost of health-care provision and their efforts to contain spending in this area, among which budget setting would appear to have been the most successful (Mossialos and Le Grand, 1999). By the late 1990s, after expenditure on old age, health represented the second largest budget head for social benefits across the Union. The Netherlands, Portugal and Ireland were the countries spending the highest proportion of their GDP on health care, although only Ireland devoted a larger percentage of its expenditure on social benefits to health than to old age, due to its relatively youthful population (Eurostat, 2000, table 3). Measured in terms of total health expenditure per head of population in purchasing power standards (PPS), Germany and Luxembourg, followed by France, were found to be spending more than all other member states on health in the mid-1990s. Their expenditure was twice the amount devoted to health in Greece, Ireland and Portugal, and overall spending was lower in countries with a national health service [3.15, 1998, table 14].

The relationship between expenditure on medical care and standards of health is not, however, straightforward, since other social, environmental and cultural factors determine quality of health and of care. Cost containment and efficiency drives may not necessarily affect health outcomes as much as was expected by their critics. Marketization can, for example, result in a rapid rise in expenditure and greater inequality in access, without bringing a significant improvement in the general standard of health care, as demonstrated by the Czech case (Kokko *et al.*, 1998, p. 305). Differences persist between member states in the incidence of certain diseases for reasons that do not appear to be directly related to spending or lifestyle. In the mid-1990s, for example, Belgium, followed by the Netherlands and France, had the highest mortality rates for cancers among men, and particularly for lung cancer in the first two cases. The Netherlands, Denmark and the United Kingdom displayed the highest death rates for breast cancer among women. Sweden, Greece, Finland and Portugal showed the lowest death rates from all cancers for men, and Greece, Spain and Portugal for women. France recorded the largest proportion of daily cigarette smokers for both men and women aged 15–34. Rates were also high for men in this age group in Portugal. Spain recorded, by far, the highest mortality rate from AIDS among men and women, while the lowest rates were found in Finland. [3.15, 1998, tables 3, 9, 11].

Moreover, satisfaction with health care is not necessarily related to the level of spending. Denmark, which devoted a relatively low proportion of GDP to health care and achieved efficiency gains in the 1980s and 1990s, recorded by far the highest level of satisfaction. High levels of dissatisfaction were found in Greece and Italy; while Greece displayed the lowest figure for spending on health, Italy figured among the countries with high *per capita* spending (Mossialos, 1998, table 4).

FROM WORKING TO LIVING CONDITIONS

One of the pessimistic conclusions drawn from analyses of the pressures working for and against social Europe is that the social dimension of the Union would become 'a fragmentary arrangement, with the Community presence confined to specific segments of the labour market' (Teague and McClelland, 1991, p. 21). Matters relating to health and safety at work or the working environment provide a good example of what readily came to be regarded as legitimate areas for European intervention, on the grounds that action was needed to provide a satisfactory level of social protection for migrant workers and to avoid distortion of competition. In the early 1990s, health and safety at work were described as the 'most active aspect of EC social policy in the employment field' (James, 1993, p. 135). The quantity of legislation on the subject would seem to confirm that the Commission has been more active in this area of social policy than in most others and has taken the initiative in setting standards across the Union.

If the terms 'approximation' and 'harmonization' were used in the Community charter with reference to living and working conditions and health and safety at the workplace, whereas they were absent from the paragraphs on social protection, it may be, at least in part, because the principle of standardizing procedures for protecting workers proved to be much less contentious, and possibly more attainable, than the setting of targets for other aspects of working conditions and public health. The Union was able to build on national precedents for health and safety at work and, when the SEA came into force in 1987, to play a central co-ordinating role, progressively bringing national legislation into line with Council directives and recommendations. The 1989 framework directive was particularly noteworthy in that it probably went further than national legislation in its requirements that employers should adapt working conditions to meet individual needs.

The restructuring of working hours and arrangements for the social protection of part-time workers, or the harmonization of national health systems, did not command the same level of acceptance as health and safety at work as an area of supranational competence. The introduction of qualified majority voting and the British opt-out from the social chapter prepared the way for an extension of Union intervention in the 1990s. Article 3 of the consolidated EC Treaty made the attainment of a high level of health protection into one of the Union's objectives, enabling it to use instruments such as action programmes, legislation and research. The new title on public health, even though it explicitly excluded any harmonization of national laws and regulations, confirmed the further extension of the Union's remit, with a view to encouraging co-operation between member states in this area. The Commission's 1998 communication built on the treaty commitment, clearly setting out plans for developing public health policy at the turn of the century [4.15].

Many reasons may help explain the shift in emphasis from health and safety at work to the quality of health protection for the whole population. Pressures to control public spending in the run-up to EMU encouraged governments to look for efficiency gains, and seek an optimal and equitable distribution of resources. These pressures for change coincided with population ageing and growing care needs, as well as the decline in the working age population, creating problems for the funding of health-care systems. At the same time, rising public expectations, advances in medical science and new threats to public health had implications for the demand and provision of services. As in other areas of social policy, member states responded by showing their support for a common commitment to achieving high standards. An important challenge for the twentieth-first century was therefore to find ways not only of reaching but also of maintaining equally high standards across an increasingly diversified Union, and in countries where the *acquis communautaire* had still to be implemented.

Box 4 Secondary legislation and official publications relating to living and working conditions

4.1 Council Directive 89/391/EEC of 12 June 1989 on the introduction of measures to encourage improvements in the safety and health of workers at work (*OJ* L 183/1 29.6.89).

4.2 Commission proposal for a Council Directive concerning certain aspects of the organization of working time (COM(90) 317 final, 3 August 1990) (*OJ* C 254/4 9.10.90).

4.3 Commission of the European Communities, Europe against cancer. Public health: initiatives and texts adopted in 1990, *Social Europe*, 1/91.

4.4 Council Directive 91/383/EEC of 25 June 1991 supplementing the measures to encourage improvements in the safety and health at work of workers with a fixed-duration employment relationship or a temporary employment relationship (*OJ* L 206/19 29.7.91).

4.5 Council Directive 91/533/EEC of 14 October 1991 on an employer's obligation to inform employees of the conditions applicable to the contract or employment relationship (*OJ* L 288/32 18.10.91).

4.6 Resolution of the Council and the Ministers for Health, meeting within the Council of 11 November 1991 concerning fundamental health-policy choices (*OJ* C 304/5 23.11.91).

4.7 Council Directive 92/85/EEC of 19 October 1992 on the introduction of measures to encourage improvements in the safety and health at work of pregnant workers and workers who have recently given birth or are breastfeeding (*OJ* L 348/1 28.11.92).

4.8 Commission of the European Communities, The regulation of working conditions in the Member States of the European Community, vol. 1, *Social Europe Supplement*, 4/92.

4.9 Commission communication on the framework for action in the field of public health (COM(93) 559 final, 24 November 1993).

4.10 Council Directive 93/104/EC of 23 November 1993 concerning certain aspects of the organization of working time (*OJ* L 307/18 13.12.93).

4.11 Council Directive 94/45/EC of 22 September 1994 on the establishment of a European Works Councils procedure in Community-scale undertakings for the purposes of informing and consulting employees (*OJ* L254/64 30.9.94).

4.12 Decision N° 645/96/EC of the European Parliament and of the Council of 29 March 1996 adopting a programme of Community action on health promotion, information, education and training within the framework for action in the field of public health (1996 to 2000) (*OJ* L 95/1 16.4.96); Decision N° 646/96/EC adopting an action plan to combat cancer within the framework for action in the field of public health (1996 to 2000) (*OJ* L 95/9 16.4.96); Decision N° 647/96/EC adopting a programme of Community action on the prevention of AIDS and certain other communicable diseases within the framework for action in the field of public health (1996 to 2000) (*OJ* L 95/16 16.4.96).
4.13 Decision N° 102/97/EC of the European Parliament and of the Council of 16 December 1996 adopting a programme of Community action on the prevention of drug dependence within the framework for action in the field of public health (1996–2000) (*OJ* L 19/25 22.1.97).
4.14 Council Directive 97/81/EC of 15 December 1997 concerning the Framework Agreement on part-time work concluded by UNICE, CEEP and the ETUC (*OJ* L 14/9 20.1.98).
4.15 Communication from the Commission on the development of public health policy in the European Community (COM(98) 230 final, 15 April 1998).
4.16 Communication from the Commission on undeclared work, (COM(1998) 219 final, 7 April 1998).
4.17 European Commission, *Employment in Europe*, OOPEC (annual publication).
4.18 European Commission, *National Transposition Measures*, OOPEC, 1998.
4.19 European Commission, *Tableau de bord*, OOPEC, 1997.

5 Family Policies

Family policy affords a good illustration of the general principle, progressively adopted by the institutions of the European Union (EU), that national governments should be left to determine how their social protection systems are framed, financed and organized. Several reasons may help to explain the reluctance of the Commission to intervene in family affairs. Most importantly, the welfare of family units has been given low priority because social policy, as laid down in the founding Treaty of the European Economic Community (EEC) [1.2], centred on workers' rather than citizenship rights. The Community therefore had no formal competence to act in the area of family affairs. In addition, and perhaps more so than in the case of policy for the young, older people or ethnic minority groups, views on the objectives and instruments of family policy are divided along ideological lines, both within and between countries. In some member states, family life is considered to belong to the private domain and is therefore forbidden territory for explicit state intervention. The resulting diversity of practices is such that the Commission would have been faced with an intractable task had it sought to extend its social policy remit to the co-ordination of policies targeted at family life.

According to the EEC Treaty [1.2, articles 51 and 122], the obligations of EU member states with regard to family units were confined to promoting freedom of movement of workers and their dependants, and to reporting on the social situation, which, from 1969, included a chapter on matters relating to the family. Nor did subsequent amended versions of the treaties [1.6–8] introduce any direct references to family policies. The Council of Europe's social charter of 1961 was much less inhibited in its approach to family welfare. For the Council, action in support of families was not contingent on the employment relationship or on freedom of movement. Rather, the social importance of families was openly recognized: 'The family as a fundamental unit of society has the right to appropriate social, legal and economic protection to ensure its full development.' The duties of the state towards individual family members, whether or not the family unit was legally constituted, were clearly set out in the social charter: 'Mothers and children, irrespective of marital status and family relations, have the right to appropriate social and economic protection.' (part I §§16–17)

Since so little attention is paid to family affairs in the Community's and Union's treaties, this chapter begins by reviewing the direct and indirect references to the family dimension of social policy in official documents, and sets them within the context of freedom of movement and socio-demographic change. Consideration is then given to the different ways in which member states have conceptualized family structures and to an analysis of the family policy-making process at national level. In conclusion, the possible implications of EU social policy for families and for the rights of children are examined. Measures for reconciling family and professional responsibilities are treated in the next chapter as an equal opportunities issue.

EUROPEAN FAMILY POLICY IN EMBRYO

The social protection systems of most of the EEC founder members were strongly influenced by the Bismarckian statist corporatist model of welfare, with its guiding principle that workers should be guaranteed benefits and a substitute income calculated from their previous earnings in return for the payment of employment-related insurance contributions (see Chapter 2). Since the main objective of the EEC Treaty was to promote economic growth and facilitate free movement of workers, goods and services, the only reference made to family members was in article 51, which extended social security rights to intra-European migrant workers and their dependants on the same basis as for nationals in the host country. Ten years later, Council Regulation (EEC) N° 1612/68 [9.2] set out the provisions to be made for family members to gain access to derived rights as dependants of a migrant worker (see Chapter 9). The preamble to the regulation explicitly stated 'that obstacles to the mobility of workers shall be eliminated, in particular as regards the worker's right to be joined by his [*sic*] family and the conditions for the integration of that family into the host country'. Article 10 went on to define the family members who fall within the terms of the regulation: '(a) his spouse and their descendants who are under the age of 21 or are dependants; (b) dependent relatives in the ascending line of the worker and his spouse'. Moreover, the provisions for the admission of migrant workers applied to all family members 'dependent on the worker referred to above or living under his roof in the country whence he comes'. The regulation specified that intra-

European migrants should be treated in the same way as workers and their families in the host country, so as to avoid any discrimination with regard to social protection, education and other forms of social support (see Chapter 9).

Moving family policy onto the Community's agenda

Despite an early reference in the 1974 social action programme to the objective of ensuring 'that family responsibilities of all concerned may be reconciled with their job aspirations' [1.9, p. 2], the Community did not develop any family-related measures in the 1970s. In 1983, however, the European Parliament formulated a resolution 'on family policy in the European Community' [5.2], with the objective of ensuring that family policy should become 'an integral part of all Community policies'. Such intervention was justified by reference to article 2 of the EEC Treaty, which gave the Community the broad task of raising living standards, and to article 235, which empowered the Council to act unanimously for this purpose on a proposal from the Commission, after consulting the European Parliament. The resolution expressed concern about the implications of the changing structure of the family, the different role being played by women in society and within the family, the growing number of lone-parent families, and what were described as '*de facto* families'. The Commission was called upon to draw up an action programme and to introduce a comprehensive family policy and, where appropriate, to harmonize national policies at Community level [5.2, pp. 116–17].

The Council did not respond immediately with any formal action. Then, prompted by a series of worrying reports on demographic trends, in 1989, the Commission drafted a communication 'on family policies', in which it reviewed the changes occurring in society and pointed to the essential role assumed by the family 'in the cohesion and the future of society' [5.3, p. 12]. Four areas of common interest were identified: the means of reconciling work and family life and sharing family responsibilities; measures to assist certain categories of families; consideration of the most deprived families; and the impact of Community policies on the family, in particular the protection of children during childhood [5.3, p. 3]. Action at Community level was justified, according to the Commission, not on the basis of ideology, but on the grounds that the family played an important economic role, serving as a 'touchstone for solidarity between generations' and a means of achieving equality between men and women. The Commission noted that action would have to be pragmatic in order to 'respect the special features of different national policies already created and the varying socio-economic contexts in which such policies play a role [5.3, p. 15]. Almost immediately the Council responded formally by reiterating most of the proposals made in the communication, although it decided to substitute the theme of equal opportunities for the reconciliation of professional and family life [5.4].

The issues raised by the Commission were not pursued in the Community Charter of the Fundamental Social Rights of Workers adopted in the same year [1.10]. Like the 1974 social action programme [1.9], the charter was primarily concerned with the employment-related rights of workers (see Chapter 1). It did take some account of the status of women as working mothers by recognizing that men and women needed support to enable them 'to reconcile their occupational and family obligations', but again on the understanding that employment status was paramount (§16).

Although the Community had legitimized its interest in family policy by the late 1980s, little progress had been made towards defining a 'comprehensive' European family policy as requested by the European Parliament in 1983. A concrete outcome of the Council's conclusions was, however, the establishment in 1989 of a network of 12 independent national experts (and later 15 when the Community was enlarged), known as the European Observatory on National Family Policies. Its brief was to monitor demographic trends, collect information on the situation of families, analyse measures relating to families taken by member states, and report back annually to the Commission [5.6], thereby contributing to the Community's knowledge base on social conditions in member states.

Keeping family policy on the European agenda

The Agreement on Social Policy, annexed to the Treaty on European Union in 1992 [1.6], did not directly address family matters. As in article 122 of the EEC Treaty, it conferred on the Commission the task of producing an annual report on social developments. Article 7 specified, however, that the report should indicate the progress made in achieving the objectives set out in article 1, and explicitly referred to the demographic situation in the Community. The same article empowered the European Parliament to invite the Commission to draw up reports on problems concerning the social situation. These provisions were incorporated into the consolidated version of the EC Treaty [1.8, article 143], thereby confirming the Commission's mandate for monitoring family structures as a component of socio-demographic change, and reporting on related social problems. At the same time, the European Parliament was given the opportunity to contribute to the social policy agenda.

The 1992 Council recommendation 'on the convergence of social protection objectives and policies' [2.1], adopted shortly after the signing of the Treaty on European Union, was much more explicit than the Agreement on Social Policy about the place of family matters on the European agenda. Not only did it set out the aims of removing 'obstacles to occupational activity by parents through measures to reconcile family and professional responsibilities', and of integrating individuals who wished to enter the labour market after bringing up children, it also advocated developing targeted benefits for categories of families in need [2.1, p. 52]. While the 1994 white paper on European social policy did not make any proposals for establishing an EU family policy by the year 2000, it did stress that the Union needed a broadly based social policy that took account of family life [1.15, p.7].

The United Nations had proclaimed 1994 the International Year of the Family, with the theme of family resources and responsibilities in a changing world, and the motto: 'Building the smallest democracy at the heart of society'. The Commission used the occasion to take a number of initiatives on behalf of the Union, including a Eurobarometer survey of how Europeans perceive the family and the policies implemented by their governments (Malpas and Lambert, 1993). The survey demonstrated convincingly that the family remained an essential value for the vast majority of Europeans. A major event was organized by the Commission in conjunction with the German presidency on the future of families. The European Observatory on National Family Policies produced a report on changing family policies in the member states (Dumon, 1994), and the unit in Directorate-General V (Employment, Industrial Relations and Social Affairs) responsible for analysing the social situation published an issue of *Social Europe* devoted to 'The European Union and the Family' [5.7], summarizing European and national trends. In the preface, Commissioner Flynn stressed the role played by the Commission in identifying similarities and differences in the ways member states react to changing family patterns, and in stimulating debate through the exchange of information and pooling of experience. Three areas were highlighted for attention: analysis of the impact Community policies can have on the family; the development of equal opportunities policies, particularly with reference to labour markets; and measures to support families, especially those at risk.

The European Parliament marked the close of the International Year of the Family with a resolution 'on protection of families and family units' [5.5], which argued for a comprehensive approach to family policy at EU level, thereby integrating the interests of families into all Community measures. Families were to be protected, irrespective of type and structure. Special attention was to be given to the needs of children, particularly in lone-parent families and underprivileged households, and measures were advocated to promote equal opportunities for women and men and to deal with domestic violence and child abuse.

The Confederation of Family Organizations in the European Communities (Coface), which had begun its work as a European action committee soon after the signing of the EEC Treaty, had contributed to the drafting of the resolution. By the 1990s, Coface embraced more than 70 family organizations across the Union and had consolidated its role as the 'voice' of families in Europe, addressing issues such as the impact of the extension of the Union's powers under the Maastricht Treaty, or the risk of a levelling-down of social standards. While the attention of the Council of Ministers was concentrated on the working population and more especially on the problem of unemployment, Coface was pressing for measures to protect the interests of children, rural families and disabled people.

Despite the high profile give to family affairs in 1994, the only reference to the family in the medium-term social action programme for 1995–97 [1.16, p. 21] was in the context of equal opportunities, where the reconciliation theme was pursued. The 1998–2000 social action programme made reference to the implications of changing patterns of family life for employment and social protection systems as one of the social challenges facing the Union that the programme was designed to meet [1.19, p. 7]. The same theme was pursued in the 1997 communication from the Commission, adopted in 1999, on the modernization and improvement of social protection in the European Union, the aim being to make tax and benefit systems, especially family benefits, more employment friendly [2.3, p. 6].

When, during the 1990s, the question of family life was addressed formally, the primary justification was not the promotion of family well-being. Rather, the main purpose was to protect the health and safety of pregnant workers [4.7], to maximize labour market flexibility [4.10], enhance competitiveness by enabling parents to reconcile employment and family responsibilities [6.13], facilitate freedom of movement of workers [9.2] or encourage greater equality of opportunity [6.16]. Little, if any, progress had been made by the late 1990s, through hard law, towards achieving the aims set in the 1980s by the European Parliament, the Commission and the Council. The Commission's demographic and social protection reports continued to reiterate the concerns expressed in the 1980s, albeit by emphasizing the effects of changing household structures on the composition of the labour force and on intergenerational relationships [2.5, 1997, pp. 32–6; 5.8, 1997, p. 18].

The launching of Economic and Monetary Union (EMU) provided a new incentive for the Commission to address family matters on the grounds that the efficacy of economic and social policy would be improved if more account was taken of its impact on families. The Commission argued that the failure to adapt social policies in response to socio-demographic change would entail economic and social costs [2.3; 10.3], that family-sensitive social policies can make a contribution to economic performance, and that social and family policies can serve as a productive factor (Hantrais, 1999b). While the promotion of family policy and the protection of the family unit had not been legitimized as formal treaty commitments, by the late 1990s the Commission had found ways of bringing family affairs within its social remit.

CHANGING FAMILIES AND FAMILY POLICIES

The focus on employment-related rights and benefits and the Council's and Commission's reluctance to intervene to harmonize national welfare systems meant that member states largely continued to develop their own policy agendas in areas, such as family life, that were not directly controlled by European legislation. As a result of the lack of consensus over the role government should play and over the possible objectives and instruments of family policy, no wholly satisfactory and generally accepted operational definition of a family, or of family policy, has been formulated at EU level. The family concept, as defined for statistical purposes in studies of changing family structure over time, emphasizes relationships within households. By contrast, the institutional definitions used to assess the legal status of family members and entitlements to social protection are more interested in relationships within families (Hantrais and Letablier, 1996, chapter 2). Nonetheless, the 1989 communication from the Commission [5.3, p. 2] and the 1992 Council recommendation 'on the convergence of social protection objectives and policies' [2.1, p. 49] identified changing family situations as one of the comparable trends across member states that may lead to common problems, thereby justifying the formulation of common objectives. Changes in family structure are, for example, likely to affect the ability of families to provide support for their members. The premises on which welfare states were based in most countries are, it has been argued [2.5, 1993, p. 119], being undermined as the intergenerational balance is upset, and the stability of marriage and family unity are increasingly disrupted.

In line with the Union's concern about demographic trends and the possible impact of social protection measures on the family, the focus in this section is on changing family structures in EU member states, and their implications for institutional definitions of the family and for family policy. Change in family structure is taken as an indicator of the extent to which common trends can be discerned and of the way that traditional assumptions about the family as a unit for social protection are being called into question.

Defining and measuring family change

Since 1973, when the Council of Ministers adopted Directive 73/403/EEC [5.1] on the harmonization of census dates and the standardization of information, data have been collected by Eurostat on the number of marriages, age at marriage, its duration, the number of births to women belonging to different generations, total period fertility rates (the number of births to women during the reproductive period of their lives), age at childbirth, household size and structure [5.9].

Attempts have been made to standardize data so that they can be used to quantify patterns of family building and structure, to record changes over time and compare trends between countries. Progressively, in recognition of changing family patterns and the growing interest in demographic trends across the Union, data collection has been extended to take account of factors that are more difficult to record, either because of social taboos or because reliable information is not readily available. For example, Eurostat collects data on the number of extramarital births, lone parenthood and cohabitation, indicators for which the definitions used in individual member states often diverge (Hantrais and Letablier, 1996, chapter 1). The European Community Household Panel (ECHP) survey, launched in 1993 under the auspices of Eurostat, seeks to provide comparable microdata over time on income, employment and the general living conditions of households and individuals in EU member states. The surveys cover health, education, housing, income, transitions between different life stages, and living and working arrangements. For census purposes,

Eurostat has adopted the United Nations' definition of the family unit, based on the 'conjugal family concept', which defines the family in the narrow sense of a family nucleus as

> the persons within a private or institutional household who are related as husband and wife or as parent and never-married child by blood or adoption. Thus, a family nucleus comprises a married couple without children or a married couple with one or more never-married children of any age or one parent with one or more never-married children of any age. (United Nations Statistical Commission/Economic Commission for Europe Conference of European Statisticians, 1987, p. 35, §131)

The term 'married couple' is taken to include couples living in consensual unions. 'Children', according to this definition, include step-children as well as adopted children, but not foster children. Data collected in national censuses generally concern private households rather than families. Households have been defined by the United Nations either as a person living alone, or as a group of persons living together, whether or not they are related, providing themselves 'with food and possibly other essentials for living', and who may pool their income (United Nations Statistical Commission, 1987, p. 33, §121).

Changing family structure

During the period since the EEC was established in 1957, the size and structure of families in member states have been transformed. Far-reaching changes have occurred in patterns of family formation and dissolution, with the result that alternative family forms and non-family households have become widespread. Family size has decreased due to the decline in birthrates and in the number of generations living together. From the mid-1960s, as effective means of contraception became more widely available, and legislation was enacted in most member states to enable the whole population, at least in theory, to have access to birth control, total period fertility rates declined steeply. By the late 1990s, rates for the 15 EU member states had fallen well below the level in the United States and were, together with those for Japan, the lowest in the world (data supplied by Eurostat). The decline in fertility rates, in combination with the increase in life expectancy, resulted in a 22 per cent fall in the proportion of the population aged 0–24 in less than 40 years [5.9, 1999, tables B-4, B-5]. By the middle of the twenty-first century, it was being predicted that only 19 per cent of the population of the EU would be aged under 20, compared to 24 per cent in 1995 (Eurostat, 1997b, table 2). The enlargement of the Union to the East may accentuate the trend: among the applicant states from Central and Eastern Europe, all except Poland and the Slovak Republic were expected to be in a situation of population decline by the year 2015 [5.8, 1997, p. 29].

Although the trends observed in fertility rates have generally been in the same direction across the Union and the gap between the most and the least prolific nations has been narrowing, important variations can be noted both between and within member states in the timing, pace, sequencing and degree of change. Portugal and the Netherlands, for example, experienced the most marked decline in completed fertility rates for the 1930–50 cohorts of women, while Sweden recorded the smallest fall. Completed fertility rates by generation had reached a particularly low level in Germany by the late 1990s, associated in West Germany with a high proportion of childless women. Italy combined an average level of childlessness with very low fertility rates, and France high fertility with a low rate for childlessness. Ireland, where abortion continued to be illegal, was alone in recording a completed fertility rate above replacement level, estimated at 2.1 children for each woman of childbearing age [5.9, 1999, tables E-13, E-16].

Across the Union, women were postponing the age of childbearing: mean age was 29 years by the late 1990s, with Austria, Portugal and the United Kingdom furthest below the EU average [5.9, 1999, table E-9]. The low figure for the United Kingdom could be attributed to the relatively high rate of teenage pregnancies: 159 per 1000 women aged 20 and under in 1998, compared to 25 per 1000 in the Netherlands (Council of Europe, 1999, tables UK-3, NL-3).

As birthrates were falling, the proportion of one-person households was growing, reaching 28 per cent of all households by the mid-1990s, and 35 per cent in Finland and Sweden, but less than 15 per cent in Portugal and Spain (Eurostat, 1998a, p. 38). This increase was due partly to the decline in the proportion of extended households (three generations). For this indicator, member states again displayed considerable diversity, ranging from barely over 1 per cent of households in Finland and Sweden to almost 22 per cent in Greece, according to data from the first wave of the ECHP (Vogel, 1997, table 12.1).

While family size was declining, marriage rates were also falling, reaching 5 per 1000 population on average by the late 1990s, compared to almost 8 per 1000 in 1960. Sweden displayed a particularly low level [5.9, 1999, table F-3]. Age at marriage was being postponed: mean age at first marriage had risen to nearly 29 years for men (32 in Denmark) and to over 26 years for women (almost 30 in Denmark) by the late 1990s, an increase of two years in each case compared to 1960 [5.9, 1999, table F-14, F-15]. Here, the gap had narrowed between the countries with the highest and lowest ages at first marriage for both men and women. The rejection or postponement of marriage does not mean, however, that couples are no longer forming partnerships. Comparisons of unmarried cohabitation rates across the Union are unreliable, because the phenomenon is conceptualized and measured differently from one society to another, and because cohabitees form a particularly unstable and heterogeneous category. Data from Eurostat (1998a, p. 40) and national data (Statistics Sweden, 1995, p. 16) indicate that unmarried cohabitation had become a widespread living arrangement in Denmark and Sweden by the mid-1990s, affecting about 25 per cent of all couples. It was especially prevalent among the younger age groups, and was increasingly associated with extramarital births, which accounted for more than 50 per cent of all live births in Sweden, over 46 per cent in Denmark, and a third or more of births in Finland, France and the United Kingdom, but for little more than 3 per cent in Greece [5.9, 1999, E-4]. Moreover, the gap between the countries with the highest and lowest rates of extramarital births had increased more than fourfold between the 1960s and 1990s.

During the same period, marriage as an institution became increasingly fragile. Much higher crude divorce rates per 1000 population were, however, recorded in some countries than in others: the Nordic states and the United Kingdom displayed the highest divorce rates, with more than 40 per cent of marriages contracted in 1980 ending in divorce, compared to less than 10 per cent in Italy and Spain. Divorce was not legalized in Ireland until 1997 but, even then, the conditions for obtaining it remained restrictive. The disparity between the countries with the highest and lowest divorce rates, excluding Ireland, doubled between 1960 and the late 1990s [5.9, 1999, table F-19].

As the proportion of marriages ending in divorce has risen, average duration of marriage has been declining. The duration of marriages ending in divorce fell most rapidly in southern European countries, where marriages contracted in the 1960s lasted longer than in other member states (Eurostat, 1997a, table 2). Whereas a century earlier lone parenthood was most likely to be the result of bereavement, and unmarried motherhood was a condition that went unrecorded in census statistics, by the 1990s lone parenthood was much more likely to be the outcome of divorce or separation. Over 10 per cent of families with children aged below 15 were living in lone-parent families, except in the Mediterranean states. Denmark and the United Kingdom recorded the highest rates, and Greece the lowest (data supplied by Eurostat).

The similarity in the general direction of the trends shown by this batch of demographic indicators does not imply that the pace of change has been the same throughout the Union. While indicators of postponement of family formation and reduction in family size would appear to be converging, those for family de-institutionalization would seem to be diverging (Hantrais, 1999a, figure 2). The Nordic states have tended to lead the field in adopting less conventional patterns of family formation, while maintaining fertility rates above the EU mean. This pattern has been followed by France and, to a lesser extent, by the Netherlands and the United Kingdom. While East Germany was, prior to unification, closer to the Nordic pattern, West Germany retained a more conventional approach to institutional forms of marriage and family building, as did Austria and Belgium. Italy, Ireland and the southern Mediterranean countries that joined the Community in the third wave of membership also remained more traditional in their approach to family institutions and, like the *Länder* of former West Germany, saw their fertility rates fall steeply during the 1990s.

The picture of family structure that emerges from the data examined in this section is not unequivocal, making it difficult to identify a single European family model to be targeted by a common family policy. However, subject to individual variations in degree, the trends identified do raise a number of policy issues that member states are addressing in accordance with their approaches to the organization and delivery of social protection (Hantrais, 1999a). The de-institutionalization and destabilization of the family unit can, for example, be considered to pose a threat to a social order founded on a commitment to marriage and to the family as a basic social institution, placing the most vulnerable groups (dependent women and children) at risk. Policy makers therefore have to decide whether or not to recognize alternative family forms in fiscal and social policy, whether to seek to promote family building, whether to try and prevent family breakdown, and whether to support families through periods of transition.

Changing legal rights of family members

Statistical representations of family structure are determined to a large extent by the institutional frameworks that set the legal parameters of the family (Desrosières, 1996). The definitions used for demographic and institutional purposes are not, however, identical, and these differences do matter for family policy. For example, policy makers may take account of marital status or the legal recognition of paternity in determining eligibility for tax relief and social security entitlements, while statistical records may not be based on the same criteria.

Many changes in family structure have gradually been given official recognition, even if they are not always written into codes of law. From the 1960s, legal frameworks were, for example, being adapted to reflect the fact that the husband was no longer the undisputed head of the family and its sole or main breadwinner. Increasingly, parental responsibility for children has been shared between married partners, and the breakdown of marriage has been legally endorsed (Hantrais and Letablier, 1996, pp. 35–9; Hantrais and Lohkamp-Himmighofen, 1999, pp. 9–19). The situation is less clear-cut in the case of unmarried cohabiting couples. The Nordic states and the Netherlands have gone furthest in recognizing the legal rights of unmarried couples. By the late 1990s, cohabiting couples in several countries could officially register their partnership. At the other extreme, in Ireland their rights were restricted, and in some member states, Greece for example, the issue had not reached the political agenda (Ditch *et al.*, 1996, p. 19; Hantrais and Lohkamp-Himmighofen, 1999, pp. 5–8).

Practices regarding the attribution of paternity and the sharing of parental responsibility in unmarried couples have continued to differ markedly from one member state to another, despite the guidelines laid down by the Council of Europe in 1975 in its European Convention on the Legal Status of Children Born out of Wedlock. By the mid-1990s, paternal recognition was a discretionary right of the father in France, whereas Nordic and German legislation pursued the father on the grounds that he has the duty to support his children. Elsewhere paternal recognition was conditional on the consent of the mother alone and/or the child (Meulders-Klein, 1993, pp. 122–33). Once paternity is established, the way is open for defining the responsibilities of parents towards one another and towards their children, and their legal right to state support. In the mid-1990s, across the Union unmarried cohabiting parents had an obligation to maintain their children, although fathers in Austria and Germany had no legal authority over their children. In the case of separation, joint custody was awarded unconditionally only in Denmark and Luxembourg. Elsewhere, if paternity had been established, it was generally subject to a court decision, and/or the mother's consent, except in Austria where it was not possible for separated couples to share parental rights (Ditch *et al.*, 1996, p. 29).

Despite the shift during the 1990s from the family or couple to the individual as the basic unit for taxation, France retained the family as the income tax unit. Under the *quotient familial*, high-income earners with large families received generous rebates, as well as allowances for childminding costs. Germany continued to operate a system, based on *Ehengattensplitting*, which favoured married couples with one high and one low-income earner. Progressively, the distinction was removed between married and unmarried households with regard to taxation by bringing the situation of married couples into line with that of unmarried cohabitees, rather than the reverse. In France, the Netherlands and Sweden, the tax levy was the same as for married couples. However, in most other EU member states in the 1990s, unmarried childless cohabitees continued to pay more tax than married couples. This was the case in Austria, Belgium, Denmark, Finland, Ireland, Italy and Portugal for couples with only one earner. In Belgium and Greece, cohabitees with two earners paid less tax (Ditch *et al.*, 1996, p. 25).

These examples show how public policy has progressively recognized changes in the structure of families, and responded to pressures to adapt and modernize legal frameworks to take account of the spread of alternative family forms. As with demographic trends, EU member states have been moving in the same direction, but the pace and momentum for change have varied, with the result that the rights of family members have continued to differ from one country to another.

Defining family policies and identifying policy objectives

Variations between countries in the way the family is defined and taken into account in legal statutes, as outlined in the previous section, reflect persisting differences not only in the principles underlying national family policies, but also in the socio-economic and political contexts in which they are formulated and implemented. A distinction has often been made between countries with explicit and implicit family policies. France, Sweden, and also Hungary and Czechoslovakia, were presented as exemplars of explicit family policies in the 1970s and 1980s, while Austria, Denmark, Finland and Germany, together with Poland, were described as having a tradition of explicit but more narrowly focused family policy (Kamerman and Kahn, 1978). Explicit family policies have been characterized as being far-reaching, coherent and legitimated. The United Kingdom has often served as an example of an EU member state with an implicit, or even negative, family policy, in the sense that governments have gone so far as to reject the idea of such a policy area. They have, nonetheless, implemented measures that are likely to have an impact on families and would elsewhere be described as belonging to family policy, which has led to British family policy being characterized as 'undeveloped' (Chester, 1994, p. 274).

In one of its early reports, the European Observatory on National Family Policies broadly defined family policy as 'measures geared at influencing families', but excluded the unintended outcomes for families of measures implemented in other policy areas (Dumon, 1991, p. 9). The 1994 report on changing family policies conferred on the observatory a much broader remit. It identified three types of family policy: policy targeting families as groups rather than individuals; the family dimension in social and fiscal law, extending to private sector provision; and the family impact of all policies (Dumon, 1994, pp. 325–6). Successive co-ordinators of the observatory were thereby allowed considerable latitude in interpreting their brief.

One of the reasons put forward at the beginning of this chapter to explain why the Union had not developed its own family policy was the problem of reaching a consensus over objectives. The aims and consequences of family policy can, like other areas of policy, be manifest or latent, direct or indirect, mutually consistent or inconsistent. Over the postwar period, governments in member states formulated their own policy objectives in line with their political ideology, their approach to policy making, and as a response to their interpretation of the needs of families in the context of the changes occurring in the economic and socio-cultural climate.

Few countries, if any, can be said to have pursued wholly coherent family policy objectives. Inconsistency may be explained to a large extent by the potential conflict of needs with which policy makers have to contend. Policies formulated in other areas, such as health, education or employment, are likely to have an impact on the family and may also lead to conflicts over objectives. For example, policies that are intended to preserve traditional family structures may be in conflict with others aimed at the pursuit of equality of opportunity. Given that resources are never infinite, choices have to be made that may involve moral judgements. These conflicts of interest raise a number of questions. Should policy concentrate support on families that conform to traditional family types, that is married couples and their legitimate offspring, or should they recognize and institutionalize new family forms, such as cohabitation and lone parenthood? In other words should they try to stem change, keep pace with it or even promote it? Within this same framework, should policy makers seek to influence family size or the timing of childbirth? Should family policy be universally applied to all families, or should it operate as a form of social solidarity and, by being selective, help only families most in need? Should attention be focused on individuals rather than on the family unit? Should women be encouraged to stay at home to look after young children, or should the state provide facilities that enable women to combine employment outside the home with childrearing?

In their attempts to deal with these questions since the signing of the EEC Treaty [1.2], EU member states have pursued three main policy objectives, reflecting the different rationales underlying their welfare regimes: income (re)distribution, pronatalism and equal opportunities. Some member states have pursued all three objectives simultaneously, albeit with different emphases depending, among other things, on the political ideology of the governments in power. Most countries have sought to use family policy as a means of redistributing income, either horizontally from individuals or couples without children to those with children, or vertically from high to low income earners, often targeting families most in need. In many cases, both horizontal and vertical redistribution has been pursued, increasingly with emphasis on helping children at risk, in line with the child-centred approach adopted in the 1990s. Policy has also been adapted to take account of the fact that young people are remaining dependent on their parents until a later age.

Some countries have been concerned about population decline and have sought to provide incentives to encourage couples to have larger families. Belgium and France pursued this objective in their family policies over the postwar period and made their pronatalist aims explicit. The United Kingdom and, until the late 1980s, the Federal Republic of Germany are examples of countries which deliberately avoided formulating policies that might be interpreted as encouraging population growth because of its expansionist connotations. The equal opportunities objective has progressively moved up national agendas as EU-level policies have been developed to take account of the need for support measures to help parents, both men and women, reconcile employment with family life (see Chapter 6).

Formulating and implementing family policies

Some governments have gone further than others in formalizing the responsibilities of the state towards families. In Finland, France, Germany, Greece, Ireland, Italy, Luxembourg, Portugal and Spain, the national constitution recognizes the family as a fundamental social institution and undertakes to afford it protection. The Portuguese constitution (article 67) goes furthest in setting out concrete measures which the state pledges to implement in order to protect the family and respond to its needs (Steindorff and Heering, 1993, pp. 136–7). The European Parliament's 1983 resolution 'on family policy in the European Community' made clear its view that society has a responsibility towards families:

> society has a duty to guarantee the family the necessary material facilities and environment for its members to fulfil their personal and social duties, and therefore the social services most suited to the harmonious development of the couple and the rearing and education of children must be available. [5.2, p. 117]

In gathering information about the composition of households and family living arrangements, in establishing the responsibilities of the state towards families, and in determining eligibility for benefits, the state inevitably encroaches on the personal lives of individuals and infringes their privacy. Public policy may thereby contravene the Council of Europe's European Convention for the Protection of Human Rights and Fundamental Freedom, signed in Rome in 1950 (Meulders-Klein, 1992), since article 8 of the convention stipulates: 'Everyone has the right to respect of his [*sic*] private and family life, his home and his correspondence.'

Government intervention in family affairs can take a number of forms. It may involve prohibitive, permissive or proactive policies. Despite strong opposition in countries with a powerful Catholic lobby, most countries have moved away from prohibitive legislation, as in the case of divorce or abortion. Permissive legislation has been extended to take account of alternative family forms, as illustrated in the previous section. Since the founding of the EEC, all member states have pursued proactive family policies. Family allowances (the term used in French-speaking and southern European countries) and child benefits (the term used in northern Europe) are selected here as the most visible and explicit measures to illustrate national differences in the formulation and implementation of proactive family policy.

In most member states where social security systems have been based on the insurance principle (see Chapter 2), family allowances were conceived as part of the wage package, and employment-related contributions were the main or sole source of funding. In a few cases (France, Italy and Luxembourg), in the 1990s employees did not pay earmarked contributions. In Greece, Portugal and Spain, both employers and employees contributed, in the two latter cases as part of the global contribution for social protection. The direct link with employment was broken in Austria, Belgium, Denmark, Finland, Germany, Ireland, the Netherlands, Sweden and the United Kingdom, where funding was solely or mainly through taxation [2.7, 1998, table II].

As in statistical data, the definition of a dependent child applied in assessing entitlement for benefit changes from one country to another, reflecting differences in policy orientations. The level of benefits varies according to factors such as family size, the birth rank of the child or the length of education, to the extent that children cannot be said to be of 'equal value'. In the late 1990s, supplements were paid for large families in Sweden, and the amount of benefit per child increased markedly with the number of children in Belgium and France. Only in the United Kingdom was the amount paid higher for the first than for subsequent children. Adjustments were made according to the age of the children in Austria, Belgium, Denmark, France, Luxembourg and the Netherlands. Benefits were targeted at low-income families in Greece and Spain, which operated an income ceiling on eligibility; the system in Italy was degressive; and Portugal also took account of income in calculating the level of allowances [2.7, 1998, table X].

In addition, the age limit for benefits varied between member states. The minimum age limit was set at 16 in Ireland, Portugal, Sweden and the United Kingdom, at 17 in Finland and the Netherlands, and at 18 in all other member states, except Austria and France where benefits were paid up to the age of 19. Most countries extended the age limit for children continuing in education and training. In Ireland and the United Kingdom, it was raised to 19, in France to 20, in Greece to 22, in the Netherlands and Portugal to 24, in Belgium to 25, in Austria to 26, and in Germany and Luxembourg to 27. No extension was granted in Denmark, Finland, Italy, Spain and Sweden. Unemployed children, or those 'remaining at home', could receive benefit up to the age of 21 in Austria and Germany, and up to 24 in the Netherlands in cases where they were not entitled to a student grant. The age limit for dependent children was raised to 21 in France for low-income supplement and housing benefit. No age limit applied for disabled children in Austria, Germany, Greece, Italy, Luxembourg and Spain [2.7, 1998, table X].

Before statistics began recording a steep rise in the incidence of extramarital births, cohabitation and lone parenthood, most countries already made some form of provision for lone parents as a result of divorce or bereavement. Never-married mothers were also catered for, primarily to ensure that their children would not suffer financially from having only one parent. By taking lone parents, and particularly lone mothers, into account as both statistical and benefit categories, the *de facto* situation of a growing number of lone parents was thus given legitimacy. Lone parents have also been identified as a target group for social work and special benefits, usually because of their low incomes. In the late 1990s, supplements to family allowances were paid to lone parents in Denmark, Finland (as well as maintenance if necessary), France, Germany (in the absence of maintenance payments from the other parent), Greece, Ireland (on a means-tested basis), Sweden and the United Kingdom [2.7, 1998, table X].

Differences in eligibility rules and in benefits rates, which ranged from 5.20 euros per child per month in Greece to 254 euros for each subsequent child after the third in Luxembourg in 1998 [2.7, 1998, table X], meant that the treatment accorded to children could vary considerably from one member state to another. Using 1996 data, the European Observatory on National Family Policies calculated the value of what it called the 'child benefit package', expressed in terms of the difference between the net income of a childless couple and that of a couple with children at the same level of earnings (Ditch *et al.*, 1998, pp. 57–68). The package combined cash benefits, tax relief and services in kind (including health, education, childcare and housing costs), designed to mitigate the costs of raising children. Measurement of the relative generosity of the assistance given to parents clearly placed Luxembourg at one extreme of the rank order and Greece at the other in relation to a European mean. France and Belgium were also among the higher ranking countries, while Spain and Italy were at the lower end. Germany, Austria and the United Kingdom preceded Denmark, Sweden, Finland, Portugal and the Netherlands in the medium rankings closer to the mean. Although the observatory noted a general shift from tax allowances to cash benefits, it found little evidence of convergence across EU member states in the policy provision for meeting the cost of raising children.

THE FAMILY IMPACT OF EUROPEAN SOCIAL POLICY

Just as the social dimension had long been subordinated to the economic interests of the European Community and Union, the welfare of the family unit was not included in the original social policy remit of the EEC. In accordance with the subsidiarity principle, family matters remained outside the competence of European institutions, except if they concerned the dependants of migrant workers, or were subsumed under measures to ensure health and safety at work, equality of opportunity between women and men, and the general improvement of living standards. Although the consolidated version of the EC Treaty [1.8] did not introduce any direct reference to family policy, by the late 1990s through these indirect routes, the topic had secured a place on the Union's agenda. In the same way that gender was eventually mainstreamed (see Chapter 6), the case could have been made for formalizing the analysis of the family impact of all EU policies as an explicit treaty commitment. Instead, it was left to the Commission to initiate action in support of families by other means, prompted by the sustained efforts of Coface and, from the 1980s, of the European Parliament.

During the 1990s, the Commission used its mandate for reporting on the demographic situation and on social problems to draw attention to family values as a stabilizing force in society, to identify the contribution that family-sensitive policies can make to economic performance and to alert governments to the costs of neglecting family factors [2.3; 5.8; 10.3]. Another clear indication of the concern at EU level with family policy is the priority given to the social and economic challenges resulting from changing family structures among the research tasks identified under the Fifth Framework Programme for 1998–2002 [3.13]. Within the horizontal programme, entitled 'Improving the human research potential and the socio-economic knowledge base', the issues to be addressed under the first research task encompassed the challenges presented by family change for welfare states, intergenerational relationships, work patterns, time use, equity and education, including lifelong learning.

The Commission has been assisted in its attempt to record and analyse changing family forms and family policies in EU member states by Eurostat, through its data collection function, and by the European Observatory on National Family Policies, through its monitoring activities. During the 1990s, the observatory carried out its task with a specific commitment to improve the quality of life for all families (Ditch *et al.*, 1998, p. v). Its national experts pooled information and ideas, advised the Commission and helped to identify and disseminate good practice. Although many of the other social policy networks and observatories created in the 1970s and 1980s were disbanded, the family policy observatory continued to operate throughout the 1990s, indicating the symbolic importance attributed to family matters, and a measure of agreement between member states over its continued funding.

From the early 1970s, Eurostat carried out its brief by constantly refining its data gathering techniques, enabling more accurate tracking of changing patterns of family formation and dissolution and of the development of alternative family forms [5.9]. Over time, the dedicated panel survey of European households (ECHP) will also make an important contribution to comparative longitudinal data on family and household change.

It is difficult to assess whether the activity of EU institutions and organizations, and the exchange of information and ideas at EU level have had an impact on national family policies, and even less so on behaviour, or to know whether a more formal Union competence would result in greater convergence of policy objectives and outcomes. Despite some similarity in policy developments, from analysis of the child benefit package, the observatory was, for example, unable to discern much evidence of convergence across EU member states in their approaches to meeting the cost of childraising (Ditch *et al.*, 1998, p. 68). Demographers, political scientists, economists and sociologists, particularly in France, have long been debating whether public policy influences demographic trends and, more especially, family structures, but without reaching a definitive answer (Hantrais, 1999b).

With reference to permissive legislation, it has been suggested in this chapter that shifts in national policy may be a response to changes in family structure, rather than the reverse. It seems unlikely, for example, that legislation on the rights of the dependants of migrant workers has substantially increased intra-European mobility (see Chapter 9), but changing family structures may have made it necessary to revise existing legislation. The definition of dependency used in Council Regulation (EEC) N° 1612/68 [9.2], although broader than in many EU member states, was restricted to the heterosexual institution of marriage, thereby excluding unmarried and same-sex cohabiting couples. Since intra-European migrant workers are, by law, entitled to the same treatment as nationals in the host country, the rights of migrants with non-conformist living arrangements may differ as they move from one member state to another. The Union's commitment to respect the diversity of national systems and its rejection of the notion of harmonization or unification mean that, in some cases, national provisions for families may contravene article 13 of the amended EC Treaty [1.8] outlawing discrimination on grounds of sexual orientation. Family policy thus continues to provide an interesting example of the complexities of the policy-making process and of the ways in which changes in living arrangements can have an impact on EU legislation.

Box 5 Secondary legislation and official publications relating to family policies

5.1 Council Directive 73/403/EEC of 22 November 1973 on the synchronization of general population censuses (*OJ* L 347/50 17.12.73).
5.2 Resolution of the European Parliament on family policy in the European Community, 9 June 1983 (*OJ* C 184/116 11.7.83).
5.3 Communication from the Commission on family policies (COM(89) 363 final, 8 August 1989).
5.4 Conclusions of the Council and the Ministers Responsible for Family Affairs, meeting within the Council of 29 September 1989 regarding family policies (*OJ* C 277/2 31.10.89).
5.5 Resolution from the European Parliament on protection of families and family units at the close of the International Year of the Family, 14 December 1994 (*OJ* C 18/96 23.1.95).
5.6 European Commission/European Observatory on National Family Policies, *National Family Policies* (annual publication to 1998).
5.7 European Commission, The European Union and the family, *Social Europe*, 1/94.
5.8 European Commission, *The Demographic Situation in the European Union*, OOPEC (annual report until 1999, then incorporated into the Commission's report on *The Social Situation in the European Union*).
5.9 Eurostat, *Demographic Statistics*, OOPEC (annual publication).

6 The Gender Dimension of Social Policy

While family life is an area in which the Commission and some national governments have been reluctant to intervene, women's rights have long been on the European policy agenda, not, it is argued, from a desire to achieve equality between the sexes, but as a means of ensuring fair competition between member states (Buckley and Anderson, 1988, p. 10; Crawley, 1990, p. 7; Hoskyns, 1996, p. 45). The initial motivation for Community intervention in gender issues was to avoid any one member state gaining a competitive edge, in this case by paying women at lower rates than men. The pressure for legislation is said to have come mainly from the French, who had enshrined the principle of equal pay in their postwar constitution of 1946 and wanted other member states to follow suit so that France would not be at a competitive disadvantage due to higher labour costs (Quintin, 1988, p. 71; Hoskyns, 1996, pp. 54–5).

In the early years of the European Economic Community (EEC), interest in equality between the sexes coincided with both second-wave feminism and the development of socio-economic conditions that were conducive to women's emancipation (Buckley and Anderson, 1988, p. 5). Economic reconstruction, expanding opportunities in education and changes in family structure all contributed to producing an environment in which national governments were receptive to proposals for promoting greater gender equality.

Progressively, Community institutions extended their remit to cover many aspects of women's economic activity. Already in the 1960s, the Commission was organizing studies and conferences, and making recommendations on the workings of article 119 of the EEC Treaty [1.2], which dealt with equal pay. In the Community's social action programme of 1974 [1.9], implementation of the equal pay principle was one of the priority actions. During the 1970s, the focus of attention broadened to encompass equal treatment in access to employment, training, working conditions and social security. From 1977, the European Social Fund (ESF) was used to support training for women over the age of 25. Exchange of information and experience was promoted through international activities, supported during the 1980s by a series of action programmes. The Commission monitored the situation, initiated research, and took action against individual governments through the European Court of Justice (ECJ), thereby building up a strong body of case law. Although, as exemplified by equal pay, the Union has clearly been influenced by national law and practice, the impetus provided by Council directives and by rulings from the ECJ served as a powerful incentive for legislative change in individual member states (Hantrais, 2000).

In the 1980s, European women were developing a strong constituency, and women's pressure groups played an active role in taking forward gender policy, both informally and through more formal channels instituted at European level. In 1981, the Commission set up an Advisory Committee on Equal Opportunities for Women and Men, with two representatives from each member state. The European Network of Women (Enow) was established in 1983 to provide a forum for non-governmental women's organizations. The European Parliament created its own *ad hoc* Standing Committee on Women's Rights in 1981 to report on the situation of women in the Community. Following the 1984 elections, it became a permanent committee of the European Parliament, with a brief for monitoring existing directives and looking into ways of extending the Community's equal opportunities legislation, while also keeping under review the impact on women of policy decisions taken in other areas. The committee has sought to be proactive in its dealings with the Commission and the Council of Ministers, and can be credited with having consolidated a large body of information about the situation of women in the European Union (EU) and with pushing forward legislation. Women have been more strongly represented at European level than in most national parliaments, with nearly 20 per cent of elected members in the European Parliament in 1989, 27 per cent in 1994, and 30 per cent in 1999. Another group that has played an important role in setting the agenda for women's affairs, and in initiating research and action is the European Women's Lobby, which began meeting in 1990, with financial support from the Commission (Vale, 1991). By the late 1990s, the lobby represented some 2700 women's organizations, including Enow, and had taken on the task of co-ordinating action to further women's interests at both EU and national level (Stratigaki, 2000).

The 1990s were marked by two important developments for gender policy: the adoption of measures at EU level to help parents reconcile their occupational and family life, and the mainstreaming of gender. Opinion has, however, been divided over the extent to which they constitute real progress for equal opportunities. Views also diverge over the impact that policy formulated at EU level can have on the everyday lives of women as workers and mothers within member states. As in other policy areas, the extent and pace of change in behaviour and in attitudes towards women's roles in society vary according to a number of factors, including the wider policy environment, the state of labour markets, and national trends in family building and structure.

This chapter begins by examining in more detail the Union's policy framework with regard to gender issues in order to gain a better understanding of the developing policy process at EU level. The impact of the implementation of European policy on national policy formation and practice is then considered, with particular reference to the characteristics of employment patterns, and the relationship between paid work and family life. In conclusion, an attempt is made to assess the interaction between EU and national gender policy and the progress made towards greater equality of opportunity.

EUROPEAN LEGISLATION AND WOMEN'S SOCIAL RIGHTS

In accordance with the overall objectives of the EEC Treaty, the attention paid to women in the Union has been primarily, and almost exclusively, in their capacity as workers (see Chapter 1). This section examines the various legal and other instruments used at EU level to promote women's labour market rights and equal opportunities at work. It analyses the gradual shift in focus towards the reconciliation of employment and family life and the introduction of the concept of mainstreaming.

Equality in the Community's and Union's treaties and charter

In the 1957 EEC Treaty under the chapter on social provisions, article 119 referred explicitly, and unambiguously, to the right of women to equal pay with men. Originally, the article had been included in a section of the treaty on the distortion of competition but, in the final stages of the negotiations, it was moved to the title on social policy, most probably with a view to strengthening the social dimension (Hoskyns, 1996, p. 57). The ground had been prepared for the equal pay principle by the adoption in 1951 of Convention 100 of the General Conference of the International Labour Organization (ILO). By the time the EEC Treaty was signed, the convention had been ratified by Belgium, France, Italy and Germany. Convention 100 concerned 'equal remuneration for men and women workers for work of equal value', whereas article 119 laid down the principle that 'men and women should receive equal pay [rendered by the broader term *rémunération* in the French version] for equal work'. The controversial phrase 'equal value' was omitted. Instead, to appease the French, pay and equal pay were defined in terms that were more specific than for any other aspect of social policy. Pay meant 'the ordinary basic or minimum wage or salary and any other consideration, whether in cash or in kind, which the worker receives, directly or indirectly, in respect of his [*sic*] employment from his employer'. Equal pay implied that 'pay for the same work at piece rates shall be calculated on the basis of the same unit of measurement' and 'that pay for work at time rates shall be the same for the same job'.

Despite its insistence on the status of women as paid workers, article 119 provided a very useful basis for developing equal opportunities legislation at European level (Crawley, 1990, p. 7). Articles 100 and 235 of the treaty enabled the Commission to prepare directives not only on equal pay but also on equal treatment. Article 100 made it possible to issue directives to approximate provisions across member states, and article 235 conferred the power to legislate by unanimous voting when action was necessary to achieve EEC objectives, and provision was not made under other articles. The treaty thus established a framework for promoting the harmonization of national legislation to the social and economic advantage of women in paid work.

Although the Commission attempted to bring forward proposals relating to the organization of life outside the workplace, the main focus of policy adopted at Council level was clearly the rights and opportunities of women as paid workers. The 1989 Community Charter of the Fundamental Social Rights of Workers [1.10, §16] reaffirmed that 'Equal treatment for men and women must be assured. Equal opportunities for men and women must be developed.' Further action was called for to ensure implementation of the equality principle, particularly in access to employment, remuneration, working conditions, social protection, education, vocational training and career development. A reference was also introduced in §16 to the need for measures 'enabling men and women to reconcile their occupational and family obligations' with a view to achieving greater equality of opportunity.

The Agreement on Social Policy appended to the Maastricht Treaty [1.6] confirmed the orientation towards workers' rights by reiterating *verbatim* the terms of article 119 of the EEC Treaty. A paragraph in circuitous wording was added, however, advising member states that they should not be prevented 'from maintaining or adopting measures providing for specific advantages in order to make it easier for women to pursue a vocational activity or to prevent or compensate for disadvantages in their professional careers' (article 6 §3). This statement has been construed to mean national governments can take positive action to counter discrimination (Cox, 1993, p. 43), an issue disputed since the 1970s (Stratigaki, 2000, pp. 39–41).

Not only did the 1997 Treaty of Amsterdam [1.7] reinstate the social chapter in the main body of the treaty, following the British opt-in, it also confirmed the Union's strong commitment to gender equality and gave it a legal base. A new paragraph was introduced referring to work of 'equal value', and §3 of article 6 in the Agreement on Social Policy was strengthened by substituting the 'under-represented sex' for 'women'. The two new paragraphs of (renumbered) article 141 in the consolidated version of the EC Treaty thus read as follows.

> 3. The Council, acting in accordance with the procedure referred to in article 251, and after consulting the Economic and Social Committee, shall adopt measures to ensure the application of the principle of equal opportunities and equal treatment of men and women in matters of employment and occupation, including the principle of equal pay for equal work or work of equal value.
>
> 4. With a view to ensuring full equality in practice between men and women in working life, the principle of equal treatment shall not prevent any Member State from maintaining or adopting measures providing for specific advantages in order to make it easier for the under-represented sex to pursue a vocational activity or to prevent or compensate for disadvantages in professional careers. [1.8, §§3–4]

In line with the objective of mainstreaming gender, a reference was added in article 2 of the revised EC Treaty to 'equality between men and women', and a catch-all paragraph was included at the end of the revised article 3 (§2), stating that 'In all the activities referred to in this Article, the Community shall aim to eliminate inequalities, and to promote equality, between women and men.' A new article inserted in the Treaty of Amsterdam (article 13 in the consolidated version) gave the Council authority to take action to combat discrimination, including that based on sex. EEC Treaty article 118 was expanded to incorporate supporting measures to integrate 'persons excluded from the labour market' and 'equality between men and women with regard to labour market opportunities and treatment at work' (amended article 137 §1).

The new title VIII on employment in the consolidated version of the EC Treaty required the Council to draw up annual employment guidelines [1.18; 1.20]. One of the four pillars in the 1998 and 1999 employment guidelines was the strengthening of equal opportunities policies. It pointed to the need to tackle gender gaps by reducing unemployment among women and the under or over-representation of women in certain sectors and occupations. It went on to highlight the need for measures to enable women and men to reconcile work and family life, referring to parental leave, part-time work, flexible working arrangements and childcare services, as well as policies to facilitate the return to work. By the late 1990s, the Union's treaty obligation to equal opportunities had thus been confirmed and extended, although the primary, if not sole, justification for action remained paid work.

Secondary legislation on women's rights

The Union has used a variety of instruments to promote greater equality of treatment and opportunity for women, ranging from the treaty commitments described in the previous section, through Council directives, Council and Commission recommendations and resolutions, conclusions and communications, to action programmes proposed and implemented by the Commission. This section examines the secondary legislation and soft law drawn up to ensure the application of the treaties in national law and practice.

In 1975, the Commission issued its first directive in the area of equal opportunities. Council Directive 75/117/EEC 'on the approximation of the laws of the Member States relating to the application of the principle of equal pay for men and women' [6.1] enlarged on the provisions of article 119. In particular, it clarified and extended the meaning of the principle of equal pay to work of equal value, as assessed by job evaluation schemes. The directive explicitly outlawed discrimination on grounds of sex, not only where an employee feels s/he is being directly discriminated against because s/he is paid less than an employee of the opposite sex, but also where conditions are imposed which exclude or impede the progress of members of one sex, and which are not essential for the job. While the directive gives employees who feel they have grounds for complaint the right to legal redress, the concepts of work of equal value and indirect discrimination remain difficult to operationalize. Over the years, a series of judgements on cases brought before the

ECJ has been necessary to help clarify the position for national legislators (Byre, 1988; Burrows and Mair, 1996, pp. 21–32).

Subsequent directives built onto the framework provided by article 119 and the 1975 directive. The following year, Directive 76/207/EEC extended the equality principle to 'equal treatment for men and women as regards access to employment, vocational training and promotion, and working conditions' [6.2]. Directive 79/7/EEC, which was adopted in 1978 and finally came into force in 1984, addressed 'the principle of equal treatment for men and women in matters of social security' [6.3]. Member states were allowed six years to implement the 1978 directive because of its complexities and the costs involved (Luckhaus, 1990, p. 12). This directive was supplemented in 1986 by Directives, 86/378/EEC [6.7] and 86/613/EEC [6.9], which extended the principle of equality of treatment to occupational schemes and self-employed men and women. The directive required that there should be no direct or indirect discrimination on grounds of sex in relation to matters such as the scope of social security schemes, conditions of access and calculation of benefits, for example with regard to retirement, in cases where a married woman's employment did not entitle her husband to benefits, or where occupational schemes were only open to men.

Although the three directives removed the automatic exclusion of women from benefit entitlements earned as full-time workers, they did not cover survivors' and family benefits, and they left open the possibility of excluding the determination of pensionable age, advantages for persons who have brought up children and the granting of increases for long-term invalidity, old age, industrial accident and occupational disease benefits for a dependent wife. Another important omission was that they did not directly address the issue of part-time or unpaid work. A draft directive on voluntary part-time work, first proposed in 1981, was not adopted until 1997 (see Chapter 4), although cases brought before the ECJ did result in some recognition of women's rights as part-time workers (Luckhaus, 1990, p. 18). While the ECJ was subsequently more liberal in acknowledging women's needs as part-time workers, its judgements signalled the intention not to interfere with this aspect of the organization of family life and the division of household labour.

A proposal for a directive, issued in 1983 and amended in 1984 [6.4], addressed the question of parental leave and leave for family reasons, but was similarly not adopted for more than a decade. However, the less binding Council recommendation 'on child care', adopted in 1992 [6.13], included special leave for parents to look after their own children, as well as measures to encourage men and women to share family responsibilities for childcare and the education of children. The recommendation was the outcome of a long process of negotiation over childcare provision within the framework of policy on equal opportunities and the reconciliation of family obligations with employment. The ground had been prepared by the European Commission's Childcare Network, which began operating in 1986. The network took as its basic premise that the inequality in the conditions under which men and women supply their labour is socially determined, and that childcare affects both women's opportunities for participation in the labour market and their general well-being, whether or not they are in paid employment. Therefore, equality is an issue for men as much as for women (European Commission Childcare Network, 1990, p. 2).

Council Directive 92/85/EEC 'on the introduction of measures to encourage improvements in the safety and health at work of pregnant workers and workers who have recently given birth or are breastfeeding' [4.7] affords another example of how the Commission handled a contentious issue by bringing forward a proposal under the framework directive as a health and safety measure. As with Directive 93/104/EC 'concerning certain aspects of the organization of working time' [4.10], it was adopted by qualified majority voting (see Chapter 4). Essentially, the working time directive sought to provide a minimum level of protection by proposing that women who are working at the time when they become pregnant, or who are registered as unemployed, are automatically entitled to 14 weeks' maternity leave with pay and without loss of employment-related rights. Another aspect of women's working conditions was tackled in a Council recommendation 'on the protection of the dignity of women and men at work' [6.12], which outlawed sexual harassment at the workplace.

In the 1994 white paper on European social policy, the Commission announced its intention to keep all these items on the agenda for the remainder of the decade. Legislation was to be pursued on part-time work. On the question of parental leave and career breaks, the possibility of a framework directive was to be examined as a measure aimed at reconciling professional and family life, with a view to establishing minimum standards [1.15, p. 31]. The implementation of the recommendation on childcare was to be monitored, baseline data were to be established on childcare infrastructures and services, and the issue of gender stereotyping was also to be addressed [1.15, p. 43].

Under the terms of the Agreement on Social Policy appended to the Treaty on European Union [1.6, articles 3–4], procedures were put in place to enable management and labour to initiate the contractual process. Council Directive 96/34/EC 'on the framework agreement on parental leave concluded by UNICE, CEEP and the ETUC' [6.16] was the first example of recourse to the new procedure. The directive made provision for leave of at least three months to be taken up to the time when the child reached the age of eight. It stipulated that the right should be granted to each parent on a non-transferable basis. Payment was not to be mandatory during the leave period, and member states were given discretion to decide under what conditions leave should be granted. Although the directive was binding with regard to the results to be achieved, it thus left member states to choose the forms and methods of implementation. The British opt-out had meant that the United Kingdom was not bound by the directive. Following the change of government and the incorporation of the Agreement on Social Policy into the Treaty of Amsterdam, an amended version of the directive (97/75/EC) was therefore adopted in 1997, extending its provisions to the United Kingdom [6.16].

While the earlier draft of the directive was written in the context of equal treatment for men and women, the 1996 version has to be situated in relation to growing pressures to increase labour market flexibility as part of the Union's employment strategy. The 1990s directives appeared to mark a shift in emphasis towards non-labour market factors in the guise of reconciliation of employment with family life, but they did not go far enough to signal a break with the employment-based origins of equality policy.

Community action programmes on equal opportunities for women

Directives are one of the more tangible and binding outcomes of the Union's activities in the area of women's rights. While legislation provides a framework for action, the Commission was aware that the law alone cannot ensure equality of opportunity. Throughout the 1960s, the Commission regularly reported on the difficulties of putting the equal pay principle into practice. One of the objectives of the 1974 social action programme was to achieve greater equality between men and women not only with regard to pay but also in access to employment, vocational training and improvements in working conditions. The programme made reference for the first time to the existence of the political will to adopt measures to ensure that family responsibilities could be reconciled with job aspirations [1.9, p. 2]. Subsequently, the Commission registered its intention to act as a prime mover in the area of equal opportunities by establishing a Women's Bureau in 1976 (renamed as the Equal Opportunities Unit in 1994), and by initiating a series of action programmes promoting equal opportunities for women. An important feature of the programmes was their effort to raise awareness, disseminate information and mobilize what were called 'equality partners', including the two sides of industry and non-governmental organizations.

The first equal opportunities action programme for the period 1982–85 stressed the need to put equal opportunities into practice, by means of positive action programmes aimed at enabling women to overcome their disadvantage in relation to men, and extending to a more equal sharing of family responsibilities [6.5]. The second action programme, covering 1986–90, addressed the consolidation of the legal rights of individuals and sought to promote positive action to overcome the non-legal barriers to the achievement of equal opportunities [6.6]. A section was devoted to the sharing of family and occupational responsibilities, proposing action to promote parental leave, childcare services and the reorganization of working time.

The Council responded to the provision made in the Community charter in its resolution 'on the third medium-term Community action programme on equal opportunities for women and men', covering the period 1991–95 [6.11]. The programme was presented against the background of the conditions and opportunities created by the completion of the internal market and the need to develop new policies and measures taking into account the social and economic changes of the 1990s and beyond. The Council recommended that 'better use should be made of women's abilities and gifts so as to permit their full participation in the process of European development'. Women's participation was, moreover, described as 'an essential factor in European economic and social cohesion' [6.11, p. 1]. Pursuing this line of argument, the Council stressed the need for measures to reconcile professional and family life. As argued in the previous chapter, the justification for extending Community policy to family affairs consistently focused on the status of individuals and their effectiveness as workers. However, the resolution mentioned not only the efforts required to improve the position of women in society, particularly at all levels in the media sector, but also the need to promote the participation of women in the decision-making process in public, economic and social life.

In accordance with the principle of complementarity and subsidiarity, the third action programme identified separately measures that fell under the Commission's responsibility and those that individual member states were expected to implement. It also provided for the integration of equality issues into general mainstream policy at EU and national level. The New Opportunities for Women (Now) initiative for the promotion of equal opportunities in the field of employment and vocational training, particularly in less developed areas, affords an example of both these principles.

The initiative was established within the framework of the structural funds and involved a partnership not only between the Union and national governments, but also between regional and local administrations, vocational training agents, socio-economic partners, research and information centres on women. To help women create small businesses and co-operatives or re-enter employment, Community support could extend to guidance and advice, technical assistance, such as awareness-raising actions, and the collection and dissemination of information on good practice and vocational training. As an enabling device, the Commission undertook to support the provision of childcare facilities, including the operating costs of facilities linked to vocational training centres and the training of childcare workers. It thereby extended its remit beyond the workplace into areas where previously – like some national governments – it had been reluctant to intervene, although the interest in childcare was, as stated in the white paper on social policy, to a large extent, motivated by its job creation potential [1.15, p. 43].

The fourth medium-term Community action programme on equal opportunities for men and women for the period 1996–2000 was adopted by a Council decision in 1995 [6.14]. Article 2 of the programme defined and gave substance to the principle of mainstreaming, which had been floated in the third action programme, stating that the intention was 'to promote the integration of equal opportunities for men and women in the process of preparing, implementing and monitoring all policies and activities of the European Union and the Member States having regard to their respective powers'. Mainstreaming implied an integrated approach and more streamlined management to ensure that equal opportunities were given a higher profile. A key term in the programme was again partnership: within the Commission, between social partners, with competent national and regional authorities, between women and men and with non-governmental organizations. The aim of this co-operative approach was to change attitudes and break down the rigidity of sex roles in all aspects of economic and social life.

As confirmation of the commitment to the principle of mainstreaming gender, a new structure was set up within the Commission, in the form of a Group of Commissioners on Equality between Women and

Men and Women's Rights, responsible for stimulating debate and ensuring that equal opportunities would be integrated into all areas of policy and action.

At the instigation of the group, the Commission further developed its approach to mainstreaming in a communication issued in 1996 [6.17], affirming the political will to act, and explaining that all policies should be scrutinized from the planning stage and evaluated from a gender perspective to take account of their possible effects on the situation of women and men. The communication said very little about the strategies and instruments to be used to implement mainstreaming. No timetable or budget was set. Reference was made to the Commission's remit for producing an annual report on the policies implemented and action taken. The reports were intended to give visibility to Community policy on equal opportunities, to contribute to the development of its strategy, and serve as a reference point both for the Commission and for present and future member states. In 1999, a follow-up report on the communication pointed out that the progress made had been piecemeal, and identified the risk that mainstreaming might result in the abandonment of policies specifically targeting women, as exemplified by the disappearance of a designated budget line in the Socrates programme for equality-oriented projects [6.17, p. 9]. The report therefore advocated retaining the dual approach by combining mainstreaming with specific measures of positive action. It also recommended devoting resources to gender-impact assessments of policies, the collection of comparative sex-disaggregated statistics, the setting up of gender-proofing procedures within the directorates-general, and the organization of training in gender analysis and assessment for officials.

By the late 1990s, through treaty commitments, secondary legislation and the Commission's action programmes, equality issues had thus achieved a prominent position on the European social policy agenda. The Treaty of Amsterdam had recognized equality between women and men as a primary political objective, a strong body of legislation had been built up on equal pay and equal treatment, and the action programmes, reports and guidelines provided a firm basis from which to move forward. However, as with other areas of social policy, it was not difficult to find an economic motivation for the equality policies that had been given such a high profile in the official rhetoric. The action initiated was confined to a single dimension of women's lives, and the information collected indicated that, despite the measures taken, equality of opportunity was far from being an everyday reality for most women and men in the Union.

THE IMPACT OF EUROPEAN LEGISLATION ON NATIONAL POLICY AND PRACTICE

Whereas in the previous chapter no clear picture emerged of what might be considered as a European family policy, this chapter has shown that, in the area of equality between men and women at work, the Union can be credited with having formulated and implemented a more coherent body of policy. Procedures have been established for monitoring its effectiveness, incentives have been introduced to ensure enactment, and penalties can be incurred for infringements. European policy may therefore have played a more prominent role in shaping national legislation than was the case for family affairs. This section begins with a review of the transposition of European equality legislation into national regulatory frameworks. Transposition does not, however, mean compliance or changes in attitudes and behaviour. Attention is therefore also given to identifying changes in the patterning of gender relations in EU member states.

Transposing European legislation into national law

In the areas of equal pay and equal treatment, some member states have been in the forefront of change, others have kept pace with European legislation, while yet others have only gradually implemented directives, generally in response to infringement proceedings [6.19, 1998, chart 3]. Cases brought before the ECJ have also helped to resolve problems arising over implementation. The much-quoted Kalanke and Marschall cases [6.18] have, for example, made clear that positive action in favour of women is compatible with European law, except in the specific case of unconditional preferential quotas.

Even though national equal pay legislation predated European law in France, where the 1946 constitution affirmed the equality principle, work of equal value was not formally defined in law until 1983. The French authorities had not, in fact, foreseen how the ECJ would interpret article 119. Nor had lawyers and policy makers been able to predict how European directives would be used to enforce the equality principle (Lanquetin *et al.*, 2000, pp. 70–6). The Italian constitution of 1947 provided for the same pay for equal work, while also offering protection to women workers to enable them to fulfil their family functions. The implementation of the equal pay principle in the 1960s was, however, an extremely conflictual process (Bimbi, 1993, pp. 147–8; Del Re, 2000, pp. 111–13). Although Germany had a basic law on equal rights dating back to 1949, infringement proceedings were avoided by belatedly adopting legislation on equal pay in 1980 [6.8, p. 16].

Several of the other founder member states were introducing legislation on equal pay for work of equal value in the early 1970s when the European directives were being drafted [6.8, pp. 9–34]. In Belgium the principle of equal pay for work of the same or equal value in the Collective Labour Agreement of 1975 was given binding force in the private sector. Luxembourg's Grand-Ducal regulation of 1974 included an equal value clause. The Netherlands followed suit in 1975. The member states that joined the Community in the 1970s were also developing appropriate legislation. Ireland's Anti-Discrimination Act of 1974 included an equal pay clause. The United Kingdom passed an Equal Pay Act in 1970, with a five-year period of voluntary compliance. The Danish equal pay law dates from 1976, but infringement proceedings were initiated against Denmark for not including the term 'equal value'.

Most member states extended their legislation to cover illegal dismissal on the basis of sex and to make provision for legal redress, with the burden of proof resting on employers. Some established monitoring procedures through organizations such as the Equal Opportunities Commission, which was set up in 1975 in the United Kingdom, or the Equality Status Council established in 1978 in Denmark.

The countries that joined the Community in the 1980s were required to bring their national legislation into line with European law which they had had no hand in drafting. In the case of equal rights and equal opportunities directives, this did not seem to present any major problems, since national legislation had been moving in the same direction. On joining the Community, the Spanish government was quick to draw up the necessary legislation in adapting its own provisions to take account of European directives. Quite radical changes had been occurring in women's legal status since the mid-1970s. The Civil Code was amended in 1975 to recognize women's full legal capacity. The Spanish constitution of 1978 enshrined equality as an essential constituent element of a legally established social and democratic state. Reference was made specifically to non-discrimination based on sex in relation to work, and this principle was also embodied in the Workers' Statute and the Basic Law on Employment. Similarly, Portugal had made profound changes to its constitution in 1976 and 1982 to grant new legal status to women. The constitution laid down the principles of equality and non-discrimination not only at work and in education but also between spouses. Greece had already included an article in its 1975 constitution establishing equal rights between the sexes, and this principle was extended by transposing the detail of Directive 75/117/EEC into national law, which came into force in 1984.

In most countries, implementation of Directive 76/207/EEC on equal treatment in access to employment, promotion, vocational training and working conditions was a longer process than for equal pay, and infringement proceedings were initiated against all the nine earlier member states over some aspect of their national legislation [6.8, pp. 69–72]. Despite the long period allowed for implementation of Directive 79/7/EEC on equal treatment in social security, not all member states had complied by the target date of 1984 [6.8, pp. 76–83]. The relevant law was adopted in Germany in 1985, and in Belgium and Luxembourg in 1986. By 1997, Directives 86/378/EEC and 96/97/EC on equal treatment in occupational social security schemes had still not been transposed into national legislation in Belgium, Denmark, Luxembourg and the Netherlands [4.18, 1998, pp. 36–8].

Austria and the two Nordic states that became members of the EU in the 1990s all had in place laws governing equal pay and equal treatment. Sweden had some of the earliest legislation dating back to the 1940s in the public sector. Austria's equal pay act was adopted in 1978, and Finland passed a law on equality between women and men in 1986. Finland and Sweden instituted Gender Equality Ombudsmen. Despite Sweden's distinguished record on equality, EU membership brought much closer scrutiny of Swedish equality law. The Gender Equality Ombudsman, the JÄMO, tested the conformity of Swedish equal opportunities law with EU legislation. As a result, the scope of the Swedish act against discrimination in employment, adopted in 1980, was extended in 1992 in a new equal opportunities act, subsequently revised in 1994. The amended law tightened up regulations on wage discrimination, made the meaning of the concept of equal work more precise and introduced regulations concerning indirect discrimination and sexual harassment (Bergqvist and Jungar, 2000, pp. 171–6).

When Directive 92/85/EEC, which provided for paid maternity leave, was adopted, all except Ireland and the United Kingdom already made some form of statutory provision. However, the Commission initiated infringement procedures against France, Ireland, Italy, Luxembourg and Sweden in 1999 for not fully or correctly complying with the stipulations laid down in the directive. By the deadline of June 1998, few member states had met the formal requirement for transposition of Directive 96/34/EC on parental leave, although all but Greece, Ireland, Luxembourg and the United Kingdom offered statutory parental leave at the end of 1997. Sweden was well advanced having instituted parental insurance as early as 1974 [4.18, 1998, pp. 47–9].

These examples suggest that European law was perhaps less effective as a force initiating reform at national level than as an instrument for accompanying or accelerating change, which is to be expected since directives are the outcome of a compromise reached between member states. However, instances of resistance can be identified when individual member states have felt that their own legislation was already adequate to cover the contingencies provided for in directives, or when they have claimed that the social and economic cost of implementation would be unreasonable. Legislation affecting working time, maternity and parental leave, and childcare was opposed, and in some cases blocked, for these reasons. The United Kingdom, in particular, developed a reputation in the 1980s for its almost systematic opposition to EU equality legislation, on the grounds that the measures proposed would entail additional labour costs for employers or endanger their flexibility to respond to market demands. Although the United Kingdom has established a good record for transposing directives in the areas of employment and social policy [1.15, table 1], in 1997 it was, with Germany whose transposition record was average, the member state that had been issued with the largest number of rulings from the ECJ on EEC article 119 and the 1970s equality directives [6.19, 1997, chart 3]. As a result of ECJ rulings, on several occasions the United Kingdom had been forced to change its own legislation to comply with European law (Burrows and Mair, 1996). By contrast, Italy, which had a very poor record for transposition, had received only one ruling from the ECJ. This may say more about the effectiveness of the British Equal Opportunities Commission in bringing cases before the courts than about the status of equal opportunities in the two countries. In any event, transposition does not necessarily imply that legislation is translated into good practice at national level.

Women's access to rights as workers and mothers

Analysis of European law as it affects women shows clearly how attention has been paid almost exclusively to their rights as workers. Gradually, EU directives have recognized that women may need special treatment in their capacity as working mothers, thereby juxtaposing the potentially competing aims of equality and difference, which have, for example, led to conflicts in France (Lanquetin *et al.*, 2000), and to paradoxes in Italy (Del Re, 2000). As argued in previous sections, the inclusion of women's rights on the European agenda has been justified by economic reasons: the flexibility required to enable parents to reconcile paid work with family life was 'employment-friendly' before being 'women-friendly'. This section looks at the way that some of the measures designed to extend women's rights as workers and as working mothers have been implemented in EU member states.

Individualized rights

A consequence of the directives on equal treatment for men and women in social security schemes has been the shift towards the individualization of rights in employment-insurance schemes. Accordingly, individuals are more often being assessed independently of their family situation with regard to social security and income tax. Women and men are thus required to pay the same earnings-related contributions and taxes. In return, they gain access to the same rights to sick pay, pensions, unemployment and other benefits arising from employment. Individualization was promoted in the white paper on social policy [1.15, p. 42] and in the Commission's communication on modernizing and improving social protection [2.3, section 2.4] as a means of removing discrimination in social protection and fiscal policy and reducing women's dependency on male breadwinners. The communication recognized, however, that direct social security rights can disadvantage women because of their lower pay, more interrupted and less secure patterns of employment, and that derived rights, such as survivors' pensions, may provide more generous entitlements for women whose former spouse earned a high income.

No EU member state operated a completely individualized system of social protection in the late 1990s. As indicated in the previous chapter, child benefits varied in accordance with family income in the Mediterranean states, and income tax systems in several instances took account of family circumstances. The most widely documented, and arguably most important, area of concern for equality policy has been pension rights, where individualization has highlighted the need for compensatory measures to take account of the shortfall in the contributions paid by women to occupational pension schemes. Most countries give some form of recognition in pension calculations for women who spend time out of the labour market performing caring duties. They cover a wide variety of arrangements. In Greece, for example, women who have raised children are entitled to bring forward retirement age by three years for each child, and in Austria time spent raising children is considered as a working period calculated at the rate of four years per child. In many cases, supplements may be added to retirement pensions for parents with dependent children. Denmark, Italy, Portugal and Spain made no special arrangements for childrearing in pension arrangements, but all countries took account of responsibilities for family dependants in assessing survivors' pensions, an area that had been excluded from the equal treatment directives on social security [6.19, 1996, chart 6] (see also Chapter 7).

Arrangements for maternity leave

When the Commission drafted a proposal for the provision of 14 weeks' statutory maternity leave on full pay in 1990, the United Kingdom reacted by claiming that the directive would cause 'a dramatic change in entitlement to paid leave from work in the UK' [6.10, p. 1]. Under national law, a working woman had no automatic right to maternity leave. Under the Employment Protection Consolidation Act of 1978, she did have the right to return to work if she fulfilled the qualifying conditions. Entitlement to maternity pay, which was separate from maternity leave and was governed by the Social Security Act of 1986, was also subject to a qualifying period. The Commission's proposal was therefore expected to have important repercussions for the amount women would receive during maternity leave, and to impact on labour costs for employers. Countries that already had more generous schemes for paid maternity leave were, by the same token, keen to have these measures extended across the Union to avoid being at a competitive disadvantage. In the event, Directive 92/85/EEC [4.7] stipulated that member states could make maternity pay conditional on a period of not more than 12 months employment and set it at a level 'at least equivalent to' the sick pay to which the woman would have been entitled (article 11 §3).

Most of the other member states did not need to make major changes to their arrangements to bring their practices into line with the directive. By the time it was due to take effect, they all had provision for at least 14 weeks' leave (though it was not necessarily called maternity leave), and Italy offered up to five months. Portugal extended the period of maternity leave from 90 days to 14 weeks in 1995 to comply with the directive. Practices varied over payment. Leave with full pay was granted in Austria, Germany, Greece, Luxembourg, the Netherlands (up to a maximum level) and Portugal. In Sweden, the limit was set at 90 per cent of earnings and, in Belgium, the rate began at 82 per cent (up to a maximum level) and was reduced over time. France awarded 84 per cent of previous earnings, Italy 80 per cent, Spain 75 per cent and Ireland 70 per cent. In Finland, the rate was 66 per cent on average. Denmark paid a flat-rate benefit (European Commission Network on Childcare and Other Measures to Reconcile Employment and Family Responsibilities, 1994, pp. 49–51). In all EU member states, mothers were protected against unlawful dismissal and given a guarantee of reinstatement after maternity leave.

Information about two of the applicant states suggests that, by the late 1990s, their provision was at least as good as that stipulated in the directive, if not better. Women workers in the Czech Republic were entitled to statutory maternity leave of 28 weeks, with an entitlement of 37 weeks for lone mothers. Poland paid a full salary during maternity leave, and the Czech Republic offered maternity benefit at 69 per cent of salary (Lohkamp-Himmighofen and Dienel, 2000, pp. 55–6).

Arrangements for paid parental leave

The proposal to harmonize provisions for paid parental leave across all member states raised similar issues to maternity leave for the United Kingdom, which had no statutory provision, although a number of firms had introduced career break schemes. Leave was provided in Ireland only under certain collective agreements. Belgium offered leave of absence in the form of a career break to look after children (European Commission Network on Childcare, 1996, table 5). By the time the parental leave directive was due to be implemented in 1998, all but four countries had put in place formal statutory arrangements for leave. More limited provision applied in Greece and Luxembourg, primarily for public sector workers (Lohkamp-Himmighofen and Dienel, 2000, pp. 56–8). Ireland had not introduced general legislation, but the United Kingdom had undertaken to comply and was allowed until the end of 1999 to do so. The length of leave ranged from ten weeks in Denmark to the time of the child's third birthday in Finland, France, Germany, Italy and Spain. In the Netherlands and Sweden, parents could take parental leave up to the time when the child reached the age of eight, in line with the proposal in the parental leave directive.

Parental leave was without pay in five countries: Greece, Luxembourg, the Netherlands, Portugal, and Spain, although in some cases, provision was made for paid leave in collective agreements. Maternity absence in the United Kingdom was also unpaid, and neither national legislation nor collective provision existed on paid parental leave in

Ireland. In countries where leave was with pay, the arrangements varied from flat-rate payments in Austria, Belgium, Denmark and France (from the second child), a combination of flat-rate and income-related pay in Finland and Sweden, to low income-related pay in Italy (European Commission Network on Childcare, 1996, table 5).

One of the intentions behind the directive was to encourage parents to share the leave between them by specifying that it should apply to men and women and be granted on a non-transferable basis. In the late 1990s, only Italy did not extend leave to fathers. Most countries made it possible for parental leave to alternate between the two parents. Austria and Sweden also offered special incentives to encourage fathers to take leave. In Austria, six months of the leave could not be transferred from one parent to the other, and were lost if one of the parents did not take the allocation. In Sweden, a minimum of one month had to be taken by the father (the so-called 'daddy month'). In Greece each parent had an individual right to three months of the leave period. Flexibility was maximized in most countries, as proposed in the directive, by making it possible for leave to be taken on a part-time basis. Only Denmark, Greece, Italy, Portugal and Spain offered leave solely on a full-time basis. Austria, Belgium, Luxembourg, the Netherlands and Sweden allowed the total period of leave to be extended if it was taken on a part-time basis (Lohkamp-Himmighofen and Dienel, 2000, pp. 56–8).

The directive specified that member states could continue to apply, or introduce, more favourable provisions than those set out in the agreement. Not only coverage but also take-up of parental leave varies across member states, as well as within countries where arrangements are decided under collective agreements. Parental leave is therefore likely to continue to be conceptualized differently from one member state to another. In Denmark, for example, relatively short parental leave has been offered to both mothers and fathers, essentially as an equality measure (Carlsen, 1993). Parental insurance in Sweden, on a non-transferable basis, is regarded, with childcare, as one of the pillars of equality policy, aimed at making it easier for both women and men to combine parenthood and employment (Bergqvist and Jungar, 2000, p. 161). In France, the childrearing allowance (*allocation parentale d'éducation*) has been considered as a means of enabling mothers to take an extended break in employment, without losing employment rights, whereas in Germany paid leave has been considered rather as a benefit, or maternal wage, for mothers who 'choose' to stay at home to look after their children (Fagnani, 1996, p. 135). When the allowance was extended to the second child in France in 1994 (previously it applied only from the third), it proved to be an attractive alternative for women who were unemployed or whose job security was limited (Afsa, 1996). In the United Kingdom, parental leave, the guarantee of reinstatement and childcare have had to be 'sold' to employers as strategies enabling them to make direct savings on training and recruitment by retaining well-qualified female workers (Home Office, 1998, p. 26).

Provision of childcare

When the Council recommendation 'on child care' was adopted in 1992 [6.13], the *Länder* of former East Germany and Denmark had by far the most extensive public provision of childcare for children aged under three, followed by Sweden (though it was not yet a member of the Union), Belgium, France and Finland. At the other end of the scale, Austria, West Germany, Greece, Ireland, Spain and the United Kingdom stood out as being particularly poor providers of publicly funded care. Ireland and the United Kingdom were also distinguished by the fact that childcare services did not give priority to the children of parents in paid employment but rather to children at risk (European Commission Network on Childcare, 1996, table 6).

Childcare provision thus confirms the picture already presented for maternity and parental leave, and benefits. Clearly, some member states have gone much further than others in supporting parents and in helping to reconcile employment with family life, albeit for different reasons and with differing effects as far as labour market activity and the sharing of family responsibilities are concerned (Hantrais, 2000). The interpretation of public childcare arrangements has also evolved at EU level. When the European Childcare Network began operating in 1986, the primary objective was to respond to the need for good quality childcare as a means of assisting working mothers, supporting the development of young children, and promoting the role of men in caring for children. By the time the Commission published a guide to good practice on the implementation of the recommendation on childcare in 1996, the network had been discontinued, and the climate had changed. In his foreword to the guide, the Commissioner responsible for Employment and Social Affairs, Pádraig Flynn, stressed the importance of removing obstacles to full participation in the labour market, and of enabling parents, and especially women, to make 'their proper contribution to economic and social life' [6.15, p. 5]. When the European Network Families and Work, which had been established in 1994, was renamed in 1997 to encompass intergenerational solidarity, its focus was new forms of work organization (including workplace nurseries), time management policies and occupational mobility, presented as practices contributing to the reconciliation of work and family.

Gender equality at work

An underlying reason for individualizing rights in the 1990s was to encourage the participation of women in the labour force, partly on the grounds that derived rights could have a negative effect on the labour supply. The progressive shift towards the reconciliation between employment and family life in equality policy also signalled the primary concern with labour market flexibility. Scrutiny of trends in employment patterns for women and men during the 1990s, in conjunction with data on the ageing of the labour force has reinforced concern about the future European labour supply. Further support for a more egalitarian sharing of employment opportunities has become necessary to ensure both the quantity and quality of the labour force. Women, it is claimed, are not being utilized to their full capacity, either because many of them spend lengthy periods out of the labour force, or because they do not work full time (Rubery and Smith, 1999, p. 7).

Although women's economic activity rates have been increasing steadily across the Union since the mid-1970s, while those of men have been falling, everywhere rates for women remain lower than for men [4.17, 1999, pp. 127–42]. Even in the younger age groups, where availability is less subject to family constraints, rates for women fall consistently below those for men, indicating that, despite equality legislation, women still experience more difficulty than men in finding initial employment and in remaining economically active. Although activity rates had increased markedly for women with children, in the 1990s they continued to be adversely affected by the age and number of children (Hantrais, 1999b, tables 3.1–2).

In addition, there is abundant evidence to show that legislation to ensure equal pay for work of equal value and to improve women's opportunities in access to training and employment has not enabled them to enter the labour market, or to advance their employment careers, on equal terms with men (Rubery *et al.*, 1999). In the 1990s, everywhere women continued to be in lower paid, less secure employment than men. In all member states, women were more likely than men to work part-time or to be employed on fixed-term contracts. Rates for part-time work were particularly high in the Netherlands, the United Kingdom and Sweden (more than 40 per cent of the labour force).

Except in Ireland, Sweden and the United Kingdom, women were also more likely than men to be unemployed [4.17, 1999, pp. 127–42].

Nor had occupational segregation disappeared, as measured by the division of paid work between what are commonly accepted as men's and women's jobs. Not only did women continue to be concentrated in the least secure and least well-paid sectors of employment, but the growing proportion of women in lower skilled service jobs also made such low-paid work even more female dominated. Although more women were entering and remaining in paid employment for longer periods, they tended to be concentrated in the caring professions and public sector employment, where working conditions were more flexible and 'women friendly', but where pay was lower than in the private sector. Analysis of occupational segregation has shown that, while it may be possible to implement legislation on equal pay for the same work, it is more difficult to prove discrimination on the basis of equal value for different work, or avoid the gendering of jobs and the potential incompatibility of flexibility and equality (Rubery *et al.*, 1999).

For so long as equal pay, equal treatment and access to social security provisions are dependent on full-time continuous working patterns, it is clear that large proportions of women in many member states will be excluded from welfare rights, or entitled to lower rates, because of their interrupted employment patterns, precarious or part-time status. As a result, in the late 1990s many women continued to be reliant on a male breadwinner for derived rights, or were obliged to resort to means-tested benefits.

THE GENDER IMPACT OF EQUALITY POLICY

Although European legislation extended the equal treatment principle to social security entitlements, it has been argued throughout this chapter that the continuing focus on paid employment prevented the Union from adequately addressing what have been described as 'the combined sources of inequality between the sexes' (Meehan, 1993, p. 194). The failure of European policy makers to tackle the question of equal rights outside the workplace has meant that women who have not gained access to welfare through their own employment status have typically received benefits as the dependants of a male breadwinner. Since women are more often than men marginalized as workers, they are over-represented among the population groups most likely to suffer in an employment-based system of social protection, thus exacerbating not only gender inequalities but also differences between groups of women and between families according to whether they contain single, dual or no-earners.

Nowhere, in the member states has the unpaid caring work done at home by women as providers of services been given the same recognition as paid work in entitlements to benefits, as might be possible in a worker-carer model of the citizen applied to both men and women (Lister, 1997, p. 168). Just as European legislation, when translated into national law and practice, may have been instrumental in narrowing differentials between men and women in terms of earnings and opportunities in sectors of the economy such as public services, the lack of a firm steer from the Union may go some way towards explaining why so little change has been recorded in the division of labour in the home (Hantrais, 1999b, pp. 47–8).

During the 1990s, European legislation constantly deferred to the subsidiarity principle in setting minimum standards that member states were invited to overstep. Although, in reports and guides, attention was drawn to examples of good practice, and there is evidence to suggest that governments did introduce legislative change to comply with directives, it would be premature to conclude that the result is convergence in provisions, as amply demonstrated by the examples quoted in this chapter. Women would still seem to fare better in member states where entitlements to benefits are provided on a universal basis of citizenship than in those where employment-insurance contributions form the basis for welfare entitlements. This assumption only applies, however, for so long as the benefit system is dependent solely on taxation and provides flat-rate payments and a high standard of care for everyone. Most countries either already have, or are moving towards, a mixed economy of welfare, enabling some groups to obtain benefits over and above a guaranteed minimum rate, generally on the basis of occupational and private schemes (see Chapter 2). In such a system women, who customarily have interrupted employment patterns and work in low-paid insecure jobs, are likely to continue to suffer disadvantages in access to welfare.

Just as mainstreaming could be interpreted as a threat to the gains made by women, unless combined with positive action, other measures promoted at EU level may also work against the interests of women, illustrating the dangers inherent in equality policies if they do not take full account of possible side-effects. The erosion of wage differentials due to equal pay legislation may, for example, have reduced the advantage to employers of taking on women, contributing to the higher rates of female unemployment and lower job security for women. The individualization of welfare and tax benefits may also work to the disadvantage of women on low incomes, as argued above. When a high standard of employment rights is targeted specifically at women, it may result in them being crowded out of the job market because of the heavy demands they are expected to make on employers. Equal rights for part-timers may mean, for example, that the low income from short part-time hours, after social insurance deductions, makes part-time work unattractive for employees, while the additional labour costs discourage employers from recruiting part-time workers. Arrangements for extended maternity and parental leave may also discourage employers from taking on women of childbearing age.

Although attempts have been made to guard against such negative discrimination at EU and national level, it has proved difficult to strike a balance between the twin goals of equality and difference, with the result that, at the turn of the century, equal opportunities policy was at a cross-roads. The Union's institutions had built up a strong regulatory framework, supported by soft law and an active women's lobby. Membership of countries such as Sweden had pushed forward the concept of mainstreaming but, at the same time, the Union had moved towards a position where it was not prepared to interfere with national social protection systems. As countries from Central and Eastern Europe take up membership, and as the emphasis on the future of the labour supply intensifies, it seems likely that gender equality is set to remain a contested policy area for the Union.

Box 6 Secondary legislation and official publications relating to gender and social policy

6.1 Council Directive 75/117/EEC of 10 February 1975 on the approximation of the laws of the Member States relating to the application of the principle of equal pay for men and women (*OJ* L 45/19 19.2.75).

6.2 Council Directive 76/207/EEC of 9 February 1976 on the implementation of the principle of equal treatment for men and women as regards access to employment, vocational training and promotion, and working conditions (*OJ* L 39/40 14.2.76).

6.3 Council Directive 79/7/EEC of 19 December 1978 on the progressive implementation of the principle of equal treatment for men and women in matters of social security (*OJ* L 6/24 10.1.79).

6.4 Commission proposal for a Council Directive on parental leave and leave for family reasons (COM(83) 686 final, 22 November

1983) (*OJ* C 333/6 9.12.83); amended proposal (COM(84) 631 final, 9 November 1984) (*OJ* C 316/7 27.11.84).

6.5 Commission of the European Communities, Equal opportunities. action programme 1982–1985, *Women of Europe Supplement*, N° 9, 1982.

6.6 Commission of the European Communities, Equal opportunities. 2nd action programme 1986–1990, *Women of Europe Supplement*, N° 23, 1986.

6.7 Council Directive 86/378/EEC of 24 July 1986 on the implementation of the principle of equal treatment for men and women in occupational social security schemes (*OJ* L 225/40 12.8.86); Council Directive 96/97/EC of 20 December 1996 amending Directive 86/378/EEC on the implementation of the principle of equal treatment for men and women in occupational social security schemes (*OJ* L 46/20 17.2.97).

6.8 Commission of the European Communities, Community law and women, *Women of Europe Supplement*, N° 25, 1987.

6.9 Council Directive 86/613/EEC of 11 December 1986 on the application of the principle of equal treatment between men and women engaged in an activity, including agriculture, in a self-employed capacity, and on the protection of self-employed women during pregnancy and motherhood (*OJ* L 359/56 19.12.86).

6.10 Commission of the European Communities, Background report: protection at work for pregnant women or women who have recently given birth (ISEC/B25/90, 5 October 1990), London.

6.11 Council Resolution of 21 May 1991 on the third medium-term Community action programme on equal opportunities for women and men (1991 to 1995) (*OJ* C 142/1 31.5.91).

6.12 Commission Recommendation of 27 November 1991 on the protection of the dignity of women and men at work (92/131/EEC) (*OJ* L 49/1 24.2.92).

6.13 Council Recommendation of 31 March 1992 on child care (92/241/EEC) (*OJ* L 123/16 8.5.92).

6.14 Council Decision of 22 December 1995 on a medium-term Community action programme on equal opportunities for men and women (1996 to 2000) (95/593/EC) (*OJ* L 335/37 30.12.95).

6.15 European Commission, Work and childcare: implementing the Council recommendation on childcare. A guide to good practice, *Social Europe Supplement*, 5/96.

6.16 Council Directive 96/34/EC of 3 June 1996 on the framework agreement on parental leave concluded by UNICE, CEEP and the ETUC (*OJ* L 145/4 19.6.96); Council Directive 97/75/EC of 15

December 1997 amending and extending, to the United Kingdom of Great Britain and Northern Ireland, Directive 96/34/EC on the framework agreement on parental leave concluded by UNICE, CEEP and the ETUC (*OJ* L 10/24 16.1.98).

6.17 Commission Communication, Incorporating equal opportunities for women and men into all Community policies and activities (COM(96) 67 final, 21 February 1996); Progress report from the Commission on the follow-up of the Communication: Incorporating equal opportunities for women and men into all Community policies and activities (COM(1998) 122 final, 4 March 1998).

6.18 Case C–450/93 Eckhard Kalanke v Freie Hansestadt Bremen [1995] ECR I–3051, on positive discrimination in the appointment and promotion of men and women; Case C–409/95 Hellmut Marschall v Land Nordrhein-Westfalen [1997] ECR I–6363, on priority for women in promotion.

6.19 European Commission, *Equal Opportunities for Women and Men in the European Union*, OOPEC (annual publication), http://europa.eu.int/comm/employment_social/equ_opp/index_en.htm

7 Policy for Older and Disabled People

The emphasis placed on workers' rights in the Community's and Union's treaties and charter signalled that European social policy was only indirectly concerned with categories of the population who did not gain entitlements to social protection as active members of the labour force. The Treaty establishing the European Economic Community (EEC) [1.2], and later the Single European Act (SEA) [1.5] and the Treaty on European Union [1.6] made no reference to older or disabled people. A statement on European policy for these two potentially disadvantaged categories of former or would-be workers was, however, introduced into the Community Charter of the Fundamental Social Rights of Workers [1.10], and a new article on non-discrimination in the Treaty of Amsterdam [1.7] identified disability and age among the areas where discrimination was to be eliminated. As with family policy (see Chapter 5), demographic factors explain why older people have moved onto the social policy agenda. Throughout the 1990s, one of the major challenges facing the Union was how to prepare for the demographic imbalance predicted for the twenty-first century, and how to tackle associated issues, such as intergenerational equity and the social and economic integration of older and disabled people. Policy makers were faced with the problems of ensuring funding for pensions and the provision of adequate and effective social services in a context of financial stringency, and where many of the premises on which welfare states had been founded were being called into question.

In this chapter, the focus is primarily on the policy implications of the ageing of the Union's population, and the related needs of elderly and infirm people. Firstly, consideration is given to the development of European social policy for older and disabled people, with reference to the Union's legal framework and the Commission's action programmes in this area. The social and economic problems associated with demographic ageing are then examined across member states. National social protection provisions for older and disabled people are analysed to determine how policy makers in member states have responded to changing needs, particularly with regard to pensions and informal caring. Finally, an attempt is made to assess the possible impact of actions taken at European level on national policy making and on intergenerational relations within member states.

THE DEVELOPMENT OF EUROPEAN SOCIAL POLICY FOR OLDER AND DISABLED PEOPLE

Changing demographic structures have given rise to a number of policy issues that have been addressed at EU level on the basis that their repercussions go beyond the realm of action of individual nations. In particular, greater life expectancy, in combination with falling birth-rates, means that the proportion of the population aged 80 or over has been growing at an unprecedented rate. Concern about the possible impact of such changes on the funding and provision of benefits and pension schemes, and thus on workers' mobility, public expenditure and international competition, helps to explain why the Union's institutions have identified ageing as an area for concerted action by member states. The social and economic integration of disabled people is of interest both on humanitarian grounds, and because their participation in a regular working environment is seen as an asset for the Union. Their exclusion from work and social life is said to constitute an underutilization of experience and talent, and a waste of resources [7.16, pp. 6, 21]. In this section, the different forms of action taken at EU level are examined with reference to these objectives and to the policy measures that have been proposed and implemented.

Provision for older and disabled people in European treaties and the Community charter

The concern that differences in the treatment of older or disabled people might prevent the effective operation of the common market was implicit in the EEC Treaty. Articles 51 and 121 made provision for migrant workers to aggregate entitlements to benefits during periods spent in other member states, and for common measures to be implemented, thereby ensuring their rights to social protection, for example in the form of an adequate pension in old age. Articles 117 and 118 on social policy referred to the expectation that member states would work closely together to achieve this overall objective by harmonizing social systems, although no specific reference was made to age or disability.

In addition to the need to ensure that differences in social protection systems would not impede freedom of movement, another reason why older and disabled people were of indirect interest to the EEC founder members was that differences in the method of funding pensions and health care might affect the competitiveness of goods, services and manpower in countries with social insurance schemes that relied heavily on employer and employee contributions. Some member states feared they might be at a competitive disadvantage because of their relatively high labour costs and more generous provision. The danger of welfare tourism, whereby nationals from one member state might be attracted by more generous social benefits elsewhere in the Community, was also relevant for older and disabled people. Similarly, according to the concept of social dumping, governments might find it financially attractive to subcontract caring to other member states with higher productive efficiency or lower labour costs (Knapp *et al.*, 1990, pp. 67–8; see also Chapters 1, 2 and 9).

More than 30 years after the signing of the EEC Treaty, although the original reasons for European intervention had not disappeared, the Community charter [1.10] formally recognized the aspirations of older and disabled people for independent living. While affirming its intention to respect national systems and leave member states to make their own arrangements, the charter made clear the obligation to ensure minimum rights for older and disabled people to help them overcome their financial and other handicaps. It recommended that, at the time of retirement, every worker should be able to enjoy 'resources affording him or her a decent standard of living' (§24) and should be entitled 'to sufficient resources and to medical and social assistance specifically suited to his [*sic*] needs' (§25). The section on disabled persons (§26) stipulated that provision should be made for 'additional concrete measures aimed at improving their social and professional integration', covering vocational training, ergonomics, accessibility, mobility, transport and housing.

Although the Agreement on Social Policy appended to the Treaty on European Union [1.6] did not make specific reference to age or disability, a new article outlawing discrimination on the grounds of age or disability was introduced into the Treaty of Amsterdam [1.7], and subsequently became article 13 in the consolidated version of the treaty [1.8]. It gave the Council the authority to act unanimously, after consulting with the European Parliament, on a proposal from the Commission, to 'take appropriate action to combat discrimination based on sex, racial or ethnic origin, religion or belief, disability, age or sexual orientation'. Article 129 enabled the Council to adopt incentive measures for developing the exchange of information and best practice in the field of employment, and article 137 (§1) gave it the power to act to promote the integration of persons excluded from the labour market. By the late 1990s, EU member states were thus committed to pursuing action in support of older and disabled people.

Secondary legislation for older and disabled people

During the 1980s before the Community charter was adopted, the situation of older and disabled people had been addressed in several resolutions from the European Parliament. Broad themes relevant to their interests had been placed on the agenda. Resolutions on the social integration of handicapped people [7.1] in 1981 and the situation and problems of older people [7.2] in 1982 were followed in 1986 by resolutions on services for older people [7.4] and measures to improve their situation in member states [7.5].

Although no binding legislation was implemented specifically for older or disabled people, directives adopted under the aegis of equal treatment for men and women (article 119 of the EEC Treaty) covered pension rights. Directive 79/7/EEC on equal treatment in matters of social security [6.3], which was extended to occupational social security schemes and to self-employed workers in 1986 [6.9], aimed to tackle an important source of inequality by giving women greater access to social security entitlements in their own right (see Chapter 6). Women, or specifically married women, had, for example, been excluded from some state and occupational pension schemes. In 1982, a Council recommendation had set out the principles of Community policy with regard to retirement age [7.3]. The document was not concerned with gender differences, but a report from the Commission in 1992 on the application of the recommendation raised the issue, and noted that it was under examination in most member states that had different retirement ages for men and women [7.9]. Flexible arrangements for retirement were considered further in a Council resolution in 1993 [7.12].

In the programme for the application of the Community charter [1.11], provision was made for action in all the areas that had been identified. Although binding legislation was still not considered appropriate, and no legislation was adopted during the 1990s, a proposal was issued in 1991 for a Council directive 'on minimum requirements to improve the mobility and the safe transport to work of workers with reduced mobility' [7.8]. The shift of emphasis in policy announced in the charter was confirmed in 1993 by a change in the name of the unit responsible for disabled people from 'Measures for the Disabled' to 'Integration of the Disabled'.

The 1992 Council recommendation 'on the convergence of social protection objectives and policies' [2.1] treated disability as 'incapacity for work'. The aim was to ensure minimum means of subsistence and social and economic integration, through benefits enabling disabled people to maintain 'their standard of living in a reasonable manner in accordance with their participation in appropriate social security schemes' [2.1, p. 51]. The recommendation also provided a clear statement of the principles governing social protection for older people [2.1, p. 52]. Building on §§24–5 of the Community charter, it placed the onus on member states to guarantee a minimum level of subsistence to all older people in accordance with provisions at national and European level. Strong guidance was offered to national governments on the measures needed to combat the social exclusion of older people. The Council recommended that workers should have the right to carry on working after minimum pensionable age. A replacement income was to be maintained throughout retirement. Entitlements were to be extended to cover workers with incomplete careers, and schemes were to be adapted in response to demographic change. The aim was again to prevent any disparities between member states in spending on care for older and disabled people that might impede workers' mobility within the Union. A justification for Council Directive 98/49/EC 'on safeguarding the supplementary pension rights of employed and self-employed people moving within the European Union' [9.22] was that it would remove one of the remaining obstacles to free movement of workers (see Chapter 9).

Action programmes for older and disabled people

Despite the absence of references in the Community's and Union's treaties to these disadvantaged groups, and the relative lack of binding legislation, programmes for older and disabled people predate the Community charter. The 1974 social action programme [1.9, p. 2] advocated measures to promote the vocational and social rehabilitation of handicapped people. Within the general context of improving quality of life for all European citizens, the Commission drew up and implemented a series of action programmes to ensure the economic and social integration of the 10 per cent or so of the population across the

Community affected by a physical, sensorial or mental handicap. Action was also initiated by the Commission to support older people.

The first action programme specifically aimed at disabled people was adopted in 1981, providing support for national efforts through technical exchanges of experience in the areas of education, training, employment, social security and care systems, communications, mobility and housing [7.1]. In 1988, the Council adopted a second Community action programme for the period 1988–91 under the title 'Handicapped People in the European Community Living Independently in an Open Society' (Helios), designed to promote social integration and an independent lifestyle for people with disabilities [7.6]. Within the programme, a computerized information system and network for disabled people in Europe was set up, under the name of Handynet, containing information about technical aids and the addresses of specialist companies and organizations. A further three-year programme was established in 1993, with the focus on the integration of young people with disabilities into ordinary systems of education and the promotion of independent living for disabled people. It made particular reference to older people and to the aim of contributing to the economic and social cohesion of the Union [7.11].

The European structural funds have served as a financial instrument at Community level to support initiatives such as Employment-Horizon for the integration of disabled people into the world of work. A European Disability Forum was launched in 1993, designed to ensure the flow of information between EU institutions, national authorities and non-governmental organizations. In a communication issued in 1996 'on equality of opportunity for people with disabilities' [7.14], the Commission stressed the importance of the aim of integration as the key to inclusion in mainstream society. Member states were to achieve greater equality of opportunity by empowering people with disabilities, by removing access barriers to participation, by opening up all spheres of activity and by making public opinion receptive to strategies on equality of opportunity for people with disabilities. The priority to be given to the employability of people with disabilities was demonstrated in the 1999 employment guidelines when the theme was moved into the first pillar [1.20].

Meanwhile, separate actions had been adopted for older people. A programme of concerted Community actions was established in 1991 by a Council decision, following a communication from the Commission on the subject [7.7]. The aim was to monitor and exchange information about demographic trends and their impact on social protection and health systems, while also looking at measures for improving the mobility of older people and for helping them to lead independent lives. Another more nebulous objective was to promote solidarity between generations. The positive contribution of older people to economic and social life was recognized, and the Commission undertook to ensure that their income would be protected.

Under the programme, an Observatory on Ageing and Older People was set up with responsibility for providing the Commission with authoritative reports about the situation of older people in each country and the policies being pursued. The observatory had a monitoring role similar to that of the European Observatory on National Family Policies (see Chapter 5). Its efforts were to be concentrated on four areas: 'living standards and way of life, employment and the labour market, health and social care, and the social integration of older people in both formal and informal settings' (Walker, 1993a, p. 2; Walker and Maltby, 1997, pp. 4–5). The working definition of social policy for older people was couched in broad terms to include the impact of social and economic policies on older people, regardless of whether they originated from the public, private or voluntary sectors. In particular, member states were to address 'the challenges resulting from present and future demographic developments and the consequences of an ageing population for all Community policies' (Walker, 1993a, p. 2), implying that the theme of ageing, like that of gender, was to be mainstreamed.

The year 1993 was proclaimed as the European Year of the Elderly and of Solidarity between Generations. The intention was to heighten society's awareness of issues concerning older people, to promote intergenerational solidarity and involve older people in the process of Community integration [7.10]. The 1994 white paper on European social policy [1.15] also focused on the theme of integration. The Commission proposed to draw up a code of good practice for employers and to introduce measures to eliminate discrimination against disabled people. Together with older people, they were identified as categories not to be excluded from the benefits of a more integrated Europe, because they were capable of making an active contribution to society [1.15, p. 49].

The Commission adopted a responsive stance, acting to promote and facilitate the exchange of knowledge and experience through support for initiatives at EU, regional and local level. Progressively, during the 1990s, it drew attention to the problems associated with population decline and ageing. In a proposal for a Council decision 'on Community support for actions in favour of older people' [7.13] covering the period 1995–99, the Commission identified four key areas for close attention: improving the situation of older women; management of an ageing workforce; the transition from work to retirement; and care and access to care for dependent older people. The proposal did not achieve unanimity at the Council, but one of the strands – the retention, reintegration and retraining of older workers – became the focus of a guide to good practice produced in 1998, building on the findings from a project co-ordinated by the European Foundation for the Improvement of Living and Working Conditions on combating age barriers (Walker, 1998).

An issue of growing concern throughout the 1990s was how to sustain pension arrangements after the year 2000. Supplementary pension schemes were of legitimate interest for the Union as an instrument for promoting freedom of movement for workers and capital. They also afforded a possible solution to the problem of how to provide retirement pensions in the longer term. Supplementary schemes were no longer a marginal phenomenon, but rather an 'indispensable "pillar" of the social protection structure' in the context of demographic, economic and social change [7.15, p. 5].

As a contribution to the United Nations' International Year of Older People in 1999, in a communication entitled 'Towards a Europe for all ages', the Commission set out its policy strategy for dealing with the implications of population ageing at the turn of the century [7.16, p. 5]. It recommended the development of measures in four areas. Firstly, action was needed to maintain the capacity of workers and to promote lifelong learning and flexible working arrangements. Secondly, attention was to be paid to reversing the trend towards early retirement, exploring new forms of gradual retirement and making pension schemes more sustainable and flexible. Thirdly, in the area of health and old age care, research and studies were to be initiated to develop adequate responses to health-care needs. Finally, the Commission was fulfilling its treaty obligations by promoting action to combat discrimination, unemployment and social exclusion among older people.

THE IMPLICATIONS OF POPULATION AGEING FOR EUROPEAN SOCIAL POLICY

In the 1980s and 1990s, all EU member states had to face rising levels of public expenditure on pensions, health and social care for a growing proportion of the population, as medical advances, better living and working conditions and improved social protection contributed to greater life expectancy. A legal age of retirement had been implemented across the Union. Occupational pension schemes were being extended to all categories of former workers, at the same time as the number of economically inactive older people was increasing. Despite longer compulsory schooling and the more widespread development of vocational training (see Chapter 3), the combination of falling birthrates (see Chapter 5), greater life expectancy and enforced retirement had shifted the balance in the dependency ratio away from younger towards older people. A dwindling labour force was thus being called upon to bear the cost of supporting a growing proportion of economically inactive older people. Not all member states had, however, been affected to the same extent by the consequences of population ageing. Policy responses also varied. In this section, different conceptions of ageing and the differential impact of the ageing process for social policy are examined across the Union.

Population ageing as a common social problem

According to Eurostat predictions, by the year 2020 the proportion of the population aged over 60 will have reached about 27 per cent, an increase of more than 70 per cent compared to 1960 (by extrapolation from [5.9, 1999, table B-7] and Eurostat, 1997b, table 5). From the mid-1980s, as the mortality rate in member states continued to fall, albeit more slowly, and in the absence of any new waves of immigration or a universal rise in the birthrate, the Union's population was beginning to stagnate and, in some member states, to decline [5.8, 1997, p. 21]. The trend towards an ageing and declining population was expected to intensify and become widespread in the first quarter of the twenty-first century, presenting a common challenge for EU member states.

During the 1990s, most member states were not, however, feeling the full impact of population ageing, since the postwar 'baby-boomers' were still actively contributing to the labour supply. Because young people are also big consumers of services, such as education, health and family benefits, the falling birthrate produced some savings in the short and medium term. In the longer term, the economic and social costs of an ageing population were expected to outweigh any advantages that may have accrued initially. The burden of supporting these two dependent population groups falls differently: while families meet a large share of the economic costs of raising children, those associated with caring for older people tend to be borne mainly by society.

Whereas in the mid-1990s, approximately 2.7 people of working age were available to support each pensioner, the figure could fall to 1.41 by the year 2050 (calculated from Eurostat, 1997b). In addition, at the time when the burden of caring for older people is expected to become most acute in the twenty-first century, as the baby-boomers reach retirement age, any savings from raising a smaller number of young people would be expended.

Some observers (for example Bourdelais, 1993) have argued that concern about the ageing of the population may, to a certain extent, be overstated. Statistics measuring demographic ageing in terms of the increase in the proportion of older people in the population generally assume that old age begins at 60, particularly if that is the legal age for retirement. They do not, however, usually take account of the biological phenomenon of individual ageing. In Western Europe, biological or physical ageing of individuals is occurring at a much older age than in the early twentieth century: being 60 in the year 2000 was very different from what it was in the 1920s or 1930s. Age, when measured solely by calendar years, can therefore be misleading as an indicator of social and physical needs. In the late 1990s, at the age of 60, men in member states could expect to live another 17.6 (Ireland) to 20 (Sweden) years, and women another 21.6 (Denmark) to 24.9 (France) years [5.9, 1999, tables G-5, G-6]. While medical advances have, undoubtedly, made it possible to prolong the lives of older people with disabilities, they also mean that a large proportion of the population reaching the age of 60 can expect to enjoy many more years of good health. Rather than disappearing, the problems of disability and frailty associated with biological ageing have been postponed to a later age. At the same time, the lowering of retirement age and greater longevity have created different categories of older people: the younger elderly, or third age, for the 50–74 age group and what is sometimes referred to as the fourth age for those over 75.

The younger elderly are more likely to be in good health and able to enjoy a relatively generous pension, particularly if they contributed during their working lives to an occupational scheme guaranteeing them a high proportion of former earnings. Their numbers were swollen during the 1990s due to the marked decline in the participation rates of men after the age of 50, which was exacerbating the imbalance in the dependency ratio (Rubery and Smith, 1999, pp. 28–30). While the growth in the male working-age population had been slowing down, the employment rates for men aged over 55 fell by more than seven percentage points in as many years, thereby further reducing the size of the labour force contributing to pensions and, at the same time, increasing the number of recipients of benefits [4.17, 1998, pp. 89–90].

In the 1990s, at least two-thirds of the disabled people in the Union were elderly. Among the fourth age population, about 10 per cent of people aged over 75 were estimated to be suffering from health problems requiring almost continuous care [2.5, 1997, p. 141]. The first wave of the European Community Household Panel (ECHP) survey recorded almost 20 per cent of women aged 65–84 reporting that they were severely hampered in their daily activities, and a slightly lower figure for men (Vogel, 1997, table 13.4). Because of the differential impact of armed conflict and the greater incidence among men of health risks associated with smoking, alcohol, road accidents and industrial hazards, women were over-represented among older people in all member states, and increasingly they were outnumbering men in the higher age groups. Already in 1995, across the Union women accounted for 56 per cent of people over the age of 75 living alone (Eurostat, 1998a, p. 38). Older people of the fourth age were therefore more likely to be women contending with failing health, often living alone in poor quality housing on a low income derived from a minimum state pension. The fourth age population also included growing numbers of women deriving entitlements from the occupational pension of a deceased spouse and, in the Mediterranean member states, a relatively large proportion of older people living in multigenerational households.

By the late 1990s, the hitherto silent revolution in the ageing structure of the European population had become increasingly audible. Population ageing was already putting pension systems and health services under strain, raising doubts about their sustainability and quality, and the need for alternative methods of funding and delivery. The issue of long-term care had also been addressed in some countries, and social protection systems were undergoing reform in an attempt to meet the care needs of dependent older people [2.5, 1997, pp. 113–51].

National differences in population ageing and its impact

The ageing process has not taken place at the same rate or to the same extent throughout the Union (Eurostat, 1997b, table 5). Countries, like (West) Germany, which began reducing their birthrates at an early stage while life expectancy was increasing rapidly due to high standards of living and of health care, were among the first to have to grapple with the problems of a relatively large proportion of elderly dependants. Countries where the postwar baby-boom continued into the mid to late

1960s, and which had maintained higher than average, albeit declining, birthrates, for example France and especially Ireland, were not expected to feel the full impact of the ageing of their populations until well after the year 2000. At the end of the 1990s, Italy, Greece, Germany, Sweden and Belgium were the countries with the largest proportions of total population aged over 60, whereas Ireland and the United Kingdom had the largest 'young' populations (Eurostat, 1997b, tables 2 and 5). Sweden, Italy and the United Kingdom recorded more than 4 per cent of total population over the age of 80 [5.9, 1999, table B-7]. It has been predicted that by 2050, every person of working age in Italy could be supporting one pensioner (calculated from Eurostat, 1997b).

When different indicators for population decline and population ageing are examined together, in the 1990s Sweden and Italy stand out as the countries most affected by population ageing, and Austria and Germany by population decline. The Netherlands and Finland were undergoing population decline, but were less affected by ageing. France, Spain, Greece and Belgium had ageing though growing populations, while Ireland, in particular, Portugal, Denmark and Luxembourg were characterized by younger and expanding populations. The United Kingdom remained close to the mean for both these composite measures (Hantrais, 1999a, figure 3). The applicant states of Central and Eastern Europe were experiencing similar overall trends, and they were registering demographic growth below that of the Union. They were, however, expected to feel the impact of population ageing at a later date than the 15 EU member states, due largely to their higher mortality rates [5.8, 1997, pp. 29–32].

Differences in demographic ageing are not necessarily closely reflected in the official retirement age. In the late 1990s, the highest age of retirement, with 67 for both sexes, was in Denmark, which did not have the greatest life expectancy either for men or women, and was below the EU average for the proportion of the population aged over 60 in the year 2000. France, the country with the lowest retirement age for men and women at 60, was close to the EU average for the group aged over 60. In Italy, the country with the highest proportion of over-60s, retirement age had been raised from 58 to 59 for women and from 63 to 64 for men in 1998. In Belgium, where the percentage of over-60s was above the EU average, retirement age for women was being increased progressively from 61 to 65 by the year 2009. Greece, with the second largest older population was also equalizing pension age at 65 for men and women. Austria and the United Kingdom were doing likewise, but with a much longer time lag [2.7, 1998, table VII].

In practice, statutory retirement age offers no more than a guide to the date at which individuals are normally eligible to begin drawing a state pension. Since the legal age of retirement does not, in most cases, take account of the physical and mental state of the individual, except where early retirement is permitted on health grounds, the age chosen to mark the end of working life is determined more by political considerations than on the basis of fitness for work. During the 1980s and 1990s, in most member states early retirement was being encouraged to release jobs, whereas biologically, socially and economically, it might have been more logical to consider postponing the end of working life. Economic activity rates started to decline as much as ten years before legal retirement age in a process of phased withdrawal from the labour market, which did not necessarily reflect ability to work.

During the 1990s, Germany, Italy and Austria were all showing a larger fall in the employment rate for men aged 50–54 than for prime working age population, while the reverse applied in Belgium, Greece and Portugal. In most member states, the employment rate for the population aged 55–59 fell steeply, and the unemployment rate increased. In the United Kingdom, however, men in this age group tended to withdraw from the labour force, rather than being registered as unemployed [4.17, 1998, pp. 89–90], and they were frequently classified as disabled rather than retired, which was also the case in the Netherlands and Finland [2.5, 1997, pp. 118]. Already in the early 1990s, in Belgium, France, Germany, Luxembourg and the Netherlands, it was estimated that only one in three or four ageing workers was entitled to a retirement pension directly on leaving employment (Guillemard, 1993, p. 38). By the late 1990s, employment rates for men aged 60–64 were as low as 11 per cent in France, whereas they reached around 50 per cent in Ireland, Portugal, Sweden and the United Kingdom, with an EU average of 31 per cent. For women, they ranged from less than 5 per cent in Belgium to over 40 per cent in Sweden, with an EU average of less than 15 per cent [3.14, 1999, table 003].

The combination of differences in the proportion of the population over retirement age and, effectively, out of the labour force helps to explain variations in the national resources devoted to older people. By the late 1990s, spending on old age was the largest item of public expenditure on social benefits in all member states except Ireland, which spent more on health (Eurostat, 2000, table 3). In Italy, the old age and survivors' function accounted for 65 per cent of total spending on social benefits. Expenditure on health and invalidity amounted to a third or more of the total in all but Denmark, Italy and Greece

(Eurostat, 2000, table 3). In relation to gross domestic product (GDP), spending on old age was already over 10 per cent in Italy, Denmark, Sweden, Germany, Austria and France by 1995, a level not reached for any other group of social benefits [2.6, 1998, tables C 1.4.1–8].

NATIONAL PROVISIONS FOR OLDER AND DISABLED PEOPLE

Despite the stated objective in the EEC Treaty of promoting harmonization of national social protection systems, the Union has not used its legislative powers to eliminate some of the most marked discrepancies in formal national provisions for older and disabled people. Although some convergence may have taken place over time as social security arrangements have been adapted to meet the common challenges facing member states, major differences remain in this area of social policy. Just as several models of social protection could be identified within the Union (see Chapter 2), arrangements for old age, retirement and invalidity pensions, disability allowances and caring can be analysed with reference to different national approaches.

Income security

Continental countries that followed the corporatist or conservative model of welfare, as developed initially by Germany, based their pension schemes on the principle of income maintenance, financed by employers, employees and the state. Although Belgium, France and Italy originally established old age pension schemes using subsidized voluntary insurance, they later adopted the German occupational scheme making old age insurance compulsory. According to this 'industrial achievement-performance' (Titmuss, 1974, p. 31) or 'income security' model (Ginn and Arber, 1992, pp. 259–60), social needs are met in proportion to work performance through mandatory social insurance. Basic disability allowances, invalidity and old age pensions are income related, ensuring that the workers with the highest incomes from earnings continue to receive higher benefits when they cease working. Differences occur within the continental income maintenance model with respect to the number of years that must be worked to qualify for a full pension. The contributions record stipulated in the late 1990s for a full pension ranged from 40 years in France and Italy to 50 in the Netherlands, which meant that relatively few workers could qualify for a full pension on retirement [2.7, 1998, table VII].

The income security system has the disadvantage that non-earners and many low earners are excluded and can only gain entitlements in their capacity as dependants either of a spouse or the state (see Chapters 6 and 8). Individuals who are prevented from working because of family responsibilities or disability have no chance of qualifying for full pensions in their own right, or of being able to achieve the high level of income that will guarantee a substantial pension on retirement. This problem has been recognized, though not solved, in most member states with employment-insurance based social security schemes. Insurance credits of between two (France) and four (Austria) years per child can, for example, be claimed for periods spent out of the labour market caring for young children [2.7, 1998, table VII].

Basic security

Member states with socialist or social democratic welfare regimes initially provided a basic state pension for all citizens, regardless of their employment record, funded from general taxation and with only a weak link to earnings. Denmark was one of the first member states to introduce an old age pension scheme in 1891. Sweden followed suit in 1913, and Finland in 1937. The Danish scheme was based on a very different principle from that in Germany: it was entirely funded from taxation, with entitlements on the basis of citizenship and universal services provided according to need. The same principle applied for invalidity pensions. By the 1990s, a full flat-rate pension was paid from the age of 67 to all citizens with 40 years of residence. This was supplemented by a compulsory employment-related scheme for all employees working more than nine hours a week. Supplementary pensions were funded from employer and employee contributions with reduced rates for part-timers, but payments were again at a flat rate [2.7, 1998, table VII]. Private occupational pensions were operated in the early 1990s by about half of all employers, and provided an additional income in retirement for about one in three pensioners (Ginn and Arber, 1992, pp. 266–8). By the late 1990s, the majority of workers were covered by supplementary pension schemes [7.15, p. 13].

At the turn of the century, Denmark was the only member state to have retained a solely tax-financed national pension scheme. In Finland and Sweden, employers contributed a percentage of the payroll. These two countries continued to share with Denmark the residence requirement and the flat-rate payment for the basic pension. Both had developed supplementary employment-related contributory schemes. For women, the basic security model had the advantage of enabling them to draw adequate pensions in their own right, and the disregard for employment record in the universal flat-rate pension meant that women were not penalized as in earnings-related schemes.

The 'institutional-redistributive' (Titmuss, 1974), 'basic security' (Ginn and Arber, 1992) or 'social democratic' (Esping-Andersen, 1990) model of welfare was initially followed by Britain. In his plan for pensions, William Beveridge opted for a basic state scheme that maintained flat-rate benefits on the grounds that the state should not be involved in making provision for income maintenance. This principle continued to be applied for invalidity pensions in the United Kingdom and Ireland in the 1990s, although the British pension system had moved towards the residual state welfare model described below for the basic pension.

The Netherlands also followed the basic security model, by instituting a first-tier pension scheme based on citizenship. In the 1990s, a national flat-rate pension still applied for all residents. While the pension arrangements ensured a basic income for women in their later years, irrespective of their employment record, the extensive private occupational pension schemes that were put in place tended to work against women due to their predominantly part-time status.

Residual state welfare

The British state pension scheme has come to serve essentially to alleviate poverty in old age and thus corresponds to what has been described as 'residual welfare' (Titmuss, 1974), or a 'liberal' welfare regime (Esping-Andersen, 1990). In such a system, state provision is minimal, while the market provides for privately funded earnings-related pensions. Compared to other member states, in the 1990s basic state pensions in the United Kingdom were relatively low. Non-earners had no guaranteed income and depended on an earner or a means-tested safety net. The United Kingdom was the first member state to operate a statutory supplementary scheme. The State Earnings Related Pension Scheme (SERPS) was introduced in the 1975 Social Security Pensions Act for workers who did not contribute to occupational schemes. SERPS made very little difference, however, to the pensions received by low income earners. For those in better paid jobs, occupational and private individual pension schemes offered more generous earnings-related benefits. By the 1990s, Britain had developed one of the most extensive second-tier pension schemes in the Union.

Women were at a particular disadvantage under the conditions operating in the United Kingdom (Ginn and Arber, 1992, pp. 261–3). Because of their interrupted employment histories and low part-time hours, which often fell below the earnings threshold for insurance contributions, many women were excluded from benefits that were dependent on employment record and level of earnings. The British social security system, as conceived by Beveridge, treated women as dependants on the understanding that male earnings should be sufficient to support a wife and children. Despite the provision of Home Responsibility Protection in 1978, which gave carers credits for years spent looking after children, sick or disabled persons, relatively few women could acquire a sufficient contributions record to enable them to claim a full pension.

Rudimentary or formative welfare

The member states that joined the Community in the 1980s – Greece, Portugal and Spain – had much less developed systems of social protection. Although their social security arrangements largely followed the continental model, in the 1990s their pension schemes were still a long way from providing the level of benefits enjoyed by most older people in the northern member states. Comparisons of income inequalities between generations suggest, however, that the material differences in living conditions between older people aged 65–84 and the 45–64 generation are much smaller in Greece, Italy, Portugal and Spain than in the rest of the Union, due largely to the sharing of resources in extended households (Vogel, 1997, p. 153). Although, as elsewhere, women may suffer from having shorter periods of contribution to pension schemes, they are less often living alone than in the northern member states. In Portugal, where women were twice as likely as men to be in the non-contributory pension scheme, rather than the general contributory scheme, and therefore entitled to lower benefits, the score registered for intergenerational inequalities was positive, a situation not found in any other member state (Vogel, 1997, table 14.3). In addition, only 30 per cent of Portuguese women aged over 75 were living alone in the mid-1990s, compared to 80 per cent in Finland (Eurostat, 1998a, p. 38). In Greece, where women were entitled to retire as early as 50 after as little as 20 years of work if they had young children, intergenerational income inequalities were more marked, and a larger proportion of older women were living alone (44 per cent) than in Portugal.

Towards common objectives for national pension systems

The exchange of information through the work of the European observatory and its contribution to the development of policies on older people was expected to 'contribute to some convergence in national policies' (Walker, 1993a, p. 1). Although their ideological and cultural origins and their administrative structures differed, the future viability of pension systems in member states, like other areas of social protection, was provoking common concerns. As demonstrated above, by the late 1990s few countries made provision for a flat-rate universal, national or state pension based on residence or citizenship. Those that did – the Nordic states and the Netherlands – had introduced a second-tier earnings-related, occupational or supplementary pension. The majority of member states operated an earnings-related insurance-based scheme and, in some, cases, a supplementary arrangement, which was either optional (Portugal) or compulsory (France). In the late 1990s, a factor encouraging exchange of information and experience, if not convergence, was the shared objective of containing the cost of pensions in the face of pressures from population ageing at a time when member states were striving to meet the criteria for Economic and Monetary Union (EMU), without imposing higher labour costs.

Pension reform was therefore on the agenda in most member states. The need to reduce the budget deficit to comply with the EMU targets undoubtedly provoked the 1993 and 1995 reforms in Italy [7.15, p. 13]. Most countries were implementing, or seriously considering, measures designed to reverse the trend towards early retirement. Spain and Sweden were imposing stricter controls on labour market exit. Austria, Germany and Greece were restricting eligibility criteria and reducing pension levels. Retirement age was being raised, and the number of years of contributions needed to qualify for a full pension was being increased in Belgium. Partial or progressive retirement was being made available in Austria, Finland, France, Germany and Luxembourg [2.5, 1997, pp. 23–5].

The financial crisis facing pension schemes provided an opportunity for a more thorough review of their rationale than had hitherto been countenanced. A report to the Commission from the EU network of experts on supplementary pension provision in 1996 analysed the case for greater involvement of the private sector in the funding and delivery of pensions [7.15]. A strong argument in favour of supplementary pensions was the negative impact on labour costs of the heavy reliance on earnings-related contributions and thus on employment. Another argument was the need to move away from the pay-as-you-go principle, on which most of the employment-insurance schemes were based, towards alternatives such as funded arrangements involving (private) institutional investors, which are less sensitive to changes in the size and composition of the labour force. The cost of introducing full funding for first-tier pensions was not, however, considered to be viable. The report expressed doubts about the willingness of employers to substitute compulsory insurance contributions for voluntary employer-sponsored supplementary provision. It anticipated that, where such arrangements were mandatory, the result might be lower pension levels, as had occurred in France, Greece and the Netherlands as a result of the curtailment of entitlements for employment-insurance based pensions.

The involvement of the private sector was an option being examined by the Italian government in the 1990s. The German government considered that the necessary measures had already been taken to protect pensions under the social insurance system, and that it should not interfere directly in any private provision. The Austrian government had paved the way for supplementary pension schemes, but was also not planning to become involved in the design or delivery of any arrangements made. Faced with the prospects of the rising costs of pensions, Portugal and Spain were receptive to the development of privately funded schemes, whereas the demand for supplementary provision had largely been met in Greece by mandatory pension funds [7.15, pp. 13–15].

Informal versus formal caring

A closely related issue that national governments were tackling in parallel to the pensions problem in the 1990s was how to meet the demand for good quality health and social care for older and disabled people. Most EU member states had been pursuing policies focusing on community care when changes in family and employment structures were imposing strains on informal care structures. The issue became more pressing during the 1990s, due not only to the increase in the number of frail and disabled people, but also to the reduction in the number of traditional carers, as a result of the 'shrinkage of the female care taker potential' (Alber, 1993, p. 54), at a time when governments were seeking to reduce the cost of formal caring.

Although the full impact of the decline in family size was not expected to be felt until after the turn of the century, in the early 1990s, the general increase in female economic activity rates was already making heavy demands on women at a stage in their lives when they had ageing relatives requiring care. Yet, women were still expected to be the main providers of care (Jani-Le Bris, 1993, p. 53; Daly and Lewis, 1998, p. 2), even when they were in employment (Eurostat, 1997d, pp. 6–7). Because women in the younger generations were more likely to be economically active outside the home, and in the absence of other close relatives able and willing to take on the responsibility for caring, most member states were being faced with the question of how to ensure the most effective level of care at the lowest cost to the public purse, and how, if appropriate, to provide incentives for informal carers.

Since the 1980s, most member states had been moving towards a policy of community care and de-institutionalization of caring. In the late 1990s, the situation across the Union continued, however, to display wide variations. Provision of care services in the Nordic countries was still recognized as a responsibility of the state, and more especially of local authorities. At the other extreme, the southern Mediterranean countries continued to place a clear legal obligation on relatives to care for older people, and formal service provision was made only in cases where no relatives were available to meet these obligations. In Italy, even in-laws and half siblings were obliged by law to provide support in proportion to income. The legal requirements in Portugal and Spain were such that family members could be taken to court or could lose their right to inheritance if they failed to comply. In Belgium and France, as in Austria, Germany, Greece and Luxembourg, adult children had a legal duty to maintain both their parents and their children. Except in France and Greece, the state could reclaim social assistance benefits from adult children for their parents. In the United Kingdom and Ireland, responsibilities were not defined in law (Millar and Warman, 1996, pp. 34–7).

Whatever the legal responsibilities of the state and of families with regard to care for older and disabled people, during the 1990s all governments were addressing the question of how to ensure support for the provision of long-term care [2.5, 1997, pp. 141–51]. Although the instruments used to implement policy differed, member states seemed to agree on a number of objectives. An important policy priority was to ensure the independence of older and disabled people for as long as possible by providing home support or sheltered accommodation. The employment-creating potential of formal subsidized caring was widely recognized, but was limited by financial considerations. Most countries were looking for ways of making savings, in some cases by rationing care through means-testing, and in others by requiring a contribution from the person concerned or by privatizing services.

The solution adopted in Germany in 1995 was to introduce a new branch of social insurance – *Pflegeversicherung* – to cover the cost of residential care or for care in the person's own home. Luxembourg was preparing a similar scheme, mainly funded from compulsory social insurance contributions. The system applied in Austria since 1993 took the form of a non-means-tested allowance – *Bundespflegegeld* – funded from general taxation and administered at the level of the provinces. The French and the Belgians had introduced an allowance to help older people remain autonomous by enabling them to meet the costs of non-medical care. In the Belgian case, funding was provided in part from a new social insurance contribution. In France, the allowance was means-tested. The Nordic states made little distinction between medical and social publicly financed care, administered at local level. Rising costs were being met by increasing taxation and social contributions, and through measures to improve efficiency and relieve the burden on the state, raising issues about the quality of care and individual choice. In the 1990s, British governments were looking to the private and voluntary sectors for solutions. The care allowance in the United Kingdom was means-tested, residential care was being privatized, and people living in residential homes were expected to pay for non-medical costs if their income and savings were above a specified level. Ireland also operated a means-tested care allowance and imposed charges for residential care. In the Mediterranean member states, public support for care-givers and receivers was limited, reflecting the strong expectation that intergenerational solidarity would continue to provide the answer to the caring needs of people in old age.

THE IMPLICATIONS OF EUROPEAN AND NATIONAL SOCIAL POLICY FOR INTERGENERATIONAL SOLIDARITY

During the 1990s, the emphasis in policy for older and disabled people shifted as awareness grew that the predicted consequences of population ageing were coming closer to being realized. Just as demographic concerns had moved family policy onto the agenda in the 1980s (see Chapter 5), the changing age structure of the population across the Union, together with the prospect of the demographic time-bomb exploding, provided an incentive for the Commission to draw the attention of EU member states to the social problems associated with the growing imbalance between the generations. Although further funding to support the Observatory on Ageing and Older People was not agreed, the remit of the European Network for Families and Work was extended in 1997 to encompass intergenerational solidarity, which became a recurring theme in Union documents. For example, the Commission's 1999 communication, 'Towards a Europe for all ages', proposed a strategy for effective policy responses to the problems arising from population ageing based on the strengthening of solidarity and equity between the generations [7.16, p. 4].

Whereas the Union's institutions did not have a formal remit for action to promote intergenerational solidarity, insofar as it was limited to intrafamilial relationships and therefore governed by the subsidiarity principle, they were able to initiate action when labour market or equality issues were involved. The preoccupation with employment, employability and EMU in the 1990s further justified interest in the contribution that older and disabled people could make to the age balance of the labour supply, and drew attention to the implications of an ageing and declining labour force for international competitiveness. The free movement of labour and capital legitimated interest in the transportability and comparability of pension arrangements and was also relevant to the question of family dependency.

The need to contain the cost of funding pensions in the context of EMU provided an incentive for looking at pension reform to ensure the longer term viability of pension schemes, while maintaining high standards of care and improving the living conditions of older and disabled people, and at the same time avoiding intergenerational conflicts. It justified reversing the trend towards early retirement, as a means not only of extending the number of years of pension contributions but also of reducing the time during which a pension would have to be paid, thereby helping to offset the growing imbalance in the dependency ratio.

The reconciliation of employment and family life had been accepted as a legitimate area for Union intervention in the 1990s, since it affected the availability of women for work. Although reconciliation measures were primarily concerned with childcare (see Chapter 6), recognition of the impact of caring for older and disabled people on the contribution of working age women to the labour supply raised important issues for equality of treatment. The equality rationale led to calls for the equalization of pension age and the individualization of pension rights between women and men. It also enabled areas of discrimination against older and disabled workers to be highlighted. For most working age women, intergenerational solidarity remained an ambivalent concept, in the absence of external and internal support to relieve the burden of caring (for young, disabled and older people) and of being cared for (in the case of fourth generation women). The shift in attitudes, as well as in financial resources, which was needed for it to become a positive concept, had not been achieved.

Two other non-labour market issues had been raised at EU level in the late 1990s and remained unresolved. Firstly, the attention that had been devoted to the financial needs of older people meant the balance had tipped more strongly towards older and away from younger people, both financially and in terms of policy interest, creating intergenerational tensions. In some countries, policies had been targeted at the most underprivileged groups of older people, often with noteworthy results. Increases in the pensions supplement in Denmark in the 1980s were, for example, targeted at pensioners on the lowest incomes. The Spanish government also focused on the level of minimum pensions as a means of raising living standards. In Italy, due to improved pension provision since the 1950s, the growth in living standards of older people was greater than for the population as a whole. The indexing of retirement pensions to wages or prices in France in the 1980s resulted in a marked decrease in the number of older people relying on the minimum pension. Elsewhere, the improvement of living standards could not be directly attributed to social policy for older people but might have been 'a "passive" by-product of increases in the scope and coverage of occupational pensions as a result of collective bargaining and pension scheme maturation' (Walker, 1993b, p. 14).

Secondly, the overall improvement in the living standards of older people has not benefited all older people equally. In countries where pensions are earnings related, income inequalities between occupational groups may be greater in retirement than during working life. Where the advantages of supplementary schemes are not equally distributed across different age groups, the inequalities among older people may also be intensified by widening the differential between those who have recently retired, and who are eligible for generous earnings-related pensions, and older people of the fourth age who are dependent on a minimum state pension.

Although EU level action in the area of old age and disability has been largely confined to awareness raising, monitoring, reporting and sharing of experience, the issues addressed by the Commission reflect and foreshadow the problems being encountered by all member states. They therefore provide opportunities for cross-border learning and to look for common solutions. During the 1990s, realization of the implications of population ageing for society and for family life brought a reconceptualization of old age and of intergenerational relations. New challenges were posed for policy makers, who were forced to rethink measures such as early exit from the labour market and their implications for intergenerational equity and solidarity in the twenty-first century.

Box 7 Secondary legislation and official publications relating to policy for older and disabled people

7.1 Council Resolution of the Representatives of the Member States of the European Community, meeting within the Council of 21 December 1981 on the social integration of handicapped people (*OJ* C 347/1 31.12.81).

7.2 Resolution of the European Parliament of 18 February 1982 on the situation and problems of the aged in the European Community (*OJ* C 66/71 15.3.82).

7.3 Council Recommendation of 10 December 1982 on the principles of a Community policy with regard to retirement age (82/857/EEC) (*OJ* L 357/27 18.12.82).

7.4 Resolution of the European Parliament of 10 March 1986 on services for the elderly (*OJ* C 88/17 14.4.86).

7.5 Resolution of the European Parliament of 14 May 1986 on Community measures to improve the situation of old people in the Member States of the Community (*OJ* C 148/61 16.6.86).

7.6 Council Decision of 18 April establishing a second Community action programme for disabled people (Helios) (88/231/EEC) (*OJ* L 104/38 23.4.88).

7.7 Communication from the Commission on the elderly, Proposal for a Council Decision on Community actions for the elderly (COM(90) 80 final, 24 April 1990); Council Decision of 26 November 1990 on Community actions for the elderly (91/49/EEC) (*OJ* L 28/29 2.2.91).

7.8 Commission proposal for a Council Directive on minimum requirements to improve the mobility and the safe transport to work of workers with reduced mobility (COM(90) 588 final, 11 February 1991) (*OJ* C 68/7 16.3.91), amended proposal (COM(91) 539 final) (*OJ* C 15/18 21.1.92).

7.9 Report from the Commission of 18 December 1992 on the application of Council Recommendation of 10 December 1982 on the principle of a Community policy with regard to retirement age (82/857/EEC) (SEC(92) 2288 final).

7.10 Commission of the European Communities, 1993: European Year of Older People and Solidarity between Generations, *Social Europe*, 1/93.
7.11 Council Decision 93/136/EEC of 25 February 1993 establishing a third Community action programme to assist disabled people (Helios II 1993 to 1996) (*OJ* L56/30 9.3.93).
7.12 Council Resolution of 30 June 1993 on flexible retirement arrangements (*OJ* C 188/1 10.7.93).
7.13 Commission proposal for a Council Decision on Community support for actions in favour of older people (COM(95) 53 final, 1 March 1995) (*OJ* C 115/6 9.5.95).
7.14 Communication of the Commission on equality of opportunity for people with disabilities. A new European Community disability strategy (COM(96) 406 final, 30 July 1996, adopted 20 December 1996).
7.15 European Commission, The outlook on supplementary pensions in the context of demographic, economic and social change. A report by the EU network of experts on supplementary pension provision – 1996, *Social Europe Supplement*, 7/96.
7.16 Communication from the Commission, Towards a Europe for all ages – promoting prosperity and intergenerational solidarity (COM(1999) 221 final, 21 May 1999).

8 From Social Exclusion to Social Inclusion

The emphasis in the Community's and Union's treaties and charter on employment-related rights and freedom of movement was motivated either by the need to protect workers against major sources of hardship due to incapacity for work as a result of ill health, disability, unemployment, old age and other contingencies, or by the efforts required to ensure access to social security on equal terms for mobile workers. At the time when the Treaty establishing the European Economic Community (EEC) was signed in 1957 [1.2], member states were experiencing a period of economic expansion. Following the German 'continental' model, their welfare regimes were based on the premise that earnings from paid employment would be maintained at a sufficiently high level to enable workers and their families to enjoy a decent standard of living (see Chapter 2). Provision was made in member states for those who temporarily 'fell through the net' by instituting non-contributory social assistance schemes, but in the postwar boom years the groups considered to be at risk were relatively limited, and unemployment was not seen as a problem area. When the EEC Treaty was signed, many older people, particularly the self-employed, had not accrued the right to generous earnings-related pensions, and not all occupations were subject to a legal age of retirement. In addition, life expectancy was shorter, and the proportion of elderly dependants was therefore relatively small (see Chapter 7). Immigration was helping to sustain the workforce (see Chapter 9), and the postwar baby boom had resulted in the rapid growth of the younger population, who had good prospects for finding employment in a buoyant economy. These attenuating factors did not mean that poverty was non-existent, but rather that it was not a political priority for the EEC founder members.

The centrality of freedom of movement and workers' rights in the EEC Treaty had tended to divert attention away from the social implications of the common market for population groups that were, for one reason or another, excluded from the labour force. It was, however, recognized that industrial restructuring, relocation and centralization, which were vital components in the Single European Market (SEM), might provoke economic dislocation, leading to polarization as the prosperous core areas benefited most, and the less favoured peripheral areas degenerated further. Institutional intervention, according to this logic, was necessary to offset the effects of market forces and curb the growth of 'new poverty' resulting from changing social and economic structures, and rising unemployment. New poverty was recognized as being qualitatively different from the poverty experienced hitherto, since it affected people from a much wider range of socio-economic groups. Whereas, in the 1970s, most of the poor were older people, by the 1990s a more pressing problem was the growing number of working age people falling into poverty, particularly the younger never-employed and the long-term unemployed. Increasingly, as a result of changing family structures, single-parent households were suffering from poverty: lone parenthood was frequently associated with low income and dependence on social assistance for long periods of time. Families with children were over-represented among poor people, but poverty was no longer essentially related to large family size. The threat presented to economic and social cohesion by the growing proportion of people of working age living in poverty served as a powerful incentive for continuing action at EU level.

This chapter examines policy to combat social exclusion and promote social inclusion, firstly with reference to the Union's legislative framework and action programmes. Attention is then given to the problems of defining, measuring and comparing poverty in member states and to assessing its extent and regional characteristics. Variations in national systems for income maintenance and in approaches to policy making for socially excluded individuals and groups are explored to provide a better understanding of the ways in which poverty and social exclusion have been conceptualized and dealt with by member states.

THE DEVELOPMENT OF EUROPEAN POLICY ON POVERTY AND SOCIAL EXCLUSION

Concern with poverty and social exclusion at EU level developed in parallel with the growing interest in social affairs in the 1970s and 1980s (see Chapter 1). The Community did not, however, introduce binding legislation as a policy instrument to alleviate poverty, for example by formulating directives imposing minimum income levels for individuals, or harmonizing the provision of social assistance for migrant workers. Rather, from the mid-1970s, the Commission initiated action programmes to combat poverty and social exclusion. By contrast, member states were bound by treaty commitments and regulations to operate the structural funds in support of labour market policies in priority regions and for underprivileged groups. During the 1990s, emphasis shifted away from Community poverty programmes under the auspices of the Commission towards (re)integration into the labour market and to society through the dispersal of the structural funds at national and regional level, in partnership with the Commission. An important consideration in the debates was the need to adapt the funds in preparation for enlargement to Central and Eastern Europe.

In this section, the development of Community policy for combating social exclusion and promoting social inclusion is tracked through the different overlapping and interconnected measures that have been introduced in an attempt to resolve what have been recognized as common social problems justifying concerted policy responses.

Social exclusion in the Community's and Union's treaties and charter

The EEC Treaty laid stress on the interests of workers not only in the provisions made for employment-related social protection, as illustrated in previous chapters, but also under the terms of the European Social Fund (ESF). In accordance with the Community's market-oriented objectives, the ESF was not concerned with socially and economically excluded categories, such as older people, lone-parent families or groups living in underprivileged areas. Rather, article 3(i) of the founding treaty established the fund 'in order to improve employment opportunities for workers and to contribute to the raising of their standard of living'. Article 123 on social policy confirmed that the ESF was intended solely for the working population, stating: 'it shall have the task of rendering the employment of workers easier and of increasing their geographical and occupational mobility within the Community'. Member states were to be eligible to receive 50 per cent of expenditure incurred in providing vocational training and resettlement allowances as a means of ensuring productive re-employment of workers following the conversion of undertakings. Funds were to be committed to measures aimed at supporting specific population groups in such a way that a safety net was created for designated regions and categories of the population, while also providing opportunities for the development of poorer areas.

By seeking to relieve the problems of uneven regional development through the ESF, the Community recognized that poverty was structural and could be caused by economic forces over which individuals and local economies have little or no control. The financial support provided was intended to tackle underlying structural problems and was therefore a necessary component for economic integration. Analysts of the possible effects of the completion of the internal market had concluded that its long-term benefits were likely to be unevenly distributed, and that income disparities might even be increased (O'Donnell, 1992, p. 25). Regions with industries that were able to make economies of scale and had the capacity to innovate would stand to draw the greatest benefits from freedom of movement of goods, services and workers. The Single European Act (SEA) of 1986 [1.5] thus introduced a new title on economic and social cohesion, reforming the structural funds.

The specific objective of the new cohesion policy was to reduce disparities in levels of development 'between the various regions and the backwardness of the least favoured regions' (article 130a). In addition to existing instruments, the Community was to achieve its objectives with support from the European Investment Bank (EIB), which grants loans on a non-profit basis, and through the structural funds: European Agricultural Guidance and Guarantee Fund, European Social Fund, European Regional Development Fund (article 130b). In particular, the fund established in 1975 to support the Community's regional policy was intended to help redress regional imbalances and enable the structural adjustment of regions that were considered to be 'lagging behind' (article 130c). The laggards were defined as regions whose *per capita* gross domestic product (GDP) was less than 75 per cent of the Community average [8.14, article 3]. The identification of priority regions was based on a common system of classification, the Nomenclature of Territorial Statistical Units (NUTS), set up by Eurostat in conjunction with national statistical offices.

Neither the Community Charter of the Fundamental Social Rights of Workers [1.10] nor the Agreement on Social Policy annexed to the Treaty on European Union [1.6] referred directly to poverty or social exclusion. Explicit reference was made under §10 on social protection in the Community charter to the duty of member states to provide sufficient resources and social assistance to individuals 'who have been unable either to enter or re-enter the labour market and have no means of subsistence', but national governments were left to make their own arrangements. In similar terms, the section on employment and remuneration in the charter recommended an equitable wage as the means of maintaining 'a decent standard of living' (§5). In cases where wages might be 'withheld, seized or transferred', it stated that provision should be made so that the worker could 'continue to enjoy the necessary means of subsistence for himself and his family' (§5).

Article 130b in the SEA was extended in the Treaty on European Union [1.6], becoming article 159 in the consolidated version of the EC Treaty [1.8], to require the Commission to report every three years to the European Parliament, the Council, the Economic and Social Committee and the newly established Committee of the Regions on the progress made towards achieving the cohesion objectives. It gave the Commission the power, if needed, to initiate actions outside the funds. A revised article 130d (article 161 in the consolidated EC Treaty) spelled out the procedure to be used for defining the tasks, priority objectives and organization of the structural funds. The Cohesion Fund was set up in 1993 for projects on the environment and trans-European transport infrastructures in the weaker member states (with GDP of less that 90 per cent of the EU average) to help them meet the convergence criteria for Economic and Monetary Union (EMU).

The concept of cohesion, which was intended to correct the most discriminatory effects of economic integration, can be seen as directly contradicting the principle of open competition on which the EEC was founded. The potential conflict between the treaty commitment to the removal of constraints on market forces and the provision made for institutional intervention to prevent regional imbalances thus reflects the underlying tension between economic and social objectives, which has characterized the Community's development (see Chapter 1). From the late 1980s, the structural funds came to represent a strong interstate bargaining counter for member states, as exemplified in the negotiations over enlargement. It has been argued (for example Allen, 2000) that the funds have been used at times of treaty reform to make 'side payments' to compensate member states for further enlargement.

Secondary legislation and social exclusion

One of the most binding forms of secondary legislation – the regulation – has been used in making provision for regional development through the structural funds. Some of the less binding forms of legislation – decisions, recommendations, resolutions and proposals – have been adopted to implement measures concerned with poverty, as was also the case for older and disabled people (see Chapter 7). This section reviews the role played by secondary legislation in the Community's and

Union's policies to combat poverty and promote social inclusion by supporting action programmes and the operation of the structural funds.

Action to combat social exclusion

By 1974, the impact of the energy crisis on employment and living standards was being felt across the Community, and the baby boom had come to an end. The new member states in 1972 – Denmark, Ireland and the United Kingdom – brought with them different welfare traditions in which social protection was based on universal citizenship rights rather than earnings from employment (see Chapter 2). The nine member states shared a conviction, however, that concerted action was needed to improve national provision for particularly disadvantaged groups (Shanks, 1977, pp. 63–4). Following the 1974 Council resolution on a social action programme [1.9], a proposal for a two-year experimental anti-poverty programme therefore received wide support.

The first poverty programme had to be approved by a unanimous vote of the Council under article 235 of the EEC Treaty, since no special provision had been made for formal action in this area. After a difficult process of negotiation in the context of the oil crisis, with the Germans in particular pressing for retrenchment, a Council decision eventually established the programme for the period 1975–76 [8.1]. The Commission undertook to launch 21 pilot or action projects, with the aim of achieving a 'balanced range of approaches' across all the Community regions. Each project contained a strong research component, including basic research into the 'dimensions and nature of poverty' (James, 1982, p. 6). Two cross-national studies were also funded for a year on attitudes towards poverty and on research methods for national sample surveys. The second phase of the programme was approved by another Council decision in 1977 [8.1] for a three-year period, extending and adding to the pilot projects. The Commission asked for national reports to be drawn up by independent research teams in each member state on the nature, cause and extent of poverty and for an assessment of the policies implemented to combat poverty.

The second European poverty programme was approved in 1984 for the period 1985–88, with an initial budget of 25 million ECU. Subsequently in 1986, a further 4 million ECU were added to extend the programme to Portugal and Spain when they joined the Community [8.5, p.10]. The Commission was authorized to undertake activities to promote or provide financial assistance for various types of action-research measures, for the collection, dissemination and exchange of knowledge and comparable data on poverty on a regular basis, the co-ordination and assessment of anti-poverty measures, and the transfer of innovative approaches between member states. Action was justified by reference to article 2 of the EEC Treaty, which required 'balanced expansion' and 'an increase in stability'. Sixty-five action research projects were selected for support, covering single-parent families, the problems of the long-term unemployed, youth unemployment, second generation migrants, refugees and returning migrants, the homeless and older people. Integrated urban action programmes were funded with the aim of providing a comprehensive approach to the needs of targeted groups of deprived individuals, by tackling the underlying problems of the social environment creating the circumstances that define poverty.

In terms of the number of projects selected, Spain and the United Kingdom were by far the greatest beneficiaries from the scheme, raising questions about the extent to which European support was being directed to the regions most in need. The criteria used for evaluating the projects – innovation, participation and cost effectiveness – may well have favoured member states that were already trying out innovatory schemes, where community structures were well developed, and where cost effectiveness of services was routinely monitored.

By the end of the 1980s, the growing awareness of the multi-faceted, relative and changing nature of poverty had made it necessary to adopt a new approach. The number of people experiencing poverty had increased, and new forms of poverty were appearing as a result of changes in economic and social structures. Within the framework of the action programme implementing the provisions of the Community charter, in 1989 a Council decision established 'a medium-term Community action programme concerning the economic and social integration of the economically and socially less privileged groups in society' [8.3]. An additional reason for the decision was the need to take preventive measures against any short-term negative effects of the completion of the internal market by the end of 1992 for the social groups most at risk. The 'Poverty 3' programme for the period 1989–94 was to provide corrective measures for groups already marginalized, with the purpose of ensuring greater economic and social cohesion, as written into the SEA and the Treaty on European Union. The funding devoted to the programme was 55 million ECU, which represented a substantial increase in relation to previous programmes, but remained a very small budget when compared, for example, with the average level of expenditure of social security departments in the wealthier member states or the ESF budget [8.11, table 5.1].

In line with developments in other areas of social policy, the Commission sought to give its action against poverty a more formal structure. A Council resolution of 29 September 1989 established an Observatory on National Policies to Combat Social Exclusion [8.4]. The observatory was set up to promote policy analysis, to stimulate the exchange of information and experience and to report back annually to the Commission. Like the observatories for family policies, older people and employment, its aim was to develop a common understanding of the policy framework and to monitor and analyse trends in member states. In recognition of the importance of the voluntary sector's contribution in combating poverty, Directorate-General V also initiated and funded a European Anti-Poverty Network comprising non-governmental organizations. The EAPN was set up in 1990 to co-ordinate efforts across member states and to act as a poverty lobby.

One of the most explicit statements of European policy in relation to poverty is to be found in the Council recommendation, issued four months after the signing of the Treaty on European Union in 1992, 'on common criteria concerning sufficient resources and social assistance in social protection systems' [8.6]. The Council stated that the fight against social exclusion was to be regarded as 'an important part of the social dimension of the internal market' (§7) and conducted 'in a spirit of solidarity' (§8), as announced in the Community charter. The recommendation recognized the multidimensional nature of social exclusion and 'the basic right of a person to sufficient resources and social assistance to live in a manner compatible with human dignity' (part IA). The implementation of such a right was to be organized by 'fixing the amount of resources considered sufficient to cover essential needs with regard to respect for human dignity, taking account of living standards and price levels in the Member State concerned, for different types and sizes of household' (part IC1a]. Although no figure was suggested for the level at which to set such a guaranteed income, the proposal stressed the importance of taking account of the availability of financial resources, national priorities and disparities between national social protection systems. The right to sufficient resources was to be individual and based on need, but subject to active availability for work or vocational training, or to economic and social integration measures, where appropriate. Such a right was not, however, confined to workers. It extended to individuals unable to enter or re-enter the labour market and to older people not entitled to a pension, with the aim of enabling economic and social integration, while at the same time ensuring the safeguarding of incentives to encourage the search for employment.

In pursuit of the objectives set out in documents such as the recommendation, and to ensure continuity of the poverty programmes, in 1993 the Commission presented a proposal for a new medium-term action programme to combat exclusion and promote solidarity for the period 1994–99 [8.8]. The new programme took account of the fact that social exclusion was continuing to increase and spread due to changes in economic, social and demographic structures. A total budget of 121 million ECU for five and a half years was sought for the programme, more than twice the amount for Poverty 3, confirming the Union's commitment to intensifying its effort in this area. Previous programmes had shown that sustained targeted action over several years could produce positive results, but that welfare systems needed modernizing. The Commission therefore called for greater co-operation between different agencies in the public and private sectors. While upholding its view that individual member states were responsible for combating social exclusion, the Commission presented its own role as contributing to the development and transfer of methods and expertise, identifying good practice and setting up and maintaining networks for sharing experience and deepening understanding of the problem. Model actions were to be used at local, national or regional level. Transnational networks of projects were to be developed, information was to be collected, and comparative studies were to be carried out as a means of furthering the understanding of social exclusion and finding ways of controlling it. The Commission proposed to focus on three keywords: partnership, active participation and a multidimensional strategy. By partnership and participation, it was referring to collaboration between government bodies, associations and the individuals concerned, since past experience had shown that integrated actions were most effective. The multidimensional strategy underlined the complexity of situations of social exclusion and the processes involved. An attempt was to be made to formulate policies that adopted a global approach to the problem of social exclusion.

The proposal for a new action programme was, however, opposed by the German delegation at a Council meeting in 1994 on grounds of cost and because the Union had no competence to act in the area of poverty. In anticipation of the programme's approval, the Commission had continued to fund projects under the relevant budget line. It was taken to the European Court of Justice (ECJ) by the United Kingdom on the basis that it had no legal competence for doing so, a case confirmed by a ruling in 1996 [8.9]. As a result, the proposal had still not been adopted in 1999 when the programme would have been due to end.

Further funding was also withheld from the Observatory on National Policies to Combat Social Exclusion, indicating that member states were reigning in on the Commission's power to initiate action at Community level in this policy area.

Regulating the structural funds

While the Commission had been taking forward programmes to combat social exclusion, between 1988 and 1999, a series of regulations was introduced, laying down general provisions for the structural funds. Following the signing of the SEA, it had been agreed that the structural funds should be doubled in size, that priority areas should be identified and that more rigorous regional development plans should be drawn up. The 1988 regulations, in particular 'parent' Regulation (EEC) N° 2052/88 [8.2], removed national quotas and replaced individual projects by integrated programmes. Its effect was to transfer resources from the wealthier member states to the laggard countries in the south. A further reform was undertaken in 1993 through Regulation (EEC) N° 2081/93 [8.7], as provided for in the title on economic and social cohesion in the Treaty on European Union.

The regulations identified priority areas for targeted funding. In the case of Greece, Ireland and Portugal, the entire country was designated as an Objective 1, or priority, region whose development was 'lagging behind'. Ten regions in Spain were included under Objective 1, and eight in Italy. Northern Ireland fell within this category for the United Kingdom and Corsica in the case of France. Objective 1 regions were eligible to receive a larger proportion – around 70 per cent – of the total expenditure, with the aim of redistributing resources in relation to need.

Objective 2 regions were identified as those seriously affected by industrial decline and were allocated about 11 per cent of total expenditure from the structural funds. Objective 3 covered regions targeted for combating unemployment and reintegrating people excluded from the labour market, through training and retraining schemes, the creation of stable jobs and self-employed activities. Long-term unemployed women, migrants and disabled people were singled out for special schemes, as were the same categories among the young. Provision was made for implementing measures at national, local, regional or sectoral level, with the aim of achieving the best match between the difficulties to be overcome and the requirements of the labour market. Objective 4 focused on the adaptation of workers to industrial change and changes in production systems. Together, Objectives 3 and 4 attracted about 11 per cent of expenditure. Objective 5 aimed at promoting structural adjustment in rural areas, with 4 per cent of the funds. In 1993, an Objective 6, with 0.5 per cent of expenditure, was added to promote the development of the thinly populated areas in Finland and Sweden following their accession [8.11, p. 9].

In preparation for enlargement to Central and Eastern Europe, a series of regulations was introduced further reforming the structural funds. Regulation (EC) N° 1260/1999 [8.14] laid down the general provisions for the funds, and together with the accompanying regulations, which were adopted jointly by the European Parliament and Council in 1999, replaced the earlier regulations. In pursuance of articles 146 on the European Social Fund and 159 on economic and social cohesion in the consolidated version of the EC Treaty [1.8], the 1999 regulations redefined the scope of the funds, and restructured and simplified their objectives.

Under Regulation (EC) N° 1262/1999 [8.15], the ESF was to be concerned with encouraging action at national level to promote social integration into the labour market and equality between men and women as part of the mainstreaming approach, while also combating social exclusion. Unlike the 1992 recommendation, the target population was confined to people of working age. For example, assistance was offered for schemes designed to promote the reconciliation of family and working life and to enable 'older workers to have a fulfilling occupation until retirement' (article 3 §2). The financing of early retirement schemes was explicitly excluded, although accompanying measures could cover provision of care services and facilities for dependants. The regulation also provided for Community initiatives, such as Equal, a new human resources initiative, to combat discrimination and inequalities in the labour market, but the main emphasis was on action at regional level to underpin the national action plans for employment (article 5 §2). The relationship between the Commission, member states and regional or local authorities, economic and social partners or other competent bodies was to be founded on partnerships between parties pursuing a common goal. Following the principle of additionality, the funds provided could not be used to replace public or equivalent structural expenditure. Any operations financed either by the funds or by the EIB had to be compatible with the treaty provisions and the Community's policy instruments. The regulation thus confirmed the tone that had been set for the twenty-first century by making sure that the onus was placed on national governments to propose innovative plans for labour-market integration measures.

The employment route to social inclusion

In addition to providing targeted resources through the structural funds to help regions undergoing economic restructuring, during the 1980s the Commission had responded to the growing problem of long-term unemployment by launching a number of active labour market initiatives, including the establishment of an Employment Observatory, documentation systems on employment and a series of action programmes, supported by the structural funds. The observatory's brief was to conduct annual surveys on employment trends, published as *Employment in Europe* [4.17]. The Network of Employment Co-ordinators (Nec) was charged with producing research reports on different themes relating to unemployment. The European System of Documentation on Employment (Sysdem) [8.16] and the Mutual Information System on Employment Policies (Misep) [8.17] reported on the measures adopted in member states, which, since the signing of the Treaty of Amsterdam, are obliged to prepare annual national action plans.

The Commission's own action programmes targeted specific groups and issues relating to employment: the Research Action and Evaluation programme (Ergo) was, for example, intended to raise awareness of the problems faced by the long-term unemployed and evaluate the actions taken; the Local Employment Development Action (Leda) was designed to promote local employment initiatives; the Support Programme for Employment Creation (Spec) aimed to provide technical and financial support for innovative regional or local employment creation projects.

The active approach to labour market policy was reinforced in the 1994 white paper on European social policy, in which the Commission described three priority themes for the ESF: access to and quality of initial training and education through the implementation of the Youth Start scheme, designed to promote the labour market integration of young people, particularly those with no basic qualifications or training; increasing competitiveness and the prevention of unemployment through a systematic approach to training; and the improvement of employment opportunities for the long-term unemployed [1.15, p. 27]. Two new programmes were launched (Employment and Adapt), targeting disadvantaged groups such as the young unemployed, disabled people, the socially excluded and women (Employment-Now), or those at risk due to industrial or technological change [8.18].

During the 1990s, the focus on employment became even stronger, as the structural funds were used to support the Union's employment strategy and the national action plans for employment, while also helping to prepare for enlargement. A communication from the Commission on 'Community structural assistance and employment' [8.10], adopted in 1996, clearly established the role that the structural funds should play in promoting employment in the context of economic and social cohesion. The funds provided support for job creation and stimulated demand for goods and services, while promoting 'balanced territorial development of the priority regions' [8.10, p. 2]. Although funding had been blocked for the Commission's action programme, in 1996 agreement was reached on the allocation for Community initiatives on employment. A new strand was added to the Employment initiative, covering integrated approaches to improving the job prospects of vulnerable groups, and the Adapt initiative was extended to take account of the social policy implications of the information society (1996 was the European Year of Lifelong Learning).

The new title VIa in the Treaty of Amsterdam [1.7] further reinforced the importance of actively promoting employment. This message was reiterated in the preamble to the employment guidelines issued in 1998 by the Council, stressing the precedence to be given to 'active employability measures rather than passive support measures' [1.18, p. 2], and in a Communication from the Commission in 1999, which referred to the 'mainstreaming of employment' [8.13, p. 1].

Solidarity in enlargement

The new waves of membership of the Community and Union, particularly to the south in the 1980s, brought with them challenges to intra-European solidarity, justifying the development of regional policy in support of weaker members. The 1988 reform of the structural funds significantly increased the transfer of resources to the less prosperous member states. The impact of the 1993 reform was less concentrated, since the coverage of Objective 1 was extended to take in the new German *Länder* and other regions to the north [8.11, p. 96]. As a proportion of gross domestic product (GDP), the countries with some of the lowest *per capita* incomes – Greece, Portugal and Ireland – were, however, the main beneficiaries of the structural funds in the periods 1989–93 and 1994–99, with the addition of Germany in the later period [8.11, table 5.2a–5.2b]. In relation to both the total budget and gross national product (GNP), Germany was by far the largest contributor to the structural funds in the late 1990s, followed by France, the United Kingdom and Italy [2.4, vol. 1, table 6].

The proposed enlargement to the East after the year 2000 meant that the Union's population would increase by more than a quarter to almost 500 million, while total GDP would rise by only 5 per cent. All the 'fast track' applicant states had a GDP well below the EU average in the mid-1990s [2.4, vol. 2, p. 62]. It was realized that the solidarity effort made necessary by enlargement would inevitably result in a deterioration of the budgetary position of all 15 EU member states. The Berlin European Council agreed to allocate 213 billion euros for structural operations in the current member states for the period 2000–06 (at 1999 prices). A further 7.3 billion euros were earmarked in pre-accession aid for the new member states and 39.6 billion euros for post-accession. It was also agreed that the effort should not go beyond 0.46 per cent of the Union's GNP, and that transfers from the structural and cohesion funds should not exceed 4 per cent of the GDP of future member states. The number of objectives was reduced from seven to three, and the percentage of the population covered by Objectives 1 and 2 was cut from 51 to 35–40 per cent. Objective 2 was redefined to bring together all measures covering regions with structural problems, and to support programmes favouring economic diversification. A new Objective 3 was designed to help member states adapt and modernize their systems of education, training and employment to make their economies competitive and safeguard the European model of society as part of the European employment strategy. Programmes were simplified and concentrated on geographical zones, and the number of Community initiatives was reduced from 14 to four, with management decentralized from the Commission. The initiatives retained were those that had proved to be most successful in translating intentions into effective action: Equal, for combating discrimination and inequality in access to labour markets; Leader, for rural development; Interreg, for cross-border, transnational and interregional co-operation; and Urban, for urban regeneration [2.4, vol. 1, pp. 15–22; 8.11, p. 111]. Enlargement can thus be seen as having provided an incentive for rationalizing the structural funds and improving their efficiency.

DEFINING AND MEASURING SOCIAL EXCLUSION

Despite the large amount of information assembled by the Commission, at the end of the 1990s, the Union was still faced with the problem of how to find definitions and measures of poverty that would be widely adopted and would yield comparable data over time and across member states. This section considers some of the definitions that have been applied and a selection of the materials collected over the years as a basis for comparing the situation in different EU member states.

Defining poverty, exclusion and marginalization

The Commission's aim in asking member states to provide national reports on levels of poverty and policies to combat exclusion was to monitor and compare the situation, and develop its own action programmes. A definition was therefore needed which could be operationalized in different national contexts. The Commission chose initially to define poverty in terms of income. Any individual with a disposable income falling below a specified level could be considered to be living in poverty. In the first poverty programme, the line was drawn at less than 50 per cent of the national average disposable *per capita* income in the relevant member state. Definitions of poverty as determined by an income poverty line are, however, problematic for both practical and ideological reasons. In practice, low income is a very crude measure of poverty, particularly from a comparative perspective. For example, services in kind, such as social housing and health care, which are unevenly distributed across member states, may affect the level of expenditure in cash. Within and between countries, households vary considerably in their ability to manage their budgets. Ideological factors are also important because the level at which a poverty line is set can be interpreted as 'a highly political act', raising issues about tax and social security benefits scales, definitions of low wages and minimum wage levels, and eligibility for assistance with education or housing costs (Brown, 1986, p. 49).

Poverty is not only relative, it is also cumulative: people on low incomes generally also experience poor housing, educational facilities, transport and communications. Poverty can therefore be defined more broadly in terms of individuals and groups whose resources are so far below the average that they are excluded from the living conditions and amenities that are widely available in the society concerned (Townsend, 1979, p. 31). The concept of exclusion was present in the first poverty programme. Article 1 of the Council decision setting up the programme in 1975 provided a definition of 'persons beset by poverty' as 'individuals or families whose resources are so small as to exclude them from the minimum acceptable way of life of the Member State in which they live'. Resources were defined as 'goods, cash income, plus services from public and private sources' [8.1, p. 34]. The evaluation made of the first poverty programme pointed to a number of inadequacies in the Council's definition (Room, 1982, pp. 159–61). The focus on individuals and families tended to obscure wider societal processes and structures. While the Council recognized that the 'minimum acceptable way of life' would differ from one member state to another, important variations were also to be found within societies. In addition, the focus on resources concealed not only the way in which poor people were excluded from social participation, but also the need for structural changes in society.

While the definition used in the second poverty programme was close to that of the first, it was extended to take account of other resources. The poor were defined as 'persons, families and groups of persons whose resources (material, cultural and social) are so limited as to exclude them from the minimum acceptable way of life in the Member States in which they live' [8.5, p. 11]. By not being confined to income poverty, this definition had the advantage that it introduced the concept of social exclusion, thereby recognizing that poverty brings with it a sense of powerlessness and marginalization, or exclusion, and engenders dependence. It did not resolve the question of how to determine what might be considered as a 'minimum acceptable way of life' or how to apply such a minimum across Europe.

The Observatory on National Policies to Combat Social Exclusion defined social exclusion in relation to social rights with reference, for example, to the right to employment, housing and health care. It asked questions about the effectiveness of national policies in ensuring access to such rights, and the barriers that exclude people from them. In its second annual report, the observatory went on to study the evidence that, 'where citizens are unable to secure their social rights, they will tend to suffer processes of generalised and persisting disadvantage and their social and occupational participation will be undermined' (Room, 1991, p. 17). The Council of Europe has attempted to find an operational definition of social exclusion by specifying that it implies 'a chronic and structured inability by individuals, and groups, to participate in social life' (Corden and Duffy, 1998, p. 117).

Although the manifestations of relative poverty may not have changed significantly – the standard of living and access to resources for the poor are by definition well below the average for the population as a whole – the nature and determinants of poverty have undergone substantial change since the mid-1970s. The term 'new poverty' was created to record the way in which poverty had extended to a much broader cross-section of the population, spanning different age groups, social and economic categories, ethnic groups and geographical areas and threatening people who had previously been in stable employment and well-paid jobs with periods of sporadic and recurrent poverty.

The terms 'polarization', 'dualization' and 'marginalization' were also introduced into the vocabulary of poverty analysts to describe the growing rift between those who are able to take advantage of the social and economic systems and those who are excluded from them. They signalled that the gap had been growing between people in work covered by generous social insurance and the unemployed, between urban and rural populations, between core and periphery, between the able bodied and those with disabilities, and between men and women. Categories of individuals can thus be identified who are living on the margins of society and require special help: the long-term unemployed, the young unemployed, older people, single-parent families, migrants and refugees, and the underprivileged in rural and urban areas.

Measuring poverty and social exclusion

Although the first national reports on poverty in member states were drawn up using a common framework and an agreed method for calculating poverty lines, the quality of the comparative data was very uneven. Some countries had a long tradition of research on poverty, for example researchers in the United Kingdom had been studying poverty for over 150 years, as testified by authoritative accounts such as those of B. Seebohm Rowntree (1901) and Peter Townsend (1979). Others had only begun to carry out research in this area in the late 1960s. While some member states had available regular data series on topics such as expenditure, earnings, social security provision, education and housing, others had given low priority to collecting and analysing data on indicators of poverty levels. Therefore, the information that could be assembled rarely lent itself to reliable comparisons across countries.

To circumvent problems of non-comparability, the Commission sought to establish a common definition of poverty, according to a European base-line of living (EBL), or the capacity to satisfy a body of needs, either by income from earnings or by other means. Attempts have also been made to collect data using a battery of indicators: what the population regards as a minimum income; what individuals consider as an absolute minimum for them; the degree of deprivation in terms of actual consumption and participation in social life; the number of people living on an income below a certain percentage of average *per capita* income; and the number of persons at or below the social assistance level used in each country.

Applying the Commission's definition of a poverty line – those persons whose disposable income is less than half of the average equivalent *per capita* income in their country – the final report of the first poverty programme estimated that in the mid-1970s the number of poor in the nine member states was about 30 million. When the three new southern European member states – Greece, Portugal and Spain – were included, the level of poverty across the Community rose to 38 million [8.5, p. 5]. By the late 1980s, according to the same definition about 52 million people, or about 15 per cent of total population, were considered to be living at or below the 50 per cent poverty threshold [8.8, p. 82].

The European Community Household Panel (ECHP) surveys of the 1990s found a similar level of income poverty. However, they were measuring only the population aged 20–84 living at or below 50 per cent of the national average adjusted disposable income, excluding students and young adults living with their parents (Vogel, 1997, table 8.1, including Finland and Sweden, but excluding Austria). If the poor are defined as the population suffering from material, cultural and social deprivation, which is even more difficult to measure, a much larger proportion of Europe's population would be identified. ECHP data on subjective poverty suggested, for example, that about 20 per cent of the EU's population aged 16–84 years had difficulty in 'making ends meet', and identified unemployed persons and lone parents as the categories experiencing the greatest difficulty (Vogel, 1997, table 9.4). In 1999, the Commission estimated at between 20 and 40 per cent the proportion of the population across the Union experiencing regular spells of deprivation, with more than 10 million people relying on social assistance schemes [10.4, p. 48].

The proportion of the population living in poverty, according to the 50 per cent poverty line for *per capita* disposable income, varies from one member state to another. Figures for the 1990s, according to the same ECHP source, show that rates were particularly high in Portugal, with more than 25 per cent of the population below the 50 per cent poverty line, followed by Greece, the United Kingdom and Ireland. The United Kingdom, however, stands out as being the member state with the largest proportion of children living in low-income households (Eurostat, 1998a, p. 143). The lowest poverty levels, with nearer to 5 per cent, were recorded in Finland, Sweden and Denmark. The ECHP found that the countries where it was most difficult to 'make ends meet' were, by far, Greece, Portugal and Spain, with Luxembourg and Germany at the other end of the scale (Vogel, 1997, tables 8.1, 9.1).

Data on relative income poverty reflect inequalities in earnings, but they say nothing about housing conditions or the impact on living standards of social services and benefits in kind. ECHP data suggest that national housing conditions are generally lower in the southern Mediterranean states and Ireland, where average household size is larger, and average dwelling size is smaller (Vogel, 1997, chapter 10). When housing allowances are taken into account, they may significantly increase the effective amounts paid to low-income households, as is the case in the United Kingdom [2.5, 1997, p. 97; 8.12, table 2].

When findings such as these are produced and compared, some national governments have objected to the basis on which they are drawn up. Their statistical validity has also been questioned. Estimates of the number of beneficiaries of social assistance, another means of calculating poverty levels, are equally unreliable and problematic for comparative purposes, since the criteria for gaining access to social assistance and the level of benefits differ from one country to another, as shown below. Take-up rates may vary too, in accordance with social attitudes and the stigma attached to means-tested welfare: in the early 1990s, in the United Kingdom, 80 per cent of those eligible to claim social assistance did so, compared with 50 per cent in Germany (Lødemel, 1992, p. 16). Take-up of the *revenu minimum d'insertion* (RMI) in France and the social assistance pension in Spain was said to be 100 per cent, but only a third of those eligible to receive family income support in Ireland were claiming benefit (Room, 1991, figure 2). Studies during the 1990s suggested that non take-up of benefits was probably more widespread than had been anticipated but remained difficult to measure with any precision (van Oorschot and Math, 1996).

Overall, ECHP data tend to confirm the national differences identified in *per capita* GDP that justified cohesion policy. In the late 1990s, the southern Mediterranean member states fell well below the EU average for most indicators of living standards, and they were relying much more heavily on intergenerational solidarity than on state welfare policies. By contrast, the Nordic states were above the EU average for most of the indicators, and households were found to be more reliant on universal state provision of benefits and services than on intergenerational support (see Chapter 7). Compared to the 15 EU member states, under socialism the accessor states of Central and Eastern Europe had experienced very low levels of income inequality, as well as low *per capita* GDP. With the exception of the Czech Republic and Slovenia, they therefore continued to fall a long way below the weakest EU member states for the latter measure [2.4, vol. 2, p. 62].

NATIONAL RESPONSES TO SOCIAL EXCLUSION

Although changing economic conditions intensified the need for greater solidarity between member states, by the 1990s no legally binding rights and obligations had been generated at EU level for common social assistance provisions. The growing recognition by the Union that poverty and social exclusion were a result of the inadequacy of cultural and social, as well as material resources, may help to explain why official statements continued to emphasize the subsidiarity principle in formulating measures to combat social exclusion. The 1992 Council recommendation on sufficient resources and social assistance [8.6] left member states to institute their own schemes to provide the necessary financial aid to bring resources up to an unspecified minimum level in accordance with national conditions. Subsequent reports commented on the importance of social transfers in reducing household poverty [8.12, p. 8]. For some 37 per cent of households, transfer payments were found to be the main source of income; without income maintenance payments, an estimated 40 per cent of households would have fallen below the poverty level in the mid-1990s [2.5, 1997, pp. 8, 79].

By the turn of the century, all member states operated unemployment insurance systems, but they had been stretched to the limit by rising unemployment. The EU unemployment rate peaked at over 11 per cent in the mid-1990s and then stabilized at a lower level, though it remained persistently high in Spain, especially among women [4.17, 1999, pp. 127, 132]. Most member states had instituted guaranteed income maintenance schemes for individuals not entitled to insurance benefits. Just as different national models of retirement and invalidity pension schemes or health services can be identified in member states due to differences in their welfare traditions (see Chapters 4 and 7), diversity is also found in arrangements for income maintenance during unemployment or other contingencies [2.7, 1998, tables XI, XII.1]. Commission reports on social protection have indicated the extent to which the impact of transfer payments varies from one country to another [2.5, 1997, chapters 3 and 4]. This section examines how insurance and social assistance benefits are organized in different welfare systems, and how they impact on low-income groups.

Income maintenance in continental welfare states

The continental, corporatist welfare regimes, which were generally derived from the Bismarckian employment-related social-insurance model of social protection, were more concerned with protecting and compensating workers through the insurance principle than with providing national minimum standards for all citizens. Unemployment benefits were insurance based and earnings related, thereby reinforcing the conceptual link with work. In the 1990s, they became more closely tied to availability for work and efforts made to find employment.

Both the levels and duration of benefits varied between member states. In Austria and Germany, claimants who had exhausted their insurance rights moved on to a form of income security, which, while being means tested, was again earnings related. The benefit was of unlimited duration so long as no suitable job was available. In France, insurance-based earnings-related unemployment benefits of fixed duration were followed by a flat-rate assistance payment for periods of six months, in some cases up to a maximum of 12 months. In Luxembourg, benefits were based on former earnings for up to 365 days, but could be extended in certain circumstances. Insurance-related benefits for the unemployed in Belgium were of unlimited duration but degressive, varying according to individual and local conditions, and subject to maximum and minimum levels. Unemployed people in the Netherlands were eligible to receive a statutory minimum benefit as well as extended benefits based on previous earnings for a varying length of time, determined by their employment record and age. Italy is an example of a country that followed the continental approach as far as contributory social insurance was concerned. Benefits were, however, paid at a relatively low level of 30 per cent of average earnings over the previous three months, compared with Luxembourg at the other end of the scale with 80 per cent of earnings.

For job-seekers, young never-employed or disabled people not eligible to receive employment-related benefits, and for those who have exhausted all other rights and whose parents or partners are unable to support them, the founder member states and Austria had all introduced social assistance schemes that remained outside social security systems. They provided entitlement to means-tested benefits, on the basis of nationality and/or residence, paid for an unlimited duration, except in France where the *revenu minimum d'insertion* was limited to three months, with a possible extension for periods of between three months and one year. Austria, Germany and Italy did not apply an age condition. Belgium and the Netherlands set the age of entitlement at 18, France at 25, and Luxembourg at 30, with some exceptions. The rate was determined at national level in Belgium, France, Luxembourg and the Netherlands. In the countries where it was decided, and paid for, at regional or local level, considerable variation could occur in the amount received by beneficiaries in accordance with local circumstances.

In the absence of a national health service (except in Italy), the continental welfare states made provision to cover health care. With the exception of Belgium, housing costs were also taken into account. By the late 1990s, most countries had introduced incentives in social assistance schemes to stimulate (re)integration into the labour market, generally in the form of an earnings disregard.

Income maintenance in Nordic and Anglo-Saxon welfare states

As in the continental welfare states, insurance-based unemployment benefits related to former earnings had been established in the three Nordic states, but in Denmark and Sweden, insurance contributions were optional. The arrangements for income maintenance in all three countries were based solely on the right to reside rather than on nationality conditions. Benefits were paid to an upper limit and for a fixed period. In the late 1990s, Denmark paid benefits of up to 90 per cent of reference earnings, and Sweden up to 80 per cent, in both cases with a maximum level. Only Finland operated a means-tested unemployment assistance scheme. No age condition was imposed in the three countries for social assistance, but in practice children under the age of 18 were considered to be the responsibility of their parents. Benefits were of unlimited duration, set and administered at national level, but with regional and local differentiation in Finland and Sweden. Denmark operated an earnings disregard to encourage labour market integration.

The United Kingdom was the only member state in the late 1990s where unemployment benefit was paid at a flat rate with no reference to former earnings. The job-seeker's allowance was instituted in 1995 to replace unemployment benefit, with the aim of easing the return to work, and enabling beneficiaries to escape from the poverty trap. Based on contributions, the allowance was paid for a maximum of 182 days in any job-seeking period. In 1988, social assistance had been reorganized into two separate state-financed schemes – income support and family credit – providing a means-tested, guaranteed minimum income for United Kingdom nationals, and some other categories residing in the country and aged 18 or over, for an unlimited period. Income support was a benefit for families and individuals with no income from work, whereas family credit was a benefit for families in work, but earning a very low income, and was designed to make people better off in work than unemployed. Family credit was replaced in 1999 by a working family tax credit, designed to guarantee a minimum income for families on low earnings, thereby lifting them out of poverty.

The unemployment benefits and social assistance schemes in Ireland shared some features in common with the United Kingdom. Unemployment insurance gave entitlement to a non-means-tested flat-rate benefit of limited duration. Beneficiaries were also eligible to receive means-tested unemployment assistance for an unlimited period. The supplementary welfare allowance was paid to individuals without other resources for an unlimited period from the age of 18, at a rate set at national level and with incentives to encourage the return to work.

It has been argued that, where the social insurance principle was not originally adopted as the basis for social protection, as in the Nordic states and the United Kingdom, reforms of social assistance have gone in two different directions, illustrated by the cases considered here. In the United Kingdom, emphasis was on creating a rights-oriented scheme to meet the needs of the large number of individuals and groups excluded from occupational insurance schemes. In the Scandinavian countries, by contrast, state-financed social insurance was extended in such a way that social assistance was confined to only a very small section of the very poorest groups in society (Lødemel, 1992, p. 16).

Income maintenance in rudimentary welfare states

The social security systems developed in the southern European countries that joined the Community in the 1980s largely followed the continental employment-related insurance model of social protection with emphasis on entitlements derived from employment. By the late 1990s, they all operated insurance-based systems. Spain and Portugal had also introduced means-tested, flat-rate assistance schemes for the unemployed who had exhausted their entitlements. Greece was the only EU member state not to guarantee a minimum income, but young people aged 20–29 who had never worked were entitled to receive unemployment benefit. The minimum age of entitlement for social assistance was 18 in Portugal and 25 in Spain, except in special circumstances. In Portugal, benefit was paid on the basis of residence. In Spain, where nationality was not necessarily a condition of eligibility, the benefit level was subject to regional variations. In both Portugal and Spain, payment was for 12 months in the first instance, and supportive measures were provided to help promote occupational integration, including an earnings disregard in Portugal.

CONCERTED ACTION FOR SOCIAL INCLUSION

Even if agreement could be reached on how to define and measure poverty and social exclusion across member states, it does not follow that the same solution could, or should, be adopted throughout the Union to deal with the problem. Until the 1990s, the main policy choice was often between concentrating resources on raising the incomes of the poorest of the poor through transfer payments and spreading resources more thinly in order to reduce the hardship of a larger number of individuals and households. By supporting projects that targeted specific groups at risk in the poverty programmes, and through the selective distribution of the structural funds, the aim was specifically to channel resources towards some of the most problematic categories. In pursuance of this policy objective, the recommendation on common criteria for sufficient resources and social assistance in social protection systems [8.6] set out to combat exclusion, primarily by encouraging the improvement of existing national benefits schemes.

As suggested by the examples quoted in this chapter, the arrangements for paying unemployment and social assistance benefits vary substantially from one member state to another in a relationship that does not always correspond closely to need. During the 1990s, two of the countries with the highest *per capita* incomes – Denmark and Luxembourg – also provided some of the most generous earnings-related unemployment benefits, while in Italy, Portugal and Spain, only a minority of the unemployed qualified for benefits [2.5, 1997, p. 73]. The combined impact of minimum incomes, family and housing benefits, expressed in purchasing power parities, was greatest in Denmark, Finland, the Netherlands and Sweden, and smallest in Portugal and Spain (no data for Greece and Italy) [8.12, table 2]. Disparities were narrowed to the greatest extent after transfers in Belgium and France, whereas income after transfers was least evenly distributed in Portugal and Greece, followed by the United Kingdom, with significant proportions of households remaining below the poverty line in all three countries. While, in Ireland and the United Kingdom, a large percentage of unemployment transfers were nonetheless going to the poorest households, this was not the case in the Mediterranean member states, partly because of the high proportion of the unemployed living in households with people in work [2.5, 1997, pp. 84–9]. In addition, many of the changes made to unemployment compensation schemes in the 1990s to contain costs had the effect of either cutting benefits further or restricting entitlement, thereby reducing their redistributive impact.

Over the decade, as confirmed by the Treaty of Amsterdam [1.7], attention had shifted decisively from passive measures for the unemployed towards active labour market policies, designed to promote social inclusion through employment and incentives to work, and supported by employment-friendly social protection systems. The danger inherent in this approach was that it tended to reinforce the divisions between work-rich and work-poor households, sidelining those excluded from the labour force for whatever reason. Just as new forms of exclusion were appearing for young people unable to obtain academic or vocational qualifications, or for those unable to benefit from the information society, the criterion of employability engendered the risk that resources would be diverted away from measures to deal with urban deprivation and other areas of social exclusion where different policies were required.

Box 8 Secondary legislation and official publications relating to social exclusion and social inclusion

8.1 Council Decision of 22 July 1975 concerning a programme of pilot schemes and studies to combat poverty (75/458/EEC) (*OJ* L 199/34 30.7.75), amended by Council Decision of 12 December 1977 (77/779/EEC) (*OJ* L 322/28 17.12.77).

8.2 Council Regulation (EEC) N° 2052/88 on the tasks of the Structural Funds and their effectiveness and on coordination of their activities between themselves and with the operations of the European Investment Bank and the other existing financial instruments (*OJ* L 185/9 15.7.88).

8.3 Council Decision of 18 July 1989 establishing a medium-term Community action programme concerning the economic and social integration of the economically and socially less privileged groups in society (89/457/EEC) (*OJ* L 224/10 2.8.89).

8.4 Council Resolution of 29 September 1989 on combating social exclusion (*OJ* C 277/1 31.10.89).

8.5 Commission of the European Communities, The fight against poverty, *Social Europe Supplement*, 2/89.

8.6 Council Recommendation of 24 June 1992 on common criteria concerning sufficient resources and social assistance in social protection systems (92/441/EEC) (*OJ* L 245/46 26.8.92).

8.7 Council Regulation (EEC) N° 2081/93 amending Regulation (EEC) N° 2052/88 on the tasks of the Structural Funds and their effectiveness and on co-ordination of their activities between themselves and with the operations of the European Investment

Bank and the other existing financial instruments (*OJ* L 193/5 31.7.93).

8.8 Commission proposal for a medium-term action programme to combat exclusion and promote solidarity: a new programme to support and stimulate innovation (1994–1999) (COM(93) 435 final, 22 September 1993).

8.9 Cases C–239/96 and C–240/96 United Kingdom of Great Britain and Northern Ireland v Commission of the European Communities [1996] ECR I–4475. Application for interim measures – Social Policy – Community measures to assist the elderly – Community measures to combat poverty and social exclusion.

8.10 Communication from the Commission on Community structural assistance and employment (COM(96) 109 final, 20 March 1996).

8.11 Commission of the European Communities, First Cohesion Report (COM(96) 542 final, 6 November 1996).

8.12 Report from the Commission to the Council, the European Parliament, the Economic and Social Committee and the Committee of the Regions on the implementation of the Recommendation 92/441/EEC of 24 June 1992 on common criteria concerning sufficient resources and social assistance in social protection systems (COM(1998) 774, 25 January 1999).

8.13 Communication from the Commission on Community policies in support of employment (COM(1999) 167 final, 21 April 1999).

8.14 Council Regulation (EC) N° 1260/1999 of 21 June 1999 laying down general provisions on the Structural Funds (*OJ* L 161/1 26.6.99).

8.15 Regulation (EC) N° 1262/1999 of the European Parliament and of the Council of 21 June 1999 on the European Social Fund (*OJ* L 161/48 26.6.99).

8.16 European System of Documentation on Employment (Sysdem) web site:
http://europa.eu.int/scadplus/leg/en/cha/c10208.htm

8.17 Mutual Information System on Employment Policies (Misep) web site:
http://europa.eu.int/scadplus/leg/en/cha/c10207.htm

8.18 Community employment initiatives web site:
http://www.europs.be/

9 Social Policy and Mobility

While the Treaty establishing the European Economic Community (EEC) [1.2] was not intended to provide a fully developed framework for social policy across member states, a major reason for promoting the social dimension and for seeking to harmonize national social protection systems was to remove obstacles to intra-European mobility. The treaty firmly endorsed the policy aim of creating the necessary conditions so that persons, services and capital could move freely between member states. This continued to be a primary objective as membership of the Community was extended from the 1970s. The Single European Act (SEA) [1.5], the Community Charter of the Fundamental Social Rights of Workers [1.10] and the Maastricht and Amsterdam Treaties [1.6; 1.7] reaffirmed that employment, adaptability, training and mobility were to be keywords for the Single European Market (SEM) and Economic and Monetary Union (EMU).

Most economists would argue that mobility of labour is determined by a whole range of factors operating at the level of the socio-economic environment. If mobility is to be encouraged, incentives are therefore needed through company law, taxation, wage systems and employment law, supported by qualifications, education, training and transferable social protection rights. Either directly or indirectly, the Community's and Union's treaties and charter have addressed all these issues. Less attention has, however, been paid in official documents to social and cultural factors that may also impede mobility.

This chapter begins by analysing the principle of freedom of movement, as embodied in primary and secondary legislation. An attempt is then made to assess the impact of Community law on intra-European migratory flows. Informal obstacles to mobility, such as cultural and linguistic differences, as well as family commitments and obligations, are examined as factors that may help to explain why only relatively small numbers of nationals across the European Union (EU) have become mobile since the establishment of the common market. At the same time as the Community was formulating policies to promote freedom of movement between member states, it was limiting immigration flows from non-EU countries. The issue of immigration from outside the Union is also discussed with reference to the Union's social policy and the concept of 'Fortress Europe'.

EUROPEAN LEGISLATION ON FREEDOM OF MOVEMENT

The EEC was premised on the assumption that the free movement of labour was necessary if the common market was to become a reality. The Community's and Union's treaties and charter have all reiterated this objective, and binding legislation has been implemented to ensure formal obstacles to mobility are removed. This section examines the development of the Union's social law with regard to migration and its underlying assumptions.

Freedom of movement in the treaties and charter

In the early years of the EEC, migration within the Community was mainly of unskilled workers moving north from the southern regions. In combination with non-EEC immigrants, many of whom came from Greece, Portugal and Spain, this mobility was a response to the needs of the labour market for low-paid manual workers. Intra-European migration served a double purpose: for the host countries, it answered the demand for manpower at a time of economic expansion and labour shortage; for the provider countries, it offered job opportunities for unskilled workers from areas of high unemployment. Italy, as the only EEC founder member with a persistent unemployment problem, had a particular interest in ensuring that unemployed workers within the Community were given preference over recruits from elsewhere (Collins, 1975, p. 99).

Articles 48–51 of the EEC Treaty contained the main clauses establishing the right to freedom of movement of workers. Article 48 reiterated the principle of non-discrimination set out in article 7: all discrimination based on nationality was prohibited with regard to 'employment, remuneration and other conditions of work and employment'. The same article confirmed the right of workers to accept an offer of employment in another member state, to take up employment under the same conditions as nationals and to remain in the territory of another member state after having been employed there, with the exception of public service employment.

Article 49 contained the measures required to ensure freedom of movement of workers, covering close co-operation between employment services, the elimination of administrative procedures and practices, and of qualifying periods previously concluded between member states. It also referred to the need for appropriate 'machinery' to facilitate a balance between supply and demand in the employment market. Article 50 made specific reference to the need to encourage the exchange of young workers. Article 51, which was subject to unanimous voting, focused on the measures required in the field of social security, covering arrangements for aggregation of all periods taken into account under the laws of the countries concerned 'for the purpose of acquiring and retaining the right to benefit and of calculating the amount of benefit', as well as 'payment of benefits to persons resident in the territories of Member States'. Article 121 under the section on social provisions assigned to the Commission the task of implementing common measures for the social security of migrant workers.

The Single European Act (SEA) [1.5] of 1986 expressly excluded the use of qualified majority voting for matters relating to free movement of persons (article 100a). However, the revised EC Treaty [1.8] prepared the ground for concerted action by member states over policies related to free movement, by gradually introducing alternative procedures avoiding the need for unanimity (articles 62, 67, 251).

In the Community charter [1.10], the priority attributed to the free movement of workers was indicated by its position at the beginning of the document. The right of workers to freedom of movement throughout the Community was reiterated. Equal treatment was to be promoted in 'access to employment, working conditions and social protection in the host country', implying 'harmonisation of conditions of residence in all Member States, particularly those concerning family reunion; elimination of obstacles arising from the non-recognition of diplomas or equivalent occupational qualifications; improvement of the living and working conditions of frontier workers' [1.10, §§1–3]. The implementation initiatives subsequently brought forward by the Commission included actions to ensure the rights of workers in frontier regions and to co-ordinate supplementary social security schemes for transfrontier workers [9.12; 9.13].

The Treaty on European Union [1.7] marked an important stage in the development of European policy on freedom of movement. A new article 8 was inserted under title II establishing the principle of 'citizenship of the Union'. In addition to freedom of movement within the territory of member states, citizens of the Union were afforded the right to vote and stand as candidates at municipal and European Parliament elections under the same conditions as nationals. It has been argued, however, that the concept of citizenship of the Union is a flag which fails to cover its cargo, on the grounds that Union citizenship cannot exist separately from national citizenship for so long as the Union is not a federal state and has no legal personality. The granting of citizenship remains a matter for the state concerned (Gormley, 1998, p. 174).

The Treaty of Amsterdam [1.7] retained article 8, which became article 17 in the consolidated EC Treaty [1.8], but amended the wording to state that citizenship of the Union complemented and did not replace national citizenship. A paragraph was also added to article 8d in the Maastricht Treaty (article 21 in the revised EC Treaty) to the effect that citizens may write to the Union's institutions in any of its 12 official languages and receive a reply in the same language. The Treaty of Amsterdam confirmed the extension introduced by the SEA to the Union's prohibition on discrimination on grounds of nationality (original EEC Treaty article 7), empowering the Council to adopt rules by qualified majority voting to prohibit such discrimination (article 12 in the consolidated EC Treaty). A new article 6a was introduced in the Treaty of Amsterdam giving the Council authority, subject to unanimous voting, to take action to combat specified instances of discrimination, including cases concerning racial or ethnic origin (revised EC Treaty article 13). A report to the European Commission from an expert group on fundamental rights in 1999 [9.24, p. 11] interpreted the new article as evidence of the Union's commitment actively to promote human rights and fundamental freedoms, as previously guaranteed in the 1950 European Convention on Human Rights, the Council of Europe's 1961 social charter and the 1989 Community charter.

Article 238 of the original EEC Treaty and article 310 in the revised EC Treaty gave the Community the power to conclude association agreements with other states or international organizations involving reciprocal rights and obligations. Between 1991 and 1996, ten such agreements were signed with Central and Eastern European countries, in principle ensuring free movement of workers under conditions similar to those pertaining between the EU member states, thus preparing the way for enlargement.

Secondary legislation regulating freedom of movement

In the years immediately following the signing of the EEC Treaty, action with regard to freedom of movement was primarily concerned with administrative procedures, the easing of restrictions on mobility (work permits, visas, labour and residence permits), and the transfer of wages and social security rights. A number of regulations – the most binding form of Community legislation – were adopted, and subsequently amended, to implement the treaty obligations, gradually creating a strong body of legislation.

Some of the earliest EEC legislation, Regulations N°s 3–4, addressed the question of social security for migrants [9.1]. A spate of preliminary measures during the 1960s culminated in Regulation (EEC) N° 1612/68 [9.2], which laid down the conditions for freedom of movement for workers within the Community, and Directive 68/360/EEC on 'the abolition of restrictions on movement and residence within the Community for workers of Member States and their families' [9.3]. The intention was to outlaw discrimination on grounds of nationality. Member states were to recognize the fundamental right of workers and their families to choose where they wished to work and reside. They could not demand visas or other entry requirements from Community nationals. Equality of treatment in gaining access to work, housing and social protection was to be ensured, as was the social integration of migrant workers and their dependants (see Chapter 5). The regulation also covered the arrangements for bringing together potential applicants and information about job vacancies through the European system for the international clearing of vacancies and applications for employment (Sedoc), which was replaced in 1993 by the European employment service (Eures) [9.27].

The EEC Treaty established the principle that workers should be suitably equipped to conduct their business in another member state, and that the conditions of employment should be at least as good as those in the country they were leaving. Therefore, accrued social security rights had to be transferable. The co-ordination and application Regulations (EEC) N°s 1408/71 [9.4] and 574/72 [9.5] replaced the 1958 regulations, and were themselves replaced in 1996 by a consolidated version, Council Regulation N° 118/97 [9.16]. These regulations provided for equal treatment in matters of social security, the nomination of one competent state to resolve conflicts of law, the aggregation (and proratization) of periods of insurance or employment records, and the exportability of social security benefits, including pensions and unemployment benefits. Council Directive 96/71/EC 'concerning the posting of workers in the framework of the provision of services' [9.17] extended the guarantee of social protection and employment rights to workers posted to another member state for limited periods. Council

Directive 98/49/EC [9.22] closed one of the remaining loopholes in social security matters by making survivors' benefits and some disability benefits payable throughout the EU, net of any taxes and transaction charges. The aim of European law, in all these cases, was not to harmonize social security systems, but rather to co-ordinate them so that workers would not be discouraged from moving within the Community (see Chapter 2).

By the end of the 1990s, member states were legally bound to observe the principle that workers should be free to move from one country to another without prejudicing their right to employment and to employment-related benefits. To facilitate the movement of labour, information had to be supplied on job availability in other countries, professional qualifications and experience had to be recognized, social security entitlements needed to be transferable from one state to another, and every effort had to be made to ensure the social and economic integration of migrant workers in the host country.

THE IMPACT OF UNION POLICY ON MOBILITY

It is difficult to assess the extent to which European social policy has encouraged the movement of workers between member states. The impact of Community policy, whether social or economic, on labour mobility is thought to have been limited in the first 25 years of the postwar period (Collins, 1975, p. 114). In practice, the labour shortage was such that the preference to be given to EEC nationals probably had little effect on mobility. Despite the lack of evidence of increased migration due to the provisions of the EEC Treaty, the need to promote freedom of movement was used constantly as a justification for policy developments in areas such as education and training, the improvement of living and working conditions, and social protection (see Chapters 3 and 4). In the context of the 1990s, when the Union's social priority was to reduce unemployment, intra-European mobility was subordinated to the aim of creating jobs by stimulating economic growth and competitiveness [1.14, pp. 35–6]. The positive view of mobility, presented by the Commission, was that it extended opportunities for workers to find jobs and for employers to find people with adequate skills, thereby enhancing employment and economic growth [9.26]. This section examines the possible outcomes of the Union's efforts to promote the movement of labour and analyses the attempts made to measure intra-European mobility.

The impact of the internal market on migratory flows

The completion of the internal market, following the signing of the SEA, was expected to provide an incentive to accelerate existing trends, such as the flow of Portuguese workers to France. Because of the changing nature of the labour market in the Community, by the end of the 1980s, the demand for unskilled workers had, however, fallen to a low level and was expected to remain so as further automation was introduced. The assumption that the completion of the internal market would bring an increase in Mediterranean migration (Greeks, Portuguese and Spaniards) to the north was also offset to some extent by the displacement of the industrial core through the withdrawal of manufacturing to peripheral areas outside the Union with lower labour costs. Some growth was recorded in non-labour migration, due to student mobility (see Chapter 3) and the attraction for pensioners and migrants with a private income of warmer climates in the Union's sun belt.

Demographic factors were also expected to have an impact on migratory movements. Already in the 1980s, due to the ageing of the population throughout Europe (see Chapter 7), a gradual fall was being predicted in the number of young people entering working life, provoking skill shortages in most member states, particularly in high technology industries with rapid staff turnover. In the short term, the expectation was that the problem would be offset to some extent by the increase in the number of women becoming economically active. In the longer term, however, non-EU migrants, or previously inactive women, were not thought likely to compensate for the shortfall in the labour supply. Another possible implication of an ageing workforce was that upward pressures would be exerted on labour costs, leading to the reduction of geographical and occupational mobility, since the young, unattached, and often lower paid, workers tended to be the most mobile (Ardittis, 1990).

Much of what was being said and written in the late 1980s was premised on the assumption that skill shortages would continue to be a major factor influencing labour markets (Lindley, 1991). As these shortages led to greater staff turnover and increased competition among employers for professional workers and managers with high levels of qualification, future migration between member states was expected to affect mainly highly qualified workers in multinational companies [4.17, 1989, p. 153], encouraging the brain drain ('brain migration' for Ardittis, 1990, p. 465). Much of the movement in this area was, however, thought likely to be short-stay resettlement.

Even before 1 January 1993 when the internal market was to come into force, predictions about increasing levels of intra-European mobility of labour were being revised downwards, except insofar as border areas were concerned, and it seemed increasingly unlikely that migration would serve as a cohesive force (Pickup, 1990, p. 106). During the 1990s, although the Commission continued to advocate active measures to encourage intra-European mobility, the free movement of workers was not a prominent issue in the run-up to monetary union. The achievement of EMU was expected to increase demand for workers and to have a particularly strong impact on labour in cross-border regions by simplifying economic transactions [9.18, p. 7]. Geographical labour mobility between regions within countries was given more attention as one of the possible ways of adjusting labour markets to changing economic conditions and, more especially, to differences in regional growth rates. It was recognized that, if controlled, such movements could contribute to higher rates of growth and a more balanced development. Union policy was not, however, intended actively to promote inter-regional migration because of the negative multiplier effect it could have on income in the regions from which people moved [4.17, 1997, p. 67]. The Commission was predicting that, in combination with EMU, demographic trends and the changing nature of working life would provide a new impetus for mobility in the twenty-first century for highly skilled workers in a single European employment market [9.18, p. 9].

Measurements of intra-European mobility

Until the mid-1980s, little information about intra-European migration was available. The Community Labour Force Survey (LFS) has since monitored migratory flows between member states on an annual basis by asking a small non-representative population sample where they were living one year previously. Data from this source are of limited value since they do not record short-term mobility and rely on individual recall. Nor do they show how many intra-European migrants are living in another country having taken up its nationality and citizenship. The cross-national comparability of data collected by other means is also restricted due to measurement problems and the non-compatibility of national sources (Singleton, 1998). Such data do, however, give some indication of trends within countries over a period of years.

Before the Union began monitoring intra-European mobility using the LFS, one means of assessing movement was by counting the number of labour permits delivered. During the ten years between 1958 and 1968 when labour permits were issued for Community nationals, the proportion taken by Italy, the country which had insisted on the need for freedom of movement for labour, and stood to gain most from it, actually decreased. By the beginning of the 1970s, probably about 1 million Community nationals were working in another member state, compared to 2.5 million non-EEC migrants, and about 2 million EEC nationals were estimated to be living in a member state other than their own (Collins, 1975, pp. 114–15).

During the 1980s, annual mobility was on average equivalent to less than 0.1 per cent of the Community's population. By the mid-1980s, fewer than 2 million Community nationals were working on a more or less permanent basis in another member state. When family members were included, foreign residents were estimated to number 12.5 million, including nearly 5.5 million Community nationals [4.17, 1989, p. 153]. The entry of Greece, Portugal and Spain, who were in the past the main suppliers of non-EEC workers, into the Community in the 1980s did not coincide with a major increase in internal migratory flows; intra-European mobility may even have decreased by comparison with the level reached in the early 1970s.

By the late 1990s, about 1.5 per cent of the Union's citizens were estimated to be living in another member state, representing some 5.8 million people (Eurostat, 1997 data, personal communication). Luxembourg was a special case with almost a third of its population composed of nationals from elsewhere in the Union. Although the proportion of nationals from another member state reached 5.5 per cent in Belgium, only in France, Germany and Ireland did it exceed 2 per cent. The lowest levels were found in the southern Mediterranean member states. In absolute figures, Germany was the country receiving the largest number of EU migrants, with a high proportion from Italy and Greece. France was also a big importer of other EU nationals, with a particularly large influx from Portugal. Most of the EU migrants to the United Kingdom came from Ireland.

During the 1990s, cross-border commuting (though not necessarily on a daily basis) was more widespread than relocation. According to the LFS, about 0.5 per cent of people (630 000) employed in the Union in the late 1990s lived in one country and worked in another. A similar number commuted to a country outside the Union, the majority to Switzerland. Belgium was the country with the highest proportion of its residents (1.5 per cent) working outside its borders, mainly in the Netherlands and Luxembourg. Belgium was also the member state with the largest proportion of commuters between regions, rising to over 18 per cent, almost double the figures for Germany and the United Kingdom, which were the next highest. In Italy, Portugal and Spain, transfrontier mobility was very limited [4.17, 1997, pp. 71–2].

Whatever the measures used and the categories considered, the striking feature is the relatively low level of labour movement within the Union and its slow growth. The impact of Community efforts to ensure priority for EU workers would seem to be minimal compared to the scale of immigration and emigration among member states before the EEC was established.

OBSTACLES TO INTRA-EUROPEAN MIGRATION

Despite the removal of administrative barriers, attempts to harmonize social protection systems and to implement directives on the mutual recognition of qualifications (see Chapter 3), intra-European mobility has not increased at the rate that might have been expected if the main obstacles to freedom of movement were legal restrictions. Numerous cases have been brought before the European Court of Justice (ECJ) where unequal treatment has resulted from inadequate adaptation of national laws and practices to Union legislation, from the narrow interpretation of regulations concerning pension rights, or the non-recognition of qualifications and skills and social security benefits (Gormley, 1998; Guild, 1999). A report from the Commission in 1999 revealed, for example, that most member states had failed to implement the requirements of Directives 90/364, 90/365 and 93/96 on social security [9.25, p. 8]. Only the Netherlands, Denmark and Spain were considered to have complied fully.

Analysis of migratory patterns suggests, however, that regulations may be only one of a number of variables influencing decisions about labour mobility. Many of the remaining practical barriers may have little to do with legal restrictions on mobility and establishment. Opportunities may be determined by the structure of labour markets as well as formal regulations (Pickup, 1990, pp. 5, 24). At EU level, factors believed to be inhibiting mobility in the late 1990s included high levels of unemployment, social and cultural barriers, practical obstacles and lack of information on opportunities [9.18, p. 7]. Personal decisions about mobility may be affected by individual factors such as health, income and qualifications, and also by the social and relational context, including the working environment and household circumstances. This section considers a range of institutional, social and cultural obstacles to mobility, which, cumulatively, may help to explain why the completion of the internal market may not have accelerated migration flows to the extent anticipated by policy makers.

Transferability of rights

According to European law, a person who has exercised the right to move within the Union may not be placed in a worse position with regard to social protection than someone who has always resided and worked in a single member state [9.19, p. 7]. Under the terms of European legislation, nationals from the Union who take up employment in another member state can expect to be covered by the social security system of the country in which they are pursuing their activity. They should be eligible to receive the same insurance-based benefits for sickness, maternity, pensions and unemployment as nationals residing and working in that country. Insurance rights already acquired in another member state are not lost but can be aggregated, as in the case of pensions. It is therefore possible to draw benefits in two or more countries at the same time. Where pensioners take up residence in another member state, like students, they must give proof of adequate financial means and health insurance. Health care is provided according to the legislation of the state of residence under the same conditions as for other residents, and not in the country where a worker (or former worker) is insured. The country of non-residence does, however, reimburse the relevant insurance fund in the country of residence.

Entitlements to rights conditional on qualifying periods may be maintained and carried over to another member state to satisfy its qualifying conditions. In the case of unemployment, benefit can, however, only be claimed from the country in which insurance contributions were paid, and for a period of up to six months (three in some countries), if the insured person registers as a job-seeker in another member state. An exception is made for frontier workers who are eligible to receive benefits from the country in which they reside. Assistance benefits – social assistance, guaranteed income for older people – are provided in the host country on the same basis as for nationals. As all member states have a residence condition for social assistance, benefits are not exportable, with the exception of Dutch nationals abroad in special circumstances [2.7, 1998, table XII.1]. In some cases, the provision may be lower in the host country as, for example, in Greece which did not operate a general social assistance scheme in the 1990s (see Chapter 8).

Education, training and recruitment

The enforcement of agreements over the mutual recognition of diplomas and qualifications, the revised EC Treaty commitment to education, vocational training and youth, and the Commission's action programmes have undoubtedly removed many of the formal and practical obstacles to intra-European mobility and encouraged young people to become mobile. They have not, however, eliminated important differences in approaches to education and training or changed their relationship with the labour market. Nor have attempts to encourage mobility among students led to a uniform product from national educational systems. Differentiation in the structure of internal labour markets may result from disparities in national systems of vocational education and training, in particular between countries with well-developed apprenticeship training schemes for skills acquisition and those where vocational training is less highly valued (see Chapter 3).

In a green paper on the obstacles to transnational mobility with regard to education, training and research [9.15], the Commission focused on issues concerned with what were seen in the late 1990s as the regulatory and administrative deficiencies falling within its competence that might discourage free movement. It identified barriers such as territorial restrictions on student grants, the lack of recognition of vocational qualifications acquired in another member state, the loss of rights to unemployment benefit and social security for job-seekers undergoing training of more than three months in another member state, and the problems of classifying voluntary work. Examples were quoted of countries that had not transposed European law into national legislation. In 1996, Directive 89/48/EEC [3.2] on the mutual recognition of qualifications had, for instance, still not been implemented in Belgium and Greece, and in some of the German *Länder* [9.15, pp. II–V, 19].

National practices followed traditionally in recruitment and training, and in the assessment of competence, skills and abilities are also important in understanding the acceptability and integration of workers who are the products of another educational system. Differences in formal and informal recruitment practices may serve as exclusionary mechanisms making it difficult for outsiders to enter labour markets in other countries. In combination with imbalances in the demand and supply of specialists, they can impede the transferability of labour.

Job information and access to employment

Lack of information about jobs is frequently mentioned as a reason why intra-European mobility has been limited. In this area, Community action did not gather momentum until the end of the 1980s. Then, Sedoc was established by the Commission in 1989 to enable the matching and clearance of jobs. In 1994, the computerized system for exchanging job vacancies under the European employment services project (Eures) began operating in conjunction with public employment services in member states. The aim was to provide detailed information on job vacancies and job applications, as well as general information on living and working conditions and labour markets, to assist both individuals looking for work and employers wanting to recruit elsewhere in the Union. A network of appropriately trained Euroadvisers were linked by an electronic mail system and were required to provide job-seekers with the guarantee of a standard of service at least the equivalent of what they would obtain if they were in the member state to which they were trying to move. Over the two-year period 1996–97, Eures reached about 1 million European citizens and, in 1997, it recorded having established some 500 000 contacts with employers and job-seekers. Most of these contacts were, perhaps not unexpectedly, concentrated in the information technology, healthcare and tourism sectors, which attracted most of the mobile workers [9.27].

Obtaining information about vacancies is only the first stage in a job search. The many complications of pursuing an application and contemplating relocation may deter large numbers of job-seekers from embarking on the process. Considerable effort has therefore been expended on the production of practical fact sheets for distribution nationally to people embarking on intra-European job searches [9.26].

Public sector employment

Despite the general agreement over arrangements to facilitate and encourage freedom of movement among employees and self-employed workers, article 48 of the EEC Treaty [1.2] explicitly excluded public servants from the freedom of movement clause. The revised article 39 in the consolidated EC Treaty [1.8] also specified that the provisions did not apply to employment in the public sector. The restriction was intended to safeguard the general interests of the state and does not therefore cover all public sector employment. Posts in the judiciary, police, armed forces and diplomatic service, as well as architects and supervisors in public administration, may be reserved for nationals, whereas access to professional employment, in nursing for example, is not restricted. The fact that civil servants may have access to more generous social security arrangements, as in Germany or France, as well as a guarantee of employment, may help to explain why governments were reluctant to extend access to public sector jobs to non-nationals in cases where national interest was not paramount. Employment in the public sector was an area where, in the late 1990s, the Commission recognized that action was still needed to open up access across the Union [9.18, p. 6], and it was not until 1998 that Council Regulation (EC) N° 1606/98 brought special schemes for civil servants within Regulation (EEC) N° 1408/71 [9.16].

Some member states – Belgium, France, Italy and Luxembourg – have invoked the nationality clause as a means of preventing nationals from other countries from entering public sector employment. By contrast, in Denmark, Greece, Ireland, the Netherlands, Portugal and the United Kingdom, already by the early 1990s, only 10 per cent of public sector jobs were not accessible to non-nationals (Gastines and Sylvestre, 1992, p. 201). Programmes such as Lingua were intended to encourage the mobility of teachers, by providing in-service opportunities for practising teachers to spend periods abroad. However, in some member states barriers to their freedom of movement in the longer term remained, since they were classified as civil servants, and were not therefore considered to be covered by mobility rules.

Language and culture

Ultimately, the reluctance of employers to recruit senior staff from other member states or for well-qualified labour to move between countries within the Union, except in the case of multinational firms, may be explained by an inadequate knowledge of foreign languages and by cultural differences. Although qualified skilled workers may be able to exercise their occupation in another country without being proficient in the relevant language, fluency (often in English) is essential for professional practice by highly qualified workers. An understanding of other cultures and an appreciation of national mores are also important prerequisites for social integration.

Justifiably, the Community has long seen language acquisition as a key to effective labour mobility and integration. Under Council Directive 77/486/EEC 'on the education of the children of migrant workers' [9.8], member states are obliged to offer suitable tuition in the language of the host state, while also being expected to promote the teaching of the mother tongue and of the culture of the country of origin, with a view to facilitating the possible reintegration of migrants returning to their country of origin. Article 149 §§1–2 of the consolidated EC Treaty [1.8] commits the Community to take action to promote the teaching and dissemination of Community languages as a component of quality education. The 1995 white paper on education and training [3.9] advocated proficiency in three EU languages for every European citizen, and a Council resolution in 1997 [9.20] recommended the early teaching of languages and their diversification.

Programmes such as Lingua may have some impact on language proficiency, but the size of the language problem continues to be daunting. By the mid-1990s, only Luxembourg had come anyway near to meeting the target for EU nationals to learn three languages. English was, by far, the most widespread foreign language taught in secondary schools across the Union, and was being studied by almost 90 per cent of secondary school pupils. In Finland, the Netherlands and Sweden, 99 per cent of all pupils were learning English at that level, and nowhere did take-up fall below 60 per cent. French, the second most widely taught language was taken by only 33 per cent of pupils, and no other language accounted for over 20 per cent (Eurostat, 1998a, p. 62). Individuals from other member states seeking employment in the United Kingdom are therefore likely to have a linguistic advantage over English native speakers contemplating migrating to other parts of Europe, except in sectors, such as international business, where the main language of communication is often English.

Language policy is an area where the Union can do little more than make recommendations about what would be desirable, and launch programmes to encourage language acquisition. Within member states that are multilingual, such as Belgium, language is already a contentious issue, and Brussels, Luxembourg and Strasbourg are prime examples of the difficulties of reaching agreement over working languages, a problem exacerbated by the arrival of new member states and by internal power struggles.

Lack of proficiency in the relevant language is often combined with an insufficient understanding of other national cultures. While the Community has been careful to record the need to respect national and regional diversity, it has also been attempting to promote a common cultural heritage (article 151 in the consolidated EC Treaty). Interpreted in the broader sense, cultural differences are a source of major problems not only for participants in international negotiations and business undertakings, who need to understand the assumptions, expectations and cues characteristic of different national and regional communities, but also for migrants wanting to settle in another member state. Understanding time-keeping, or what is acceptable behaviour in terms of employment practices and social interchange may, for example, affect the ability of migrants to adapt to living in countries which, as members of a political and economic Union, might be expected to have shared cultural norms. In this respect, it may be that media and other communications networks can have more of an impact on cultural integration than any action at EU level. In the absence of an agreed European culture, the concern in audiovisual policy has been primarily to promote the production and distribution of European works through the Media programmes, which included support for linguistic diversity [9.28].

Personal and family factors

Workers, particularly in dual career couples, may be constrained by personal and family factors that the completion of the internal market in itself could probably do little to change. Reasons frequently put forward by well-qualified workers for not being mobile are their concern about their children's education or about finding employment for a spouse. The Commission has recognized the possible restraining effect on labour mobility of the increased participation of women in the labour force and the reduction of gender imbalances, which mean that couples have to consider their joint careers [9.18, p. 9]. Despite legislation on equal treatment, the social and economic position of women, and attitudes towards female economic activity and the provision of support for families vary from one member state to another (see Chapters 5 and 6). In addition, the much higher cost of living in some member states and problems of finding suitable accommodation in what are often very different market conditions may reduce the attractiveness, feasibility and financial viability of moving to another member state.

Many of the personal factors determining the relative stability of the internal labour force are also likely to explain low intra-European mobility rates [4.17, 1997, pp. 70–1]. Public sector workers with security of employment, particularly dual earners with children, are more stable than single employees in the private sector and the unemployed. The male population aged 35–55 is therefore less mobile than the female and younger population. Owner occupation of housing, which increases with age, also tends to reduce geographical mobility.

UNION POLICY ON NON-EUROPEAN IMMIGRATION

At the beginning of the 1990s, the increasing participation of women in paid employment was continuing to offset the decline in the size of the working population [4.17, 1992, p. 10]. During the 1990s, employment rates for men were falling, while those for women were rising. However, a growing proportion of the jobs being created were part time [4.17, 1999, p. 127]. The issue of labour shortages was not high on the Community's agenda. Rather, the immediate concern was how to resolve the problem of unemployment and underemployment. Meanwhile, the Commission was developing policy responses to the predicted longer term downturn in the labour supply (Rubery and Smith, 1999), and to the need to modernize social protection systems to cope with the consequences of accelerated population ageing [2.3]. Measures to encourage non-EU immigration, the solution to labour shortages adopted in the postwar period, were not being advocated. In the revised EC Treaty (title IV), the Union had confirmed its treaty commitment to regulate the flow of migrants from outside its borders, but it was also taking action to ensure that race and ethnic origins were not a source of discrimination (article 13). In this section, these two potentially conflicting approaches are examined with reference to questions concerning nationality, citizenship and social protection rights.

Policy on non-EU immigration

Freedom of movement, as provided for in the original EEC Treaty, did not apply to non-EEC nationals. While the freedom of movement clause outlawed discrimination based on nationality (article 48 §2), it said nothing about racial discrimination against non-EEC nationals. The issue of non-EU migration moved onto the social agenda in 1976 when Council Regulation (EEC) N° 311/76 was adopted 'on the compilation of statistics on foreign workers' [9.6], and an action programme was launched for migrant (both EC and non-EC) workers and their families [9.7]. From the mid-1980s, the need was accepted for a Community policy on immigration. A Council resolution 'on guidelines for a Community policy on migration' [9.9] was followed in 1985 by a joint declaration from the European Parliament, Council and Commission 'on attitudes and organisations motivated by racism and xenophobia' [9.10]. Immigration and associated issues were recognized as problems the Community should address. The declaration outlawed all forms of discrimination and expressions of racism, calling on member states to adopt measures to protect the identity and dignity of everyone in society, regardless of race, religion, nationality or ethnic group, to prevent or eliminate discrimination and raise awareness of the dangers of racism and xenophobia.

Provision was made in the Maastricht Treaty [1.6] under the title on justice and home affairs for co-operation in areas of common interest, extending to asylum and immigration policy and to policy regarding nationals of third countries, covering conditions of entry and residence, family reunion and employment and efforts to combat unauthorized immigration (article K.1). The Treaty of Amsterdam [1.7] gave the Council the power, acting unanimously (with provision subsequently for qualified majority voting), to 'determine the third countries whose nationals must be in possession of a visa when crossing the external borders of the Member States' (revised EC Treaty article 62 §2). In the negotiations leading up to the signing of the Treaty on European Union [1.6], the Council had been looking for ways of easing migratory pressure by improving the economic position of developing countries [9.14], for example in the Lomé Convention between the Community and 69 African, Caribbean and Pacific countries. Other programmes had been established for the Mediterranean countries and for Central and Eastern Europe.

While the Council seemed unsure about its competence in the area of migration, as indicated by the decision to leave a number of issues concerning immigration in abeyance in the Maastricht Treaty, two agreements were being negotiated independently by member states. The Schengen Agreement on asylum and visas was signed in 1985, initially by the EEC founder members, except for Italy. It had been ratified by all member states except Denmark, Ireland and the United Kingdom by the time it was due for implementation in 1994. Essentially, the intention of the signatories was to harmonize frontier controls and procedures over asylum-seekers, and abolish internal border controls. Since questions of drug trafficking and terrorism were also on the agenda, the expectation was that the group would favour tight restrictions and would do little to protect the rights of legal refugees and immigrants (Rex, 1992, p. 116). The Dublin Convention on the right of asylum was signed in 1990 by all member states. One of its objectives, as in the Schengen Agreement, was to ensure that an application for asylum could not be submitted in several member states at the same time. Both agreements raised important issues concerning national sovereignty, since they implied that a decision reached in one member state should be accepted without renegotiation in another.

Significantly, the Treaty of Amsterdam shifted visa, immigration and asylum policy from the intergovernmental third pillar to the first pillar, which meant that asylum and immigration matters were brought within the competence of the Union's institutions and, more especially, the jurisdiction of the ECJ. Title IV (articles 61–9 of the consolidated EC Treaty) covered visas, asylum, immigration and other policies related to free movement of persons, with the aim of establishing an 'area of freedom, security and justice', by adopting appropriate measures over a five-year period from the entry into force of the treaty (article 61). Ireland and the United Kingdom were not bound by any such measures, and they also remained outside the protocol integrating the Schengen *acquis* into the framework of the Union. Denmark's situation was almost as anomalous as that of the United Kingdom. Although technically a signatory, Denmark did not accept the integration of the Schengen *acquis* into the Union, which meant that it could choose whether or not to adopt any legislation that was binding on the other 12 member states (Duff, 1997, pp. 31–2).

With the Treaty of Amsterdam [1.7], member states thus reached what was almost a common position over third-country migrants. Symbolically, 1997 was designated European Year against Racism, and the following year, the Commission presented an action plan against racism, intended to pave the way for legislative initiatives, mainstream the fight against racism, develop and exchange new models and strengthen information and communication [9.21].

National policies on non-EU immigration

While the rights to freedom of movement were being actively developed at EU level for migrants within the Community in the 1980s, individual member states were tightening controls over non-European immigration and extending visa requirements, lending a social justification to the description of the Community as 'Fortress Europe'. In the absence of Community jurisdiction for third-country nationals, member states had continued to pursue their own immigration policies. Four national policy regimes could be identified across the Union in the early 1990s (Baldwin-Edwards, 1991). Belgium, France, Germany, Luxembourg and the Netherlands conformed to the Continental or Schengen model, characterized by a move towards stricter control over immigration in the traditional labour-importing industrialized countries. The United Kingdom had shifted away from its former liberal policy and had also enforced stricter controls. Denmark, in common with other Nordic states, continued to pursue more liberal policies. Greece, Italy, Portugal and Spain, as well as Ireland, represented the semi-peripheral or Mediterranean regime. These countries had in common their emigratory histories. They had not therefore needed to develop infrastructures for absorbing immigrants, although Portugal, Italy and Spain had all undergone the process of introducing visa controls.

As approaches to immigration vary historically across the Union, this is not an area where concerted action is easy to achieve. France, Germany and the United Kingdom were, for example, all major importers of non-EU immigrants, but each developed its own ideology and approach. France, which became a country of immigration in the mid-nineteenth century, sought to assimilate its immigrants and therefore made French nationality relatively easy to obtain. The French approach to citizenship has been described as illustrating the 'inclusionary republican or civic model', whereby all residents were entitled to citizenship, whatever their ethnic origin (Mitchell and Russell, 1998, pp. 84–5). Since French policy left little room for cultural diversity, the major tensions in French society were ethnic and cultural rather than racial (Rex, 1992, p. 110). Germany developed a combination of 'the ethnic nationalist and the guest-worker ideologies' (Rex, 1992, p.111), whereby its foreign workers were considered as temporary guest workers who would return home in due course. They did not therefore need to be assimilated and were excluded from many citizenship rights. At the same time, however, a liberal policy was adopted towards asylum-seekers, especially with respect to ethnic Germans (*Aussiedler*), at least until 1991 when a bill was drawn up to end automatic right of entry. The United Kingdom pursued a policy of encouraging and absorbing immigration from its colonies, particularly after the Second World War, and demonstrated its intention to create a multicultural society, accommodating cultural and ethnic differences, by setting up a Commission for Racial Equality in 1976.

Under the terms of the consolidated EC Treaty, nationality and citizenship rules remained within the competence of member states, but were subject to any bilateral international agreements that may have been concluded. In the 1990s, as a result of different national traditions, practices varied considerably across the Union. In the United Kingdom and France, nationality had been attributed traditionally on the basis of the place of birth (*jus soli*). In 1983 and 1993 respectively, the British and French governments moved to make their national legislation more restrictive. German and Italian law favoured the acquisition of nationality on the basis of descent (*jus sanguinis*) or parental nationality, but Italy applied the *jus soli* rule in exceptional cases, and a shift in that direction was under consideration in Germany. Where *jus sanguinis* applies, and naturalization is difficult to achieve, second and third generation 'migrants' may still not be able to obtain nationality of the country where they were born. For many years, the European Parliament had been pressing for greater uniformity of nationality rules and for the *jus soli* principle to replace *jus sanguinis* as a way of removing obstacles to naturalization (O'Leary and Tiilikainen, 1998).

The number of years of residence required before naturalization becomes possible has also been variable. In the early 1990s, the requirement ranged from five years in France, Ireland, Italy, the Netherlands and the United Kingdom to ten in Germany, Luxembourg and Spain (Baldwin-Edwards, 1991, table 8). Germany also imposed strict requirements concerning language, attitude and employment before granting naturalization, whereas the Netherlands were much more liberal. The United Kingdom gave officials making decisions great discretion, and offered six categories of nationality, but only one that conferred the right to reside in the country. Nationality does not therefore necessarily coincide with citizenship. Differences in nationality laws mean that, depending upon the place of birth and the country to which they or their parents migrate, the children of immigrants may, or may not, be able to acquire another nationality and the citizenship rights that it confers.

Measuring migratory flows from non-EU member states

Since the mid-1970s, borders have progressively been closed, particularly for unskilled workers. In 1987, Belgium, Denmark, Germany and the United Kingdom introduced legislation to impose fines on airlines carrying passengers without the necessary papers. France and Germany also tried to reverse the flow of migrants by providing incentives to encourage them to return home, sometimes in the form of forced repatriation for unemployed immigrant workers. Policies such as these would seem to have slowed down the flow of non-EU migrants, although precise figures are difficult to obtain for a number of reasons. Many immigrants are not legally registered. Just as it is difficult to measure the extent of intra-European mobility because many migrants become citizens of the country in which they take up residence, foreign born residents who have been naturalized in a member state are no longer recognized as non-European. Variations in the arrangements for attributing nationality and citizenship also make comparisons of the size of non-EU migrant populations in member states unreliable.

Analysis of the demographic situation in the mid-1980s suggested that, following decisions taken in 1973 and 1974 by the main host countries, immigration into the Community had been halted, although residual immigration was continuing through reunion of families, the arrival of political refugees and illegal entry [9.11, p. 6]. Family reunion thus became a dominant source of immigration, while the number of asylum-seekers rose, particularly towards the end of the decade following German unification. Meanwhile, illegal immigration into southern Europe, especially from North Africa, increased largely due to demographic pressures in the countries supplying immigrants and to the inadequate control of some of the Union's external borders.

During the 1990s, net international migration fell below 1 million per year, but it still contributed almost 75 per cent to the Union's population growth, a postwar record. Without international migration, it was estimated, for example, that Germany, Italy and Sweden would have registered negative population growth (Eurostat, 1999, pp. 1, 3).

Not only was non-European immigration of a different intensity from one member state to another, it also varied with regard to regional origins. Almost 30 per cent of all non-nationals within the EU were from a Mediterranean country. Germany received the largest proportion of all migrants from this source (45 per cent), predominantly from Turkey, followed by France (34 per cent), where they came primarily from Algeria and Morocco (Eurostat, 1998b, pp. 2, 5). International migration to Belgium, the Netherlands and Portugal was mainly from Africa, whereas Asia supplied most non-European migrants to Denmark, Sweden and the United Kingdom (Council of Europe, 1997, pp. 16–17). When these differences are combined with intra-European mobility, and the varied nature of the reasons why population groups cross international borders, it is clear that the practical and political issues raised are not easily amenable to common policy solutions.

FREEDOM OF MOVEMENT IN A MULTISPEED EUROPE

The Treaty of Amsterdam confirmed that EU policy on freedom of movement was engaged simultaneously on several different, and potentially conflictual, tracks. Propelled by the need to meet the convergence criteria for EMU, efforts had been made to complete the regulatory framework removing barriers to the free movement of workers and their families within the Union, and to grant EU citizenship. The treaty had also reinforced the commitment of member states to securing agreement on controls over the entry of non-EU migrants while, at the same time, outlawing discrimination on grounds of race and ethnicity.

The numerous loopholes in the regulations governing social protection rights for intra-European migrants were being closed, but legislation designed to secure the rights of nationals of EU member states was serving as an exclusionary mechanism insofar as it limited access to benefits and services for non-EU nationals. Access to social welfare benefits had thus become a source of discrimination, and the divisions highlighted in previous chapters had been reinforced, contributing to a multispeed Europe. Workers who had earned entitlement to social protection and the rights conferred by nationality, residential and employment status as citizens of the Union were well provided for, whereas others were excluded or discriminated against because of an accident of birth or the enforcement of strict rules on naturalization.

Although attempts to encourage mutual recognition of social protection systems had resulted in transferability of rights for EU nationals from one member state to another, systems had not been harmonized across the Union, and provisions had become more restrictive for non-EU nationals who did not meet the criteria for eligibility. Where access to social protection and citizenship rights is not applied equally, intra-European migrants can seek legal redress as citizens of the Union. Non-EU citizens do not automatically have the same rights. By the late 1990s, entitlement to a basic minimum income was not, for example, subject to any nationality requirements in Denmark, Finland, Luxembourg, Portugal and Sweden. Other member states, including France, Ireland, Italy, the Netherlands and the United Kingdom, imposed nationality and residence requirements for non-EU migrants. In Austria, the situation varied from one *Land* to another [2.7, 1998, table XII.1]. Whereas all long-stay intra-European migrants were automatically entitled to a residence permit and the many rights associated with it throughout the Union, non-EU nationals entering a member state were required to obtain prior authorization and a residence permit, which could be subject to the holder having the offer of employment.

In the 1990s, the Union was described as being characterized by 'an emergent European immigration regime', which, for pragmatic reasons, was far more complex than implied by the term 'Fortress Europe' (Mitchell and Russell, 1998, pp. 75–6). Despite the introduction of more restrictive measures, immigration had not ceased, mainly because the effectiveness of border controls was limited, and many member states still depended on migration to meet the demand for unskilled labour. By the end of the decade, the argument still held that a passport conferring citizenship of a country in the Union was a valued possession for immigrants from third-world countries, because it brought 'relatively generous safeguards of existence' (De Swaan, 1990, p. 19). Amid concern that economic refugees might take advantage of the situation to profit from welfare provision in member states where access was more readily granted, the conflicts in the Balkans gave a renewed impetus to the search for a common approach at EU level to the problems of accommodating refugees and asylum-seekers. Thus, the 1998 general budget of the Union contained a budget line within the field of social policy on the integration of refugees [9.23].

The dual approach was also being pursued at national level, as most member states sought a balance between policies designed to tighten up controls on entry for 'undeserving', illegal, economic migrants or bogus refugees, and the promotion of socio-cultural, political and economic integration for 'genuine' migrants and refugees on liberal and humanitarian grounds. The events of the late 1990s served to highlight the dilemma being faced by governments and the pressures being exerted by public opinion, but it also reinforced the need for member states to recognize that enlargement might create new problems which could probably be more readily resolved if existing member states were able to adopt a common approach.

Box 9 Secondary legislation and official publications on social policy and mobility

9.1 Regulations N°s 3–4 on social security for migrants (*Journal officiel*, N° 30, 1958).
9.2 Regulation (EEC) N° 1612/68 of the Council of 15 October 1968 on freedom of movement for workers within the Community (*OJ* L 257/2 19.10.68).
9.3 Council Directive 68/360/EEC of 15 October 1968 on the abolition of restrictions on movement and residence within the Community for workers of Member States and their families (*OJ* L 257/13 19.10.68).
9.4 Council Regulation (EEC) N° 1408/71 of 14 June 1971 on the application of social security schemes to employed persons, to self-employed persons and to members of their families moving within the Community (*OJ* L 149/2 5.7.71).
9.5 Council Regulation (EEC) N° 574/72 of 21 March 1972 laying down the procedures for implementing Regulation (EEC) N° 1408/71 (*OJ* L 74/1 27.3.72).
9.6 Council Regulation (EEC) N° 311/76 of 9 February 1976 on the compilation of statistics on foreign workers (*OJ* L 39/1 14.2.76).
9.7 Council Resolution of 9 February 1976 on an action programme

for migrant workers and members of their families (*OJ* C 34/2 14.2.76).

9.8 Council Directive 77/486/EEC of 25 July 1977 on the education of the children of migrant workers (*OJ* L 199/32 6.8.77).

9.9 Council Resolution of 16 July 1985 on guidelines for a Community policy on migration (*OJ* C 186/3 26.7.85).

9.10 Joint Declaration by the European Parliament, the Council and the Commission on attitudes and organisations motivated by racism and xenophobia (COM(85) 743 final, 19 December 1985).

9.11 Economic and Social Consultative Assembly, Demographic situation in the Community: information report (CES 602/84 fin, 1986).

9.12 Communication from the Commission on the living and working conditions of Community residents in frontier regions, with special reference to frontier workers (COM(90) 561 final, 27 November 1990).

9.13 Communication from the Commission on supplementary social security schemes: the role of occupational pension schemes in the social protection of workers and their implications for freedom of movement (SEC(91) 1332 final, 22 July 1991).

9.14 Commission of the European Communities, Background report: immigration (ISEC/B26/93, 29 September 1993), London.

9.15 Commission of the European Communities, Green paper, Education – training – research. The obstacles to transnational mobility (COM(96) 462 final, 2 October 1996).

9.16 Council Regulation (EC) N° 118/97 of 2 December 1996, amending and updating Regulation (EEC) N° 1408/71 and Regulation (EEC) N° 574/72 of 21 March 1972 (*OJ* L 28/1 30.1.97); amended by Council Regulation (EC) N° 1606/98 of 29 June 1998 to cover special schemes for civil servants (*OJ* L 209/1 25.7.98).

9.17 Directive 96/71/EC of the European Parliament and of the Council of 16 December 1996 concerning the posting of workers in the framework of the provision of services (*OJ* L 18/1 21.1.97).

9.18 Communication from the Commission on an action plan for free movement of workers (COM(97) 586 final, 12 November 1997).

9.19 European Commission, *Your Social Security Rights when Moving within the European Union: a practical guide*, OOPEC, 1997.

9.20 Council Resolution of 16 December on the early teaching of European Union languages (*OJ* C 1/2 3.1.98).

9.21 Communication from the Commission, An action plan against racism (COM(1998) 183 final, 25 March 1998).

9.22 Council Directive 98/49/EC of 29 June 1998 on safeguarding the supplementary pensions rights of employed and self-employed

persons moving within the Community (*OJ* L209/46 25.7.98).
9.23 Proposal for a Council Decision establishing a Community action programme to promote the integration of refugees (COM(1998) 731 final, 16 December 1998).
9.24 European Commission, *Affirming Fundamental Rights in the European Union: time to act. Report of the Expert Group on Fundamental Rights*, OOPEC, 1999.
9.25 Report from the Commission to the Parliament and the Council on the implementation of Directives 90/364, 90/365, 93/96 (Right of residence) (17.3.99).
9.26 European Commission, web sites on freedom of movement:
http://europa.eu.int/comm/employment_social/fundamri/movement/index_en.htm
http://europa.eu.int/citizens
9.27 Eures web site:
http://europa.eu.int/comm/employment_social/elm/eures/en/indexen.htm
9.28 Audiovisual policy web site:
http://europa.eu.int/scadplus/leg/en/lvb/l24104b.htm

10 Assessing European Social Policy

After serving for three years as Director-General for Social Affairs at the Commission in the 1970s, Michael Shanks could still ask: 'does the European Community have a role to play in the social field...over and above that of its member-States? If so, what is it? If not', he wondered, 'what is the degree of social diversity...which the European Community can tolerate and survive?' (Shanks, 1977, p. 9). The next two decades brought many signs that the Community was actively developing a social dimension, but that social diversity was increasing rather than diminishing. A spate of social action programmes was initiated in the 1970s, followed in the 1980s by strong statements in support of a social space from the President of the Commission, Jacques Delors, culminating in the signing of the Community Charter of the Fundamental Social Rights of Workers [1.10] in 1989. The three new waves of membership in the 1960s, 1980s and 1990s had brought into the Community countries with very different welfare traditions. The 1990s were, however, dominated by a common concern across member states with persistently high levels of unemployment, at a time when governments were looking for ways of controlling public spending in the run-up to Economic and Monetary Union (EMU), and were preparing for further enlargement to the East. Rather than eclipsing social issues, the challenges facing the European Union (EU) at the turn of the century and beyond provided a new impetus for social action and for a concerted strategy at EU level to modernize social protection systems.

Whether the growing interest in the social dimension of the internal market and the apparent extension of Union competence in social affairs are sufficient to justify calling its actions in the social area a 'social policy' has become a matter for academic debate. Despite the use of the title 'Social Policy' in the Treaty establishing the European Economic Community (EEC) in 1957 [1.2], no clear consensus existed in the 1950s about the need for social intervention, the form it might take and the instruments that might be used to carry it out (see Chapter 1). The objectives of the EEC Treaty were therefore defined in economic terms, implying that any harmonization of social policies between member states could be justified only insofar as it was likely to support and strengthen economic policies. Reference was made in the founding treaty to harmonization of social protection systems on the grounds that disparities in provision might impede freedom of movement and distort competition (see Chapter 2). Despite the subsequent name change to the European Communities (EC) under the 1967 Merger Treaty [1.4], the focus of attention in the European Council remained resolutely on economic concerns and on the rights of mobile workers. Categories of the population who were not full-time members of the indigenous labour force, or undergoing training or retraining for employment, were totally neglected under the terms of the original EEC Treaty, and the harmonization of systems remained a distant goal.

From the early 1970s, awareness was growing, however, that economic developments were resulting in regional inequalities. 'Social' intervention was called for at supranational level as a means of redressing the balance. At the same time, differences in approaches to social protection among the founder members were exacerbated as new countries joined the Community in the 1970s (see Chapter 2). The social problems with which member states were beginning to grapple were brought to the fore by the energy crises of the mid-1970s. They were further intensified as the less economically and socially developed states of southern Europe became members in the early 1980s, making the prospects for harmonizing social systems seem ever more remote and unrealistic, while the need for a concerted effort to deal with social problems became all the greater.

The social action programmes of the 1970s had already heightened awareness of the problems of poverty and the needs of disabled people, marginalized and socially excluded groups who had not benefited from the postwar economic boom, and whose interests had been neglected in the drive for efficiency, increased productive capacity and competitiveness. The late 1970s and early 1980s saw a burgeoning of new action programmes, together with binding legislation to promote equal opportunities between men and women. A series of national observatories and networks was created with responsibility for collecting and coordinating information about trends and for monitoring the social situation, so that policy makers would be in a stronger position to recommend appropriate measures.

The charter [1.10] can therefore be seen as the logical outcome of many years of monitoring and negotiation, affording the Community an opportunity to make a clear statement on its social policy aims and objectives, and to raise the social dimension to a more elevated status. In the event, the solemn declaration on the Fundamental Social Rights of Workers was much diluted in its final stages and, even then, was adopted by only 11 member states, highlighting the persisting differences in policy-making objectives and styles.

Three years later, after considerable debate in national parliaments and referenda in Denmark, France and Ireland, the Treaty on European Union [1.6] was signed in Maastricht in 1992, but only after the chapter on social policy had been removed from the main body of the text on the insistence of the United Kingdom. The commitment to social policy had been undermined. The British opt-out, the emphasis in the charter and treaty on the principles of subsidiarity and proportionality, and the need for unanimous voting on legislation regarding social protection, whereas other social areas, such as health and safety required only qualified majority voting, meant that many initiatives from the Commission on social affairs could still be easily blocked or rendered ineffectual. Doubts about the ability of member states to agree over social policies had been confirmed. The competence of the Union to take policy decisions had been called into question, and member states had demonstrated that they were not prepared to forego national sovereignty in the interests of greater European social solidarity.

Economic and political developments in the late 1990s, particularly EMU and plans for enlargement to Central and Eastern Europe, in combination with persistently high levels of unemployment and the prospect of population decline and ageing, had created a climate in which the modernization of social protection systems moved onto the political agenda. A new salience was given to social issues, providing an incentive for member states to look for common ground. In 1997, following the British opt-in under the New Labour government, the Agreement on Social Policy was reinstated in the body of the Treaty of Amsterdam [1.7]. The consolidated version of the EEC Treaty [1.8] considerably extended the Union's social affairs remit, signalling that, in the 40 years since the signing of the original treaty, member states had reached agreement that social rights should be protected as an important component of the *acquis communautaire*, setting standards that accessor states would have to adopt if they were to conform to the European social model.

Although the revisions to the EEC Treaty undoubtedly strengthened the Union's social policy remit, at the same time its competence to act independently from member states continued to be contested and constrained. Most of the social clauses contained a reference to the consultation process and to the requirement that member states should be free to introduce their own measures according to their own circumstances, in conformity with the subsidiarity and proportionality principles (Protocol N° 30). Despite these safeguards and, as argued by several political analysts (Marks *et al.*, 1996; Leibfried and Pierson, 2000), even though national welfare states still appeared to retain their control over the social policy area, their sovereignty had been substantially eroded by market integration, and their autonomy had been progressively constrained within the multitiered pattern of governance that had developed.

In this concluding chapter, the materials and policy areas discussed throughout the book are drawn together in an attempt to unravel four complex and interrelated questions. Firstly, to what extent have the parameters of European social policy been constrained by questions concerning economic integration and workers' rights? Secondly, how has competence in the formulation and implementation of social policy been shared between different policy actors? Thirdly, to what extent has national sovereignty been placed under threat as the Commission has seized the initiative in the social policy area? Finally, how has the European social model developed, and what are its prospects in the twenty-first century, in light of the demographic and institutional challenges the Union is facing?

THE PARAMETERS OF A EUROPEAN SOCIAL POLICY

Opinions as to whether or not the Union has progressively established a coherent social policy of its own depend to a large extent upon definitions. If a broad definition of social policy is applied, it would probably be difficult to deny that EU institutions have developed a social policy competence, although, as argued below, doubts could still be expressed about its coherence, autonomy and redistributive powers. Social policy broadly defined, following Richard Titmuss (1974, pp. 23–32), might be described in terms of the principles governing actions directed towards achieving specified ends, through the provision of welfare, minimum standards of income and some measure of progressive redistribution in command over resources, in such a way as to shape the development of society. In seeking to ground social policy more firmly in social theory, Ramesh Mishra (1977) also needed a broad definition. He defined social policy as 'those social arrangements, patterns and mechanisms that are typically concerned with the distribution of resources in accordance with some criterion of need' (Mishra, 1977, p. xi). Definitions of social policy are generally understood to mean that the state will ensure provision is made to meet major welfare needs, although quite how this role is interpreted has been subject to many variations over time and space, leading to the development of concepts such as welfare pluralism and the welfare mix (see Chapter 2). Whether the Union can, or should, be a provider of welfare in this sense remains a much disputed question.

In this section, the parameters identified by the two broad definitions presented above, and generally adopted in the social policy literature, serve as a framework for retracing the themes that recur throughout the book. The relationship between social and economic policy is reviewed and also the scope of EU-level institutions in establishing and implementing welfare principles. The theme of redistribution is considered both in this context and with reference to the citizenship versus worker's rights debate over welfare provision and delivery.

The changing relationship between the economic and social dimensions

In the early years of the EEC, a complementary relationship existed between economic and social policy objectives, but the dominant partner was undoubtedly the economic dimension. The social aspects of the Community were gaining salience in the mid-1980s, as testified by the assertion in the preamble to the 1989 charter [1.10] that, in the context of the internal market, 'the same importance must be attached to the social aspects as to the economic aspects', which were to 'be developed in a balanced manner'. This approach was not, however, substantiated by other statements in the same text that spoke of top priority being given to employment development and creation in the Single European Market (SEM), and of the action necessary to counter the possible adverse spillover effects for the social area of the completion of the internal market. Measures were advocated to ensure that the SEM resulted in improvements in the social field for workers, especially in the areas that had, long before, been identified in the EEC Treaty: freedom of movement, living and working conditions, health and safety at work, social protection, and education and training. With a view to ensuring equal treatment, member states were enjoined to combat all forms of discrimination on grounds not only of sex, as in the EEC Treaty and directives of the 1970s and 1980s (see Chapter 6), but also with reference to colour, race, opinions and beliefs. The fight against social exclusion, which had been pursued since the 1970s through social action programmes, was to be continued 'in a spirit of solidarity'.

The charter did not develop these themes or reproduce the emotive language of the preamble, and it did not, in itself, turn out to be a strong policy document demonstrating a commitment by member states to social affairs on a par with their support for economic cohesion. The social consensus was limited to strengthening the competitiveness of undertakings and contributing to the creation of employment. Social policy was, in sum, to be a prerequisite and a support for economic integration, rather than an equal partner. It was a facilitator, though also an essential condition for ensuring sustained economic development.

The genesis of the social dimension in the Single European Act (SEA) [1.5] and the Treaty on European Union [1.6] can perhaps best be understood within the context of the debate in the 1980s about the impact of economic dislocation resulting from the completion of the internal market on regions in the less developed areas of the Union. The aims of the Maastricht Treaty were broadened out so as 'to promote economic and social progress which is balanced and sustainable...through the strengthening of economic and social cohesion' (article B). According to this interpretation, the social dimension was a response (or spillover) to the growing concern among member states about the regional imbalance that would stem from the free play of the market and ultimately be to the detriment of the whole Union. Intervention through social policy at EU level was therefore justified as a means of redressing the balance, assisting labour mobility and maintaining the supply of social benefits and services on efficiency grounds.

The relationship between the economic and social dimensions, as presented in the Community's and Union's treaties and charter, has been aptly summarized in terms of 'the trade-off between equity and efficiency' (Gold and Mayes, 1993, p. 35). The equity argument was another recurring theme in the debate over the relative importance of the social and economic dimensions of the internal market, and contributes to an understanding of the Union's social policy objectives. Intervention at Community level was advocated on the grounds that, by giving free rein to market forces, the SEM would produce a two-speed Europe with some regions falling behind. Supranational intervention to assist priority areas was therefore justified to offset the harmful effects of economic dislocation.

Another economic argument used in support of social policies was that disparities between social protection systems would result in social dumping if nations with higher labour costs sought to move production to countries where labour was cheaper. This argument lost some of its force in the early 1990s in a situation where national governments in all member states were looking for ways of containing the cost of social spending and reducing unemployment because of their negative effects on productivity and competitiveness in non-European markets. Any relocation of industry on the basis of social costs was therefore more likely to be in third-world countries where labour was still relatively cheap and workers were afforded little or no social protection.

A cynical view of the reason why social aspects were built into the economic integration package is that the intention was 'to ease the transition into the internal market by reassuring workers that there will be a social dimension; and to assist the casualties of the process of economic restructuring which is at the heart of the whole integration project' (Kleinman and Piachaud, 1993, p. 10). This view found some support in the opening remarks to the 1994 white paper on European social policy [1.15], in a reference to the vital part to be played by social policy at European level in underpinning the process of change. Solidarity was juxtaposed to competitiveness as shared values, and high social standards were presented as a 'key element in the competitive formula' [1.15, pp. 9–10]. Assumptions such as these continued to be incorporated into policy statements throughout the 1990s, for example in the social action programmes [1.16; 1.19]. However, the Commission appeared to be gaining confidence in promoting the social dimension as an essential component of an inclusive social model and as a productive factor, rather than simply an appendage to economic policy [2.3]. Official documents in the late 1990s presented economic and social progress as mutually reinforcing. A high standard of social protection was described as an integral part of what had come to be known as 'the European social model' [1.18, p. 8; 2.3, p. 1; 10.3, p. 5].

Another term that had entered the Union's vocabulary as part of the integrative approach to social policy was 'mainstreaming', not only with reference to gender issues (see Chapter 6). A services working paper, issued in 1999 by Directorate-General V (Employment, Industrial Relations and Social Affairs, DGV), bore the title 'Mainstreaming disability within EU employment and social policy'. In 1999, the Commission was planning the 'mainstreaming of employment policies' [8.13, p. 1]. The fight against racism was also to be mainstreamed [9.21, p. 3]. A communication from the Commission in 1997 spoke of 'mainstreaming the social dimension of the information society' in Community policies on employment, equal opportunities, health and safety, public health and education and training [10.1, p. 16].

A further communication from the Commission in 1999 on a concerted strategy for modernizing social protection recognized that

> strong social protection systems are an integral part of the European Social Model which is based on the conviction and evidence that economic and social progress go hand in hand and are mutually reinforcing factors. Social protection provides not only safety nets for those in poverty; it also contributes to ensuring social cohesion by protecting people against a range of social risks. It can facilitate adaptability in the labour market and can thus contribute to improved economic performance. Social protection is a productive factor. 'Modernising' social protection means to make best use of its potential as a productive factor. [10.3, pp. 6–7]

This new-found confidence in the ability of the Union's institutions to carry forward the process of mainstreaming social policies and modernizing social protection systems was reflected in the written replies given to the European Parliament's committees in August 1999 by the Commissioner designate for Social Affairs, Anna Diamantopoulou. She reiterated the view that social policy and social solidarity should not be seen as a burden on society, but rather as productive factors, with social reforms contributing to the optimization of economic performance. Indeed, she went so far as to declare that: 'Competition without solidarity would have reduced us to the law of the jungle. Solidarity without competition would have been a recipe for stagnation' [10.2, p. 13].

By the late 1990s, it could be claimed that a social space had been negotiated as a legitimate concern of the Union and had been consecrated by its treaties, becoming more than simply a spillover of market integration. The extent to which the shift in emphasis was not solely rhetorical and an attempt to justify the Union's new-found social policy confidence remained to be put to the test in the face of the challenges and opportunities the Union was facing at the turn of the century. The recognition and acceptance of the need to modernize social protection could, moreover, be taken to signal that a large degree of consensus was emerging across member states about the justification for a concerted strategy to ensure that high levels of social protection can go hand in hand with more efficient public provision of services.

Developments in the citizenship versus workers' rights debate

Commissioner designate for Social Affairs, Anna Diamantopoulou, was also aware of the need to move on from the focus on the rights of workers to 'a charter for all citizens' [10.2, p. 22]. The priority given, constantly and justifiably, in the EEC Treaty to economic objectives has been accompanied by an emphasis on workers' rather than citizenship rights. If social policy is, by definition, universally applicable and redistributive, then the focus on workers could be seen as creating a serious deficit in coverage.

The preamble to the 1989 Community charter [1.10] and the action programmes for its implementation [1.11] suggested that intervention at Community level should extend beyond the needs of workers. At the last minute, however, largely for pragmatic reasons, the term 'workers' had been substituted in the charter for 'citizens'. Accordingly, every section of the charter makes reference to workers, working life or employment. Freedom of movement applied to workers (§§1–3). A decent standard of living was to be achieved for workers through equitable wages from employment (§5). Improvements were sought in working conditions for all workers (§§7–9). Social protection was with reference to labour market activity (§10). Freedom of association applied to workers (§§11–14). Vocational training was to be provided for every worker throughout working life (§15). Equal treatment for men and women applied in the realm of employment (§16). Information, consultation and participation were intended for the working population (§§17–18). Provision for health protection and safety was at the workplace (§19), and even protection of children and adolescents was intended to ensure that they were properly prepared for work and that young workers were provided with suitable working conditions (§§20–3). Workers were to be guaranteed sufficient resources in retirement (§§24–5), and disabled persons were to be assisted in their social and professional integration (§26).

The continued emphasis on workers can be explained by three main reasons. Firstly, the social protection systems in the founder member states were derived from the employment insurance-related model characteristic of continental Europe rather than being based on universal access as of right, such as applied generally in the Nordic states, or in national health services, as operated in the United Kingdom (see Chapters 2, 4). Social protection rights had therefore been conceptualized with reference to employment and labour markets. Secondly, since the EEC had been established as an economic community, the justification for any interest in human and social rights was a consequence of the need to ensure the free movement of labour as an important component in factor mobility. Subsequently, the objectives of creating the conditions for economic restructuring and monetary stability in the context of the SEM and EMU were also premised on criteria that prioritized economic performance and freedom of movement, and hence the working (productive) population. Thirdly, national governments were more willing to acquiesce to supranational measures regulating the technical aspects of working conditions than they were to allow any interference in the provision and delivery of social welfare services that could best be dealt with at local level.

Some account was taken in the Treaty on European Union [1.6] of the need 'to strengthen the protection of the rights and interests of the nationals of its Members States through the introduction of a citizenship of the Union' (article B). Member states also undertook to 'respect fundamental rights, as guaranteed by the 1950 European Convention for the Protection of Human Rights and Fundamental Freedoms (article F). The rights of 'citizens of the Union', as set out in the consolidated EC Treaty [1.8], were limited to political representation and dependent on citizenship of a member state; social citizenship rights did not figure in the treaty. Two new social policy areas were, however, introduced which made no reference to workers. In a section on culture (title XII, article 151), the signatories to the treaty asserted their intention to encourage the 'flowering of the cultures of the Member States, while respecting national and regional cultural diversity and at the same time bringing the common cultural heritage to the fore'. Under the heading for public health (title XIII), article 152 stated that high levels of human health protection and co-ordination of health policies were to be promoted, but provision and delivery of health services and medical care, and therefore conditions for access, remained the responsibility of member states (see Chapter 4).

The chapter on social provisions (articles 136–45) continued to focus resolutely on workers as, for example, in article 137 §1, which referred to the 'integration of persons excluded from the labour market', but said nothing about minimum levels of social protection for non-workers. Although the theme of equal treatment was present in the EEC Treaty and was reiterated in both the Community charter and the consolidated EC Treaty, emphasis was again on labour market opportunities and treatment at work. The Community charter [1.10] did attempt to take some account of the status of women as mothers, by proposing that help should be given to both men and women to enable them to reconcile family and employment responsibilities (§16), but this theme was not pursued in the revised EC Treaty [1.8], therefore missing the opportunity to broaden the scope of the Union's action to the rights of non-workers.

The emphasis on workers meant that the needs of large sectors of the population were not addressed in the obligations laid down in treaty commitments. During the 1990s, the proportion of the Union's population classified as being in employment had been falling: from just over 41 per cent in 1991 to below 40 per cent in 1997. The percentage of the population of working age in employment had also declined: from nearly 63 per cent in 1991 to 61 per cent in 1997, due primarily to the fall in the employment rate for men from 75 per cent in 1991 to 71 per cent by 1998 [4.17, 1999, p. 127]. Less than a third of the Union's female population were in employment throughout the period, accounting for just over 50 per cent of women of working age, compared to around 70 per cent for men, with much larger proportions of women being employed on a part-time basis. Women were therefore more likely than men to be marginalized by the employment model of welfare (see Chapter 6). In addition, since women were more often than men in low-paid precarious forms of employment, a larger proportion of women not only lacked the benefits of a reasonable and secure income from paid work, but they were also denied access to their own pensions, sickness benefits and other payments that accrue from long-term employment. Their situation was compounded by their caring role (for children, older and disabled people), which further impacted on their eligibility for employment-related benefits (Chapter 7).

Non-European immigrants were another group excluded from the provisions of the original EEC Treaty (see Chapter 9). Although freedom of movement of workers was laid down as an essential prerequisite for the efficient functioning of the internal market, for the purposes of the Community's and Union's treaties migrant workers were understood to be nationals of member states. From the 1970s, external borders were being closed to immigrants from third countries. While paying lip service to integration policies, member states were tightening up their nationality laws, lending weight to the notion of a 'Fortress Europe', where non-European migrants had become an underclass, often deprived of nationality and citizenship rights. The Treaty of Maastricht [1.6] demonstrated that some measure of agreement had been reached by member states over the need for a common asylum and immigration policy for third-country nationals (article K.1). In the consolidated EC Treaty [1.8], the insertion of a combined title on visas, asylum and immigration into the first pillar acknowledged the issue was a Union rather than an intergovernmental concern.

In line with the more integrated and inclusive approach to social policy being advocated in the 1990s, attempts were made to demonstrate that the Union was concerned not only with working conditions but also with the quality of life for people outside work and for categories suffering discrimination. The question was how to marry economic imperatives with the image of a Community that cared not only for workers but also for older and disabled people, its youthful population, the long-term unemployed and third-country nationals.

In the event, the Treaty of Amsterdam reflected the climate of the 1990s by highlighting employment, and thus the population in work, as the route to greater integration and cohesion. Prompted by the Swedish government, the treaty had introduced a new title on employment, which became title VIII in the consolidated version of the EEC Treaty [1.8]. The Swedes were looking for a way of balancing monetary stability with growth and job creation, whereas the Germans, Dutch and British insisted that employment should be coupled with competitiveness, and that the Swedish target of 'full' employment should be modified to 'high' employment (Duff, 1997, p. 63). The ensuing employment guidelines, as required by the consolidated EC Treaty [1.8] under article 128, made clear that active policies were to be adopted by member states to promote employability, adaptability and integration into the world of work through the creation of more and better jobs [1.18; 1.20]. Rather than preparing the way for a social policy based on citizenship rights, at the end of the 1990s member states were seeking to draw a larger proportion of the population into the protected labour force for economic and humanitarian reasons. The primary aim was to reduce public expenditure by moving people off welfare and into work. The additional income from social insurance contributions and taxes was expected to sustain social protection systems.

In each of the areas examined in this book, the conclusion has been reached that European social policy was designed primarily for workers employed in the regular or formal economy. Education and training, and lifelong learning were intended to ensure the employability and adaptability of young as well as older people (Chapter 3). Legislation on living and working conditions was aimed at maximizing the productive capacity of workers (Chapter 4). Equal opportunities between women and men concerned the efficient operation of the workplace. The reference added in the 1999 employment guidelines [1.20] to the importance of an equal sharing of family responsibilities was justified because it meant that women (and men) could continue their participation in the labour market uninterrupted by family obligations (Chapters 5 and 6). Older and disabled people were to be encouraged to remain in employment to reduce the burden on pensions and welfare benefits. In the case of older people, the trend towards early retirement was to be reversed to bolster the labour supply and reduce the cost of pensions (Chapter 7). The route out of poverty was through integration into the labour force and the formal economy (Chapter 8). The purpose of promoting the mobility of labour lay in its contribution to the competitiveness of markets for labour (Chapter 9).

The problem with policies based on the assumption that employment and income from paid work are the preferred, if not only, answer to the challenges facing postindustrial societies is that they leave no place for people who are unable or unwilling to work. For example, young people who 'drop out' of the formal education system without qualifications tend to be categorized as socially inadequate and are likely to be excluded from mainstream employment. In addition, the efforts to absorb larger numbers of workers into the labour force during the 1990s meant that many of the jobs created did not correspond to the image of work as full-time long-term relatively secure employment that most male workers had come to expect and had previously experienced over the postwar period.

One of the arguments used to justify public support for the provision of child and eldercare was its job-creation potential [1.15, p. 43]. The jobs in question were essentially 'peripheral', low status, low paid and often part time, even if they were 'protected' on a *pro rata* basis as a result of European legislation [4.14]. The development of the social economy (co-operatives, mutual benefit societies and associations), which already accounted for over 5 per cent of all employment in Europe in the late 1990s [10.2, p. 25], can be seen as part of the same trend. Paradoxically, the active approach to employment policy, with its emphasis on employability and workfare as defining criteria for social inclusiveness, was thus helping to reinforce the divisions within societies between work-rich and work-poor households, and to devalue the contribution made to society and to the economy by unpaid workers, former workers, those unable to work and informal workers. From this perspective, the member states appeared to be opting collectively for an employment-based model of social protection, while reluctantly accepting that provision had to be made through residual schemes at national level to ensure sufficient resources for the 'unemployable' (see Chapters 2 and 8).

This shift in emphasis towards employment was further endorsed when the Commission's directorates-general were renamed in 1999, and the numbering system was replaced by acronyms. DGV became Employment and Social Affairs under the acronym EMPL.

EUROPEAN SOCIAL POLICY AS A SHARED COMPETENCE

The changes introduced in the Treaty of Amsterdam [1.7] not only reinstated social policy in the supranational core of the treaty, but they also removed some of the political, structural and institutional constraints that had hitherto prevented the Union from extending its social policy remit. Common to the analyses by political scientists of European social policy is the interest in the distribution of power and responsibility between member states and Community institutions. This section tracks the shifts in competence between supranational and national actors in the social policy area. It examines whether European social policy has become more than simply an aggregate of the social policies of its member states. Attention is given to identifying the possible impact of supranational intervention for national sovereignty and the constraints exercised over the Union's social policy competence. The question is also asked to what extent the Union, and more especially the Commission, adds value by responding to common social problems and to needs that cannot be satisfied at national level, while respecting the principles of subsidiarity and proportionality.

Social policy as a contested policy area

Political scientists are divided about the extent to which changes in the treaty may lead to a significant development of social policy after the turn of the century. Intergovernmentalists (for example Moravcsik and Nicolaïdis, 1999, pp. 83–4) have challenged the view that Intergovernmental Conferences have become ineffective forums. They argue that the Treaty of Amsterdam did not signal an end to the underlying divergence and ambivalence of national interests. Earlier, structuralists (for example Rhodes, 1995, with reference to the SEA and the Treaty on European Union) had reached a similar conclusion on the grounds that the Union did not offer a viable supranational alternative. Social policy was, in any case, still limited to a small number of areas considered crucial for market integration. It was only of secondary interest in a context where the growth of international capital and the free market ideology at global level had resulted in the weakening of the nation state and national labour movements. By contrast, neofunctionalists were predicting that EMU would have important spillover effects for social policy, while the impact of EMU for social Europe was seen by some critics (for example Teague, 1998) as negative and socially unfriendly. Institutionalists (for instance Nugent, 1994) have argued that the strengthening of its institutions, especially the European Parliament, would help to consolidate the Union's social policy-making powers. On the basis of case studies in the social policy area, Robert Geyer (1996) points out that one of these theories cannot alone explain the complex development of the Union's social policy.

It can be argued that, if the sole motivation for including social policy in the EEC Treaty had been to make provision for migrant workers, the need could have been met by establishing the Union as a social state in its own right (Leibfried, 1992, p. 97). The 'thirteenth state', a solution suggested by Danny Pieters (1991, pp. 186–8) before the accession of Austria, Finland and Sweden, would have involved superimposing an additional European scheme on top of existing national arrangements. To be effective, it is argued, such a scheme would need to cover all risks and be at least as attractive as national social security systems and as advantageous as the system offering the most favourable arrangements. Benefits could be funded by employers' and employees' contributions and subsidized by the Union. In the longer term, such a 'federal social security system' might be extended to other categories of workers or to whole member states. In the absence of a supranational or federal social protection system, the Union does provide social security entitlements for its own employees, but they represent only a minute proportion of the total population of the Union. No single programme covers all European citizens for any one risk, whether it be health, disability, old age, unemployment, poverty or family responsibilities.

Some analysts (for example Majone, 1996b) maintain that the Community will never be more than a regulatory state for so long as its budgetary powers are held in check, and member states bear the cost of implementing policy. This is not to underestimate the advantages of a supranational regulatory power in terms of social rights, since the Union can insist on more stringent regulation and enforcement than might be politically acceptable at national level. If the Union's social policy competence is judged by the extent of its control over actions directed towards achieving specified social ends, then it is clear that the regulatory framework governing action in the social policy area has been considerably expanded over the years. The consolidated version of the EC Treaty [1.8], following the Maastricht and Amsterdam amendments, comprised 42 articles on social measures out of a total of 314, compared to 16 out of 248 in the original EEC Treaty. Directly or indirectly, they covered almost all the areas usually falling within the remit of national ministries for social affairs.

In addition to the expanded chapter on social policy, education, vocational training and youth (title XI, articles 136–50), and on free movement of workers (title III, chapter 1, articles 39–42), the revised treaty contained two articles on discrimination (12, 13), sections on citizenship of the Union (part 2, articles 17–22), visas, asylum and immigration (title IV, articles 61–9), employment (title VIII, articles 125–30), culture (title XII, article 151), public health (title XIII, article 152), economic and social cohesion (title XVII, articles 158–62) and environment (title XIX, articles 174–6). The extent to which such a broad remit can be translated into binding legislation and implemented in member states is clearly dependent on the agreement reached between national governments. Where qualified majority voting has been introduced, blocks of legislation have been moved forward (see Chapter 4), but important areas of social policy continue to be restrained by the need for unanimous decision making, in particular social security and the protection of workers when their contract is terminated, the conditions of employment for third-country nationals, and the financial contributions for promotion of employment and job-creation (article 137 §3 in the consolidated EC Treaty). In most of these cases, a caveat was introduced to the effect that national diversity was to be respected, and that governments in member states should be free to apply their own more stringent standards or to implement legislation with regard to national circumstances and practices.

Although the Union can impose sanctions for non-compliance with European law, the main reason why it does not qualify as an autonomous social policy actor is that the lack of funds limits its power to redistribute resources directly. An increasing proportion of the EU budget has been devoted to priority regions. However, the amount distributed through structural action remained well below that devoted to the Common Agricultural Policy (CAP) until the late 1990s, when it reached almost 36 per cent of the EU budget, compared to 46 per cent for the CAP [8.11, table 5.1]. Together, the two budget heads accounted for over 80 per cent of Community resources, but the cohesion and structural funds still constituted only 0.46 per cent of the Union's total GNP in 1999 [2.4, vol. 1, p. 15]. Giandomenico Majone (1996b, p. 131) has argued that, from the outset, the structural funds 'were viewed less as redistributive measures than as side payments to obtain unanimous approval of efficiency-enhancing reforms of the Community system', For Gary Marks *et al.* (1996, p. 354), however, the SEA transformed the funds from side payments into 'an interventionist instrument of regional economic development'. These two views are not incompatible. The structural funds have undoubtedly served as a means of compensating member states for concessions made in intergovernmental negotiations over issues such as enlargement, completion of the internal market and monetary union, and they have also given the Union resources of its own. The amount involved, however, remains extremely small in relation to national expenditure on social protection and is subject to tight controls. In addition, the resources available for spending on the poverty programmes and other social actions were far too limited to have an enduring and truly redistributive impact on social problem areas and underprivileged population groups.

In defence of national sovereignty and diversity

The substantial social spillover of market integration at Community level is widely acknowledged and documented by economists and political scientists, but so too is the strong resistance of national governments to the erosion of national sovereignty in the social policy area. Constraints on the Union's ability to act do not mean that the sovereignty of national governments has not been placed under threat. The Treaty of Amsterdam further reduced institutional barriers and formalized a process of gradual erosion of national autonomy in the social policy area, which had already been accelerated in the 1980s by the SEA and was prefigured in the Community charter. However, opinions differ over the extent to which control of social policy has shifted from nation states to supranational institutions. Stephan Leibfried and Paul Pierson (2000) build a convincing case in support of the argument that member states have lost more autonomy and control over national welfare policies than the EU has gained in transferred authority. In particular, they demonstrate how European law, backed by decisions of the European Court of Justice (ECJ), has operated on the pretext of pursuing market integration to undermine the authority of national governments.

The Union's regulatory competence was considerably extended during the 1990s, as were the interventionist powers of its institutions, notably the Commission and the European Parliament. With the introduction of direct elections in 1979 and the extension of its powers under the SEA in 1986, the European Parliament saw its influence in social affairs expand. Although national interests are directly represented at the European Council and the Council of Ministers and, less directly, through the European Parliament, national governments have limited control over the ECJ. Member states have not only been taken before the ECJ for infringing European law, but they have also been forced to surrender control over their own law-making powers, in some cases even where they had themselves pushed for legislation at European level (Lanquetin *et al.*, 2000). Examples abound, particularly with reference to equal treatment for women and men, flexibility in working time or the social security rights of mobile workers (Burrows and Mair, 1996), where contentious legislation has been passed despite the opposition of individual member states, and where the ECJ has provided an expansive interpretation of European social law, thereby consolidating its influence and further impinging on national autonomy in the social area.

At the same time, national policies and interests, especially those of the more powerful countries, have clearly restricted the Union's ability to develop its own social policy. Many examples have been quoted throughout this book of the ways in which proposals to extend the Union's social policy remit, to introduce directives affecting working conditions, or to initiate action programmes have been delayed or shelved, due to the veto of individual member states or the court cases they have brought against the Commission. National governments have, for example, blocked proposals for legislation on living and working conditions. In 1994, they prevented funds being allocated to the Observatories on Ageing and Older People and National Policies to Combat Social Exclusion (see Chapters 7 and 8). As qualified majority voting has been extended, the principle of subsidiarity has assumed greater importance and serves as evidence of the continued resistance to pressures for uniformity in the social area. The effect of the multilevel system of governance may have been to erode national sovereignty, but as Gary Marks *et al.* (1996, p. 372) have argued, '[t]he complex interplay among these contending institutions in a polity where political control is diffuse often leads to outcomes that are second choice for all participants.'

The efforts by national governments to protect their own interests may not be the only reason for their resistance to supranational intervention. The failure of the Union's institutions to take sufficient account of national welfare traditions and the appreciative settings in which the policy process unfolds may also help to explain why the record on implementation and compliance with European law has been uneven, and why a level playing field of minimum standards was still on the agenda in the late 1990s. Numerous examples have been cited in this book of national differences in the approach to policy formation and practice, with the result that an EU citizen moving around the

Union would still experience quite disparate living and working conditions from one member state to another. Since one of the two reasons (the other was to enhance competitiveness) for promoting the harmonization of social protection systems was to facilitate freedom of movement within the Community, the persistence of diversity could be seen as a sign of the failure to achieve the original EEC Treaty objectives.

In the area of education and training, attempts to align systems were eventually abandoned in favour of mutual recognition, with the effect that arrangements for schooling, higher education and training, curricula and teaching methods continue to create problems for young people transferring from one national system to another (Chapter 3). Analysis of policies to improve living and working conditions reveal fundamental disparities in attitudes towards flexibility, the employment relationship and the provision of health services (Chapter 4). All member states have been adapting their legislation to take account of changing family forms, but the pace and degree of change have varied. Differences in the policy styles of governments have meant that similar measures, for example child benefits, fiscal or leave arrangements, are not necessarily used in the same way or to achieve the same ends (Chapter 5). Although all member states were obliged under European law to address issues concerning equality of pay and treatment, the conceptualization of women as mothers and workers and the approaches of national governments to the question of reconciling employment with family life have had a differential effect on the labour market opportunities of women from one country to another (Chapter 6). Despite the attempts to reach agreement over pension arrangements at EU level and to address questions of social and medical care, old age and disability can be experienced very differently, depending not only on the regulations in force in the country in which the person concerned has spent most of his or her working life, but also on the strength of intergenerational relationships and their interaction with public provision (Chapter 7). Similarly, different national systems for ensuring sufficient resources have meant that being poor or socially excluded did not have the same impact from one country to another (Chapter 8). Being a non-EU immigrant is also experienced differently in terms of social citizenship and welfare rights across the Union, which may help to explain some of the variation in the intensity of international migratory flows (Chapter 9).

Many of the differences identified can be attributed to the principles according to which welfare is funded and organized. The original EEC founder members had in common their preference for an employment-based insurance welfare model, within which harmonization did not appear to be a wholly unrealistic goal. The increasing diversity brought by subsequent waves of membership did, however, make the goal more distant (Chapter 2).

The overriding objectives in the social area, as set out in article 136 of the revised 1997 EC Treaty [1.8], were to promote employment, improve living and working conditions, ensure proper social protection, dialogue between management and labour and the development of human resources. The measures to be implemented to achieve these objectives were to take account of national practices, particularly with regard to contractual relations, and of the need to maintain the competitiveness of the economy. Although the term still figured in the revised treaty article as a possible outcome, it was clear that the harmonization of national social protection systems was no longer on the agenda. The Council recommendation of 1992 'on the convergence of social protection objectives and policies' [2.1] acknowledged that harmonization was an unattainable objective and that it did not have the support of member states. Subsidiarity had already become a key concept by the time the Treaty of Maastricht was signed in 1992 (article 3b). It was given fuller recognition by being appended to the consolidated EC Treaty in 1997 as a protocol (N° 30). Once again, member states resolutely confirmed that they were not prepared to relinquish national sovereignty in the social area.

Article 118 of the original EEC Treaty [1.2] had introduced another concept that was not far removed from the position eventually reached in the 1990s: close co-operation in the social field. Although the title of the 1992 recommendation focused on convergence, co-operation might have been a more accurate description of the Council's intentions. The 'convergence strategy' being promoted was aimed at setting 'common objectives able to guide Member States' policies in order to permit the co-existence of different national systems and to enable them to progress in harmony with one another towards the fundamental objectives of the Community' [2.1, p. 50]. In this context, convergence would be *de facto*. Community action was justified on the grounds that comparable trends were leading to common economic and demographic problems: ageing of the population, changing family situations, the persistence of high levels of unemployment and the spread of poverty. These problems required common, or at least co-ordinated, responses in order to reduce any disparities that might impede freedom of movement. Article 137 in the revised EC Treaty empowered the Council to adopt measures to encourage, rather than promote as in the original treaty, co-operation between member states in areas concerned with health and safety at work, working conditions, information and consultation of workers, the integration of persons excluded from the labour market, and equality of opportunity and treatment between men and women at work. The initiatives authorized were to be aimed at improving knowledge, developing exchanges of information and best practice, promoting innovative approaches and evaluating experience. While this form of co-operation might result in some alignment of systems, member states preserved at least a semblance of autonomy by being able to maintain or introduce their own more stringent protective measures (article 137, §5).

During the 1990s, the spillover effects from the convergence criteria established for EMU were also creating pressures for member states to co-operate more closely in the social area. The Commission's social action programme for 1998–2000 referred, for example, to the convergence of employment policies as a complement to the convergence process leading to EMU [1.19, p. 9]. Driven by economic imperatives and in their search for ways of curbing public spending, all member states were reviewing the funding and provision of welfare [2.5, 1998, pp. 19–27]. The Netherlands and Sweden, in particular, were tightening the qualifying conditions for entitlement to benefits. Austria, Finland and Spain were extending the length of the period of contributions to gain entitlement to benefits, while Belgium, Denmark and the United Kingdom had reduced the duration of benefit payments. Measures were being implemented in Austria, Belgium, Germany, Greece and Spain to reverse the trend towards early retirement (Chapter 7). Efforts to contain the cost of public spending on health care included shifting payments from social insurance funds to patients in Germany, and resorting to market mechanisms in Italy, the Netherlands, Spain and the United Kingdom (Chapter 4). Alternative sources of funding were being sought across the Union for supplementary pensions (Chapter 7). Increasingly, resources were being targeted at those most in need. Child benefits were directed towards low-income families in Greece, Italy, Portugal and Spain (Chapter 5). Across the Union, efforts were being made to introduce active policies to move people off benefits and into work, and to create work incentives, particularly in the United Kingdom (Chapter 8).

Whether these policy shifts will, in the longer term, result in greater uniformity between systems and, if so, what sort of European welfare system will emerge are still open to debate. The 1992 Council recommendation on convergence was non-committal on the question of the model towards which systems might converge. While it referred to the need to ensure maximum efficiency and effectiveness and to guarantee a minimum means of subsistence, enabling people at risk to maintain their standard of living in a reasonable manner, member states were left to make their own choices about how these objectives could be achieved. The 1994 white paper on European social policy emphasized the need for minimum standards of social protection, which would not overstretch the economically weaker member states. The intention was to avoid any levelling down while not preventing the more developed countries from implementing higher standards [1.15, p. 12].

The many safeguard clauses built into the treaties and secondary legislation imply that, in theory at least, member states can continue to implement European law in accordance with their own national practices. The sheer volume of legislation that emanates from Brussels, most of it at the request of member states, and the diminishing autonomy of national parliaments or governments as law makers (Majone, 1996a, pp. 265–6) mean, however, that their room for manœuvre is increasingly constrained.

The Commission as a promoter of a European social model

While the Union's institutions have been relentlessly encroaching into an area long seen as the preserve of national governments, and the ECJ has become a force to be reckoned with, views about the Commission's contribution to the building of social Europe have been divided. In the 1970s, Shanks described 'the role the Commission has been able to play in the social policy field…as a catalyst, an educator and influencer, a co-ordinator of research, a data-bank and a standard-setter' (Shanks, 1977, p. 84). Almost 20 years later in the context of social exclusion, another Commissioner for Social Affairs, Pádraig Flynn (1993, p. 3), used very similar terms to describe the Commission's role as 'a clearing house for information and catalyst for action'.

From the outside, Neill Nugent (1994, p. 98) has summarized the Commission's wide-ranging powers under six major headings: 'proposer and developer of policies and of legislation, executive functions, guardian of the legal framework, external representative and negotiator, mediator and conciliator, and the conscience of the Union'. He concludes that, even if the Commission might not have developed quite into the motor force originally intended, its role has been 'both central and vital to the whole EU system' (Nugent, 1994, p. 122). For Laura Cram (1997, p. 6), the Commission acts as a 'purposeful opportunist' in the social area. It has managed to maximize its room for manœuvre in the policy process at the same time as avoiding direct conflict with member states, thereby extending its scope for action without alienating national governments.

This book has relied heavily on the impressive array of reports, policy statements and communications from the Commission, and more especially from DGV, to document and analyse the development of the Union's social policy. Even if the output of binding social policy legislation is relatively limited both in quantity and scope, the Commission has exploited the ambiguities and lack of precision in the treaties to take forward non-binding legislation and soft law (Cram, 1997, pp. 28–9). The Treaty of Amsterdam further strengthened the Commission's right of initiative by incorporating new provisions, as noted above. In the area of employment, for example, the Commission was given not only a monitoring and reporting role but was also charged with drawing up employment guidelines and ensuring they were implemented by national governments (article 128 in the consolidated EC Treaty). As the outgoing Commissioner for Employment, Industrial Relations and Social Affairs in 1999, Pádraig Flynn expressed the view that the Treaty of Amsterdam, which he described 'as the social treaty of our time', had given the Commission the wherewithal to translate its good intentions into effective action [10.4, p.4].

As demonstrated throughout this book, the Commission was not prevented by the absence of a clear treaty mandate from intervening actively in the areas of education and training, health, living and working conditions, social protection, equal pay and treatment of workers, the protection of children, older and disabled people, regional development and social exclusion. It made policy recommendations, brought forward proposals for legislation, monitored their implementation, and took national governments before the ECJ for non-compliance. It liaised closely with the social partners following Jacques Delors' overtures and, through the Val Duchesse talks and the social dialogue, strengthened the involvement of management and labour in the Union's social dimension.

In addition to its own programmes in the areas of vocational training, disability, unemployment, poverty and equal opportunities for women, the Commission monitored social developments through its observatories on social exclusion, older people, family policies and employment, its networks on childcare, women in the labour market, education, vocational training, local employment, job vacancies and employment policies, and social protection systems. It set up specialized institutions such as the European Centre for the Development of

Vocational Training (Cedefop), the European Foundation for the Improvement of Living and Working Conditions and the European Agency for Health and Safety at Work, as well as committees and expert groups. Its capacity for data collection and analysis, in conjunction with Eurostat, and for evaluation of its own programmes became prodigious.

Scrutiny of the social action programmes from the 1970s, and more especially for the 1990s, the green and white papers on social policy, the network and observatory reports, the Commission's own reports on the demographic and social situations in the Union, and the many studies it has commissioned from researchers around the Community on social topics, provides extensive evidence of the way in which the Commission has worked within the constraints imposed by the treaties. Often, the Commission's operations have been behind the scenes, which may help to explain the accusations of lack of transparency, the questions raised about its legitimacy, and why it was discredited in 1999, when the whole Commission was forced to resign. While member states were agonizing over the wording of the charter and social chapter, proposals were being drafted for recommendations that went beyond the terms of the Community charter and Agreement on Social Policy. While the 1997 Intergovernmental Conference in Amsterdam was searching for a means of appeasing electorates over the employment issue, and was struggling to reach consensus, the Commission was using its data collection and monitoring powers to identify trends and was looking beyond the politicians' horizon. Demographic predictions after the year 2005 were suggesting that the impact of population decline and ageing would be to reduce the size of the labour force (Eurostat, 1997b, p. 8). Therefore, the Commission was perhaps less concerned with finding solutions to the immediate problem of unemployment than with the implications of an ageing labour force for the sustainability of social protection and for the quality of the future labour supply [10.3, p. 10].

Together, the documents issued by the Commission constitute a more comprehensive and coherent statement of the Union's social policy than is to be found in the more widely publicized formal texts, reflecting the Commission's ability to act as the conscience of the Union. The 1974 social action programme [1.9], the white paper on European social policy [1.15] and the Commission's communications on the modernization of social protection [2.3; 10.3] provide a coherent overview of the Union's social policy thinking. While the white paper on European social policy placed jobs at the top of the agenda, the aim was to achieve a broadly based, innovative and forward looking social policy capable of underpinning the process of change and ensuring 'a unique blend of economic well-being, social cohesiveness and high overall quality of life' [1.15, p. 7]. It identified the shared values that formed the basis of the European social model as 'democracy and individual rights, free collective bargaining, the market economy, equality of opportunity for all and social welfare and solidarity' [1.15, p. 9].

The challenge outlined in the Commission's communication on 'modernising and improving social protection in the European Union' [2.3] was how to adapt social protection as a core component of this model so as to sustain high standards of provision in a context of population ageing, changing family structures, a new gender balance and enlargement, without abandoning the values of solidarity and cohesion. By acting as the Union's conscience, the Commission sought to justify supranational intervention by formulating objectives and proposing the means of achieving them, without infringing the principles of subsidiarity and proportionality. A European social model based on shared values afforded an attractive and more readily acceptable alternative to member states resistant to any pressures to change national social protection systems.

THE FUTURE SHAPE OF EUROPEAN SOCIAL POLICY

As shown throughout this book, after more than 40 years of action at European level, resulting in a proliferation of legislative texts, few areas of social life remain untouched by official regulations, directives, decisions, recommendations, resolutions, communications or memoranda. Negotiations over the Community charter of the Fundamental Social Rights of Workers and the social chapter of the Treaty of Maastricht demonstrated that the United Kingdom was not alone in its concern about the pervasiveness of the Union's powers, as confirmed by the national debates surrounding ratification. The 1994 white paper on European social policy [1.15], the subsequent social action plans [1.16; 1.19] and communications on the modernization of social protection [2.3; 10.3] did not, however, signal that the Commission would be reducing the scope of its action. Rather, they highlighted the need for it to seek a common response to meet the challenges that the Union would be facing in the twenty-first century.

The Commission presented the changes creating the need for a concerted strategy as opportunities [10.3]. The process of deepening economic integration, with the introduction of the single currency from 1 January 1999, was expected to create an environment conducive to monetary stability, economic growth and sustainability of public finances, both demanding and allowing for the restructuring of expenditure on social protection. The agreement reached between governments, and institutionalized through a treaty commitment, over the need for an active and coherent approach to employment was seen as a means of securing the future viability of social protection systems in the context of demographic ageing, while making them more employment friendly. Employment was also to be the instrument for achieving an inclusive society through the promotion of family-friendly policies, designed to increase the participation of women in the labour market, and of age-friendly policies (though the term was not used) to achieve the objective of adding life to years and making active ageing a reality [7.16, p. 21; 10.3, p. 10]. The third challenge, enlargement, was also presented as an opportunity, opening up the way to enhanced trade and economic activity, and giving a new impetus to European integration, while also extending the Union's cultural diversity [2.4, vol. 1, p. 6].

Enlargement has always been an important incentive for member states to engage in reflection about the future shape of the Union's institutions and policies. The prospect of enlargement to the countries of Central and Eastern Europe after the year 2000 was no exception. The accession of as many as ten new states was expected to have a greater impact for social policy than previous waves of membership. Together, the population of these accessor states would amount to 105 million, equivalent to about 28 per cent of the Union's population in the late 1990s, but their combined gross domestic product (GDP) would reach less than 4 per cent of EU GDP [2.4, vol. 2, p. 62]. They would bring with them rising levels of unemployment, poverty and deprivation, but would be required to modernize their own social protection systems, while taking on the *acquis communautaire* in the social field [10.3, p. 11].

Enlargement was expected to entail a thorough reform of the Union's institutions before the accessor states joined, including, for example, the reweighting of votes in the Council, the extension of qualified majority voting to all areas, and a reduction in the number of commissioners to one per member state. Since social policy has often proved to be a contentious area, the extension of qualified majority voting was being promoted as a more flexible way of integrating further variants of the welfare mix. To meet the unprecedented challenges presented by accelerated demographic decline and ageing, the Commission proposed to 'modernize' social protection. The objectives were to make work pay while providing income security, to make pensions safe while ensuring the sustainability of pension systems, and to promote social inclusion at the same time as guaranteeing high quality and sustainable health provision.

Although no proposals were put forward for a European social union, during the 1990s reference was made increasingly in policy statements to a European social model, which was progressively taking shape, despite the resistance of member states to any convergence of systems. Such a model was presented as one of the achievements of the Community. Rather than taking the form of a welfare system made up of the sum of its parts, the European social model was depicted as embodying core values, to which member states were committed and which they were prepared to nurture and protect. Whether national social protection systems were based on employment-related insurance or universal benefits funded primarily from taxation, and the extent to which they were controlled by, and depended on, central government or the market were largely irrelevant. What mattered was that policies were being pursued with a common objective, namely 'to promote a decent quality of life and standard of living for all in an active, inclusive and healthy society that encourages access to employment, good working conditions, and equality of opportunity' [1.19, p. 8]. The major challenge for the twenty-first century was whether the enlarged Union would be able to sustain the European social model that it had taken so long to establish.

Box 10 Secondary legislation and official publications relating to the assessment of European social policy

10.1 Communication from the Commission on the social and labour market dimension of the information society (COM(97) 390 final, 23 July 1997).

10.2 Hearings with the European Parliament, Written replies given to the European Parliament's committees in August 1999 by the nominee Commissioner Anna Diamantopoulou.

10.3 Communication from the Commission, A concerted strategy for modernising social protection (COM(99) 347 final, 14 July 1999).

10.4 European Commission, *Forum Special: 5 years of social policy*, OOPEC, 1999.

Bibliography

Abrahamson, P. (1992) 'Welfare pluralism: towards a new consensus for a European social policy?', *Cross-national Research Papers*, 2 (6), pp. 5–22.

Afsa, C. (1996) 'L'activité féminine à l'épreuve de l'allocation parentale d'éducation', *Recherches et prévisions*, N° 46, pp. 1–8.

Alber, J. (1993) 'Health and social services', in A. Walker, A-M. Guillemard and J. Alber (eds), *Older People in Europe: social and economic policies. The 1993 Report of the European Observatory*, Brussels: Commission of the European Communities, pp. 52–68.

Alcock, P. (1998) 'The discipline of social policy', in P. Alcock, A. Erskine and M. May (eds), *The Student's Companion to Social Policy*, Oxford/Malden, Massachusettes: Blackwell, pp. 7–13.

Allen, D. (2000) 'Cohesion and Structural Funds', in H. Wallace and W. Wallace (eds), *Policy-making in the European Union*, Oxford: Oxford University Press, 4th edn, pp. 244–65.

Ardittis, S. (1990) 'Labour migration and the Single European Market: a synthetic and prospective note', *International Sociology*, 5 (4), pp. 461–74.

Baldwin-Edwards, M. (1991) 'Immigration after 1992', *Policy and Politics*, 19 (3), pp. 199–211.

Beck, W., van der Maesen, L. and Walker, A. (eds) (1997) *The Social Quality of Europe*, The Hague/London/Boston: Kluwer Law International.

Beretta, D. (rapporteur) (1989) *Social Aspects of the Internal Market. European Social Area*, Brussels: European Communities, Economic and Social Committee.

Berghman, J. (1990) 'The implications of 1992 for social policy: a selective critique of social insurance protection', *Cross-national Research Papers*, 2 (1), pp. 9–17.

Bergqvist, C. and Jungar, A-C. (2000) 'Adaptation or diffusion of the Swedish gender model?', in L. Hantrais (ed.), *Gendered Policies in Europe: reconciling employment and family life*, London: Macmillan/ New York: St. Martin's Press, pp. 160–79.

Bimbi, F. (1993) 'Gender, "gift relationship" and welfare state cultures in Italy', in J. Lewis (ed.), *Women and Social Policies in Europe: work, family and the state*, Aldershot: Edward Elgar, pp. 138–69.

Bosco, A. and Hutsebaut, M. (eds) (1997) *Social Protection in Europe: facing up to changes and challenges*, Brussels: European Trade Union Institute.

Bourdelais, P. (1993) *Le nouvel âge de la vieillesse. Histoire du vieillissement de la population*, Paris: Éditions Odile Jacob.

Brown, J. (1986) 'Cross-national and inter-country research into poverty: the case of the First European Poverty Programme', *Cross-national Research Papers*, 1 (2), pp. 41–51.

Buckley, M. and Anderson, M. (1988) 'Introduction: problems, policies and politics', in M. Buckley and M. Anderson (eds), *Women, Equality and Europe*, London: Macmillan, pp. 1–19.

Burrows, N. and Mair, J. (1996) *European Social Law*, Chichester: John Wiley & Sons.

Buti, M., Pench, L.R. and Franco, D. (eds) (1999) *The Welfare State in Europe: challenges and reforms*, Cheltenham/Northampton, MA: Edward Elgar.

Byre, A. (1988) 'Applying Community standards on equality', in M. Buckley and M. Anderson (eds), *Women, Equality and Europe*, London: Macmillan, pp. 20–32

Carlsen, S. (1993) 'Men's utilization of paternity leave and parental leave schemes', in S. Carlsen and J. Elm Larsen (eds), *The Equality Dilemma: reconciling working life and family life, viewed in an equality perspective. The Danish Example*, Copenhagen: Danish Equal Status Council, pp. 79–90.

Chester, R. (1994) 'Flying without instruments or flight plans: family policy in the United Kingdom', in W. Dumon (ed.), *Changing Family Policies in the Member States of the European Union*, Brussels: Commission of the European Communities, DG V/European Observatory on National Family Policies, pp. 271–301.

Chisholm, L. (1992) 'A crazy quilt: education, training and social change in Europe', in J. Bailey (ed.), *Social Europe*, London/New York: Longman, pp. 123–46.

Clasen, J. (ed.) (1999) *Comparative Social Policy: concepts, theories and methods*, Oxford: Blackwell.

Clasen, J. and Freeman, R. (eds) (1994) *Social Policy in Germany*, London: Harvester Wheatsheaf.

Collins, D. (1975) *The European Communities. The social policy of the first phase*, vol. 2 *The European Economic Community 1958–72*, London: Martin Robertson.

Corden, A. and Duffy, K. (1998) 'Human dignity and social exclusion', in R. Sykes and P. Alcock (eds), *Developments in European Social Policy: convergence and diversity*, Bristol: The Policy Press, pp. 95–124.

Council of Europe (1997) *Recent Demographic Developments in Europe, 1997*, Strasbourg: Council of Europe Publishing.

Council of Europe (1999) *Recent Demographic Developments in Europe, 1999*, Strasbourg: Council of Europe Publishing.

Cox, S. (1993) 'Equal Opportunities', in M. Gold (ed.), *The Social Dimension: employment policy in the European Community*, London: Macmillan, pp. 41–63.

Cram, L. (1997) *Policy-making in the European Union: conceptual lenses and the integration process*, London/New York: Routledge.

Crawley, C. (1990) 'The European Parliament Committee on Women's Rights', *Cross-national Research Papers*, 2 (3), pp. 7–9.

Daly, M. and Lewis, J. (1998) 'Introduction: conceptualising social care in the context of welfare state restructuring', in J. Lewis (ed.), *Gender, Social Care and Welfare State Restructuring in Europe*, Aldershot/Vermont: Ashgate, pp. 1–24.

De Swaan, A. (1990) 'Perspectives for transnational social policy. Preliminary notes', *Cross-national Research Papers*, 2 (2), pp. 7–22.

Deacon, B. (1993) 'Developments in East European social policy', in C. Jones (ed.), *New Perspectives on the European Welfare State in Europe*, London/New York: Routledge, pp. 177–97.

Del Re, A. (2000) 'The paradoxes of Italian law and practice', in L. Hantrais (ed.), *Gendered Policies in Europe: reconciling employment and family life*, London: Macmillan/New York: St. Martin's Press, pp. 108–23.

Delors, J. (1985) 'Preface', in J. Vandamme (ed.), *New Dimensions in European Social Policy*, London: Croom Helm, pp. ix–xx.

Desrosières, A. (1996) 'Statistical traditions: an obstacle to international comparisons?', in L. Hantrais and S. Mangen (eds), *Cross-national Research Methods in the Social Sciences*, London: Pinter, pp. 17–27.

Ditch, J., Barnes, H. and Bradshaw, J. (1996) *A Synthesis of National Family Policies 1995*, York: Social Policy Research Unit/European Observatory on National Family Policies.

Ditch, J., Barnes, H., Bradshaw, J. and Kilkey, M. (1998) *A Synthesis of National Family Policies 1996*, York: Social Policy Research Unit/European Observatory on National Family Policies.

Drake, K. (1994) 'Policy integration and co-operation. A persistent challenge', in OECD (ed.), *Vocational Education and Training for Youth: towards coherent policy and practice*, Paris: OECD, pp. 143–68.

Duff, A. (ed.) (1997) *The Treaty of Amsterdam: text and commentary*, London: The Federal Trust.

Dumon, W. (ed.) (1991) *National Family Policies in EC-Countries in 1990*, Brussels: Commission of the European Communities/European Observatory on National Family Policies, V/2293/91-EN.

Dumon, W. (ed.) (1994) *Changing Family Policies in the Member States of the European Union*, Brussels: Commission of the European Communities/European Observatory on National Family Policies.

Edwards, N., Hensher, M. and Werneke, U. (1998) 'Changing hospital systems', in R.B. Saltman, J. Figueras and C. Sakallarides (eds),

Critical Challenges for Health Care Reform in Europe, Buckingham/Philadelphia: Open University Press, pp. 236–60.

Esping-Andersen, G. (1990) *The Three Worlds of Welfare Capitalism*, Cambridge: Polity.

European Commission Childcare Network (1990) 'Childcare in the European Communities 1985–1990', *Women of Europe Supplements*, N° 31.

European Commission Network on Childcare and Other Measures to Reconcile Employment and Family Responsibilities (1994) *Leave Arrangements for Workers with Children: a review of leave arrangements in the Member States of the European Union and Austria, Finland, Norway and Sweden*, Brussels: European Commission Directorate General V, V/773/94-EN.

European Commission Network on Childcare and Other Measures to Reconcile Employment and Family Responsibilities (1996) *A Review of Services for Young Children in the European Union 1990–1995*, Brussels: European Commission Directorate General V.

European Institute of Social Security (1988) 'The role of social security in the context of the completion of the internal market by 1992', unpublished report for the Commission of the European Communities, Louvain: European Institute of Social Security, V/1653/EN-88.

Eurostat (1997a) 'About one marriage in four in the EU ends in divorce', *Statistics in Focus. Population and social conditions*, N° 14.

Eurostat (1997b) 'Beyond the predictable: demographic changes in the EU up to 2050', *Statistics in Focus. Population and social conditions*, N° 7.

Eurostat (1997c) 'Education in the European Union: opportunities and choices', *Statistics in Focus. Population and social conditions*, N° 4.

Eurostat (1997d) 'Family responsibilities – how are they shared in European households', *Statistics in Focus. Population and social conditions*, N° 5.

Eurostat (1997e) 'Taxes and social contributions in the European Union – first results for 1996', *Statistics in Focus. Economy and finance*, N° 28.

Eurostat (1998a) *Living Conditions in Europe: selected social indicators*, Luxembourg: Office for Official Publications of the European Communities.

Eurostat (1998b) 'Migration between the Mediterranean Basin and the EU in 1995', *Statistics in Focus. Population and social conditions*, N° 3.

Eurostat (1999) 'Population and living conditions', *Statistics in Focus. Population and social conditions*, N° 15.

Eurostat (2000) 'Social protection in Europe', *Statistics in Focus. Population and social conditions*, N° 2.

Fagnani, J. (1996) 'Family policies and working mothers: a comparison of France and West Germany', in M.D. García-Ramon and J. Monk (eds), *Women of the European Union: the politics of work and daily life*, London/New York: Routledge, pp. 126–37.

Ferge, Z. (1992) 'Social policy regimes and social structure: hypotheses about the prospects of social policy in Central and Eastern Europe', in Z. Ferge and J.E. Kolberg (eds), *Social Policy in a Changing Europe*, Frankfurt am Main: Campus Verlag/Boulder, Colerado: Westview Press, pp. 201–22.

Ferge, Z. (1997) 'A central European perspective on the social quality of Europe', in W. Beck, L. van der Maesen and A. Walker (eds), *The Social Quality of Europe*, The Hague/London/Boston: Kluwer Law International, pp. 165–81.

Figueras, J., Saltman, R.B. and Sakallerides, C. (1998) 'Introduction', in R.B. Saltman, J. Figueras and C. Sakallarides (eds), *Critical Challenges for Health Care Reform in Europe*, Buckingham/Philadelphia: Open University Press, pp. 1–19.

Flora, P. and Alber, J. (1984) 'Modernization, democratization, and the development of welfare states in Western Europe', in P. Flora and A.J. Heidenheimer (eds), *The Development of Welfare States in Europe and America*, New Brunswick: Transaction Publishers, pp. 37–80.

Flynn, P. (1993) 'Preface', in 'Towards a Europe of solidarity: combating social exclusion', *Social Europe Supplement*, 4/93, pp. 3–4.

Gardiner, F. (ed.) (1997) *Sex Equality Policy in Western Europe*, London/New York: Routledge.

Gastines, B. de and Sylvestre, J-M. (1992) *Le guide SVP de l'Europe*, Paris: Éditions SVP.

George, V. and Taylor-Gooby, P. (eds) (1996) *European Welfare Policy: squaring the welfare circle*, London: Macmillan.

Geyer, R. (1996) 'EU social policy in the 1990s: does Maastricht matter?', *Revue d'intégration européenne/Journal of European Integration*, 20 (1), pp. 5–33.

Geyer, R. (2000) *Exploring European Social Policy*, Oxford: Polity Press.

Ginn, J. and Arber, S. (1992) 'Towards women's independence: pension systems in three contrasting European welfare states', *Journal of European Social Policy*, 2 (4), pp. 255–77.

Gold, M. and Mayes, D. (1993) 'Rethinking a social policy for Europe', in R. Simpson and R. Walker (eds), *Europe: for richer or poorer?*, London: CPAG, pp. 25–38.

Gormley, L.W. (ed.) (1998) *Introduction to the Law of the European Communities: from Maastricht to Amsterdam*, 3rd edn, London/The Hague/Boston: Kluwer Law International.

Guild, E. (ed.) (1999) *The Legal Framework and Social Consequences of Free Movement of Persons in the European Union*, The Hague/Boston/London: Kluwer Law International.

Guillemard, A-M. (1993) 'Older workers and the labour market', in A. Walker, A-M. Guillemard and J. Alber (eds), *Older People in Europe:*

social and economic policies. The 1993 Report of the European Observatory, Brussels: Commission of the European Communities, pp. 35–51.

Hannequart, A. (1992) 'Economic and social cohesion and the Structural Funds: an introduction', in A. Hannequart (ed.), *Economic and Social Cohesion in Europe: a new objective for integration*, London/New York: Routledge, pp. 1–18.

Hantrais, L. (1999a) 'Socio-demographic change, policy impacts and outcomes in social Europe', *Journal of European Social Policy*, 9 (4), pp. 291–309.

Hantrais, L. (ed.) (1999b) *Cross-national Research Papers*, 5 (1) 'Interactions between Socio-demographic Trends, Social and Economic Policies'.

Hantrais, L. (ed.) (2000) *Gendered Policies in Europe: reconciling employment and family life*, London: Macmillan/New York: St. Martin's Press.

Hantrais, L. and Letablier, M-T. (1996) *Families and Family Policies in Europe*, London/New York: Addison Wesley Longman.

Hantrais, L. and Lohkamp-Himmighofen, M. (1999) *Cross-national Research Papers*, 5 (3) 'Changing Family Forms, Law and Policy'.

Hantrais, L. and Mangen, S. (eds) (1996) *Cross-national Research Methods in the Social Sciences*, London/New York: Pinter.

Heclo, H. (1984) 'Toward a new welfare state?', in P. Flora and A.J. Heidenheimer (eds), *The Development of Welfare States in Europe and America*, New Brunswick: Transaction Publishers, pp. 383–406.

Hervey, T. (1998) *European Social Law and Policy*, Harlow: Addison Wesley Longman.

Holloway, J. (1981) *Social Policy Harmonisation in the European Community*, Farnborough: Gower.

Home Office (1998) *Supporting Families: a consultation document*, London: Home Office.

Hoskyns, C. (1996) *Integrating Gender: women, law and politics in the European Union*, London/New York: Verso.

James, E. (1982) 'From Paris to ESCAP', in J. Dennett, E. James, G. Room and P. Watson, *Europe against Poverty: the European Poverty Programme 1975–80*, London: Bedford Square Press/NCVO, pp. 3–13.

James, P. (1993) 'Occupational health and safety', in M. Gold (ed.), *The Social Dimension: employment policy in the European Community*, London: Macmillan, pp. 135–52.

Jani-Le Bris, H. (1993) *Family Care of Dependent Older People in the European Community*, Luxembourg: Office for Official Publications of the European Communities.

Jones Finer, C. (1999) 'Trends and developments in welfare states', in J. Clasen (ed.), *Comparative Social Policy: concepts, theories and methods*, Oxford: Blackwell, pp. 15–33.

Jones, H. (1990) 'New European challenges for education – the impact of 1992', IBM Annual Lecture 1990, London, 11 July.

Kamerman, S.B. and Kahn, A.J. (eds) (1978) *Family Policy: government and family in fourteen countries*, New York: Columbia University Press.

Kirsch, J-L. (1998) 'Low training levels on European labour markets: convergence and contrasts', *Training and Employment*, N° 34, pp. 1–4.

Kleinman, M. and Piachaud, D. (1993) 'European social policy: conceptions and choices', *Journal of European Social Policy*, 3 (1), pp. 1–19.

Knapp, M., Montserrat, J. and Fenyo, A. (1990) 'Inter-sectoral and international contracting-out of long-term care: evidence on comparative costs and efficiency from Britain and Spain', *Cross-national Research Papers*, 2 (2), pp. 46–73.

Kokko, S., Hava, P., Ortun, V. and Leppo, K. (1998) 'The role of the state in health care reform', in R.B. Saltman, J. Figueras and C. Sakallarides (eds), *Critical Challenges for Health Care Reform in Europe*, Buckingham/Philadelphia: Open University Press, pp. 289–307.

Lanquetin, M-T., Laufer, J. and Letablier, M-T. (2000) 'From equality to reconciliation in France?', in L. Hantrais (ed.), *Gendered Policies in Europe: reconciling employment and family life*, London: Macmillan/New York: St. Martin's Press, pp. 68–88.

Leibfried, S. (1992) 'Europe's could-be social state: social policy in European integration after 1992', in W. J. Adams (ed.), *Singular Europe: economy and polity of the European Community after 1992*, Ann Arbor: University of Michigan Press, pp. 97–118.

Leibfried, S. and Pierson, P. (1992) 'Prospects for social Europe', *Politics and Society*, 20 (3), pp. 333–66.

Leibfried, S. and Pierson, P. (eds) (1995) *European Social Policy: between fragmentation and integration*, Washington D.C.: The Brookings Institution.

Leibfried, S. and Pierson, P. (2000) 'Social policy: left to courts and markets', in H. Wallace and W. Wallace (eds), *Policy-making in the European Union*, Oxford: Oxford University Press, 4th edn, pp. 267–92.

Letourneux, V. (1998) *Precarious Employment and Working Conditions in Europe*, Luxembourg: Office for Official Publications of the European Communities.

Lewis, J. (ed.) (1997) *Lone Mothers in European Welfare Regimes*, London/Philadelphia: Jessica Kingsley.

Lewis, J. (ed.) (1998) *Gender, Social Care and Welfare State Restructuring in Europe*, Aldershot/Vermont: Ashgate.

Lindley, R. (1991) 'Interactions in the markets for education, training and labour: a European perspective on intermediate skills', in P. Ryan (ed.), *International Comparisons of Vocational Education and Training for Intermediate Skills*, London/New York: The Falmer Press, pp. 185–206.

Lister, R. (1997) *Citizenship: feminist pespectives*, London: Macmillan.

Lødemel, I. (1992) 'The poor and the poorest in European income maintenance', *Cross-national Research Papers*, 2 (7), pp. 13–23.

Lohkamp-Himmighofen, M. and Dienel, C. (2000) 'Reconciliation policies from a comparative perspective', in L. Hantrais (ed.), *Gendered Policies in Europe: reconciling employment and family life*, London: Macmillan/New York: St. Martin's Press, pp. 48–67.

Luckhaus, L. (1990) 'The social security directive: its impact on part-time and unpaid work', *Cross-national Research Papers*, 2 (3), pp. 11–19.

Majone, G. (1996a) 'A European regulatory state?', in J.J. Richardson (ed.), *European Union: power and policy-making*, London/New York: Routledge pp. 263–77.

Majone, G. (1996b) 'Which social policy for Europe?', in Y. Mény, P. Muller and J-L. Quermonne (eds), *Adjusting to Europe*, London: Routledge, pp. 123–36.

Malpas, N. and Lambert, P-Y. (1993) 'Europeans and the family', *Eurobarometer*, N° 39.0, V/72/94-EN.

Marks, G., Hooghe, L. and Blank, K. (1996) 'European integration from the 1980s: state-centric v. multi-level governance', *Journal of Common Market Studies*, 34 (3), pp. 341–78.

Meehan, E. (1993) 'Women's rights in the European Community', in J. Lewis (ed.), *Women and Social Policies in Europe: work, family and the state*, Aldershot: Edward Elgar, 194–205.

Merle, V. and Bertrand, O. (1993) 'Comparabilité et reconnaissance des qualifications en Europe. Instruments et enjeux', *Formation emploi*, N° 43, July–September, pp. 41–56.

Meulders-Klein, M-T. (1992) 'Vie privée, vie familiale et droits de l'homme', *Revue internationale de droit comparé*, 44 (4), pp. 767–94.

Meulders-Klein, M-T. (1993) 'The status of the father in European legislation', in Danish Ministry of Social Affairs/European Commission, Report from the Conference *Fathers in Families of Tomorrow*, Copenhagen: Ministry of Social Affairs, pp. 107–50.

Millar, J. and Warman, A. (1996) *Family Obligations in Europe*, London: Family Policy Studies Centre/Joseph Rowntree Foundation.

Milner, S. (1998) 'Training policy: steering between divergent national logics', in D. Hine and H. Kassim (eds), *Beyond the Market: the European Union and national social policy*, London/New York: Routledge, pp. 156–77.

Mishra, R. (1977) *Society and Social Policy: theoretical perspectives on welfare*, London/Basingstoke: Macmillan.

Mitchell, M. and Russell, D. (1998) 'Immigration, citizenship and social exclusion in the new Europe', in R. Sykes and P. Alcock (eds),

Developments in European Social Policy: convergence and diversity, Bristol: The Policy Press, pp. 75–94.

Moravcsik, A. and Nicolaïdis, K. (1999) 'Explaining the Treaty of Amsterdam: interests, influences, institutions', *Journal of Common Market Studies*, 37 (1), pp. 59–85.

Mossialos, E. (1998) *Citizens and Health Systems; main results from a Eurobarometer survey*, Luxembourg: Office for Official Publications of the European Communities.

Mossialos, E. and Le Grand, J. (eds) (1999) *Health Care and Cost Containment in the European Union*, Aldershot/Vermont: Ashgate.

Mullard, M. and Lee, S. (eds) (1997) *The Politics of Social Policy in Europe*, Cheltenham/Lyme: Edward Elgar.

Nielsen, K. (1996) 'Eastern European welfare systems', in B. Greve (ed.), *Comparative Welfare Systems: the Scandinavian model in a period of change*, London: Macmillan, pp. 185–213.

Nugent, N. (1994) *The Government and Politics of the European Union*, 3rd edn, London: Macmillan.

O'Donnell, R. (1992) 'Policy requirements for regional balance in economic and monetary union', in A. Hannequart (ed.), *Economic and Social Cohesion in Europe: a new objective for integration*, London/New York: Routledge, pp. 21–52.

O'Leary, S. and Tiilikainen, T. (1998) *Citizenship and Nationality Status in the New Europe*, London: Institute for Public Policy Research/Sweet & Maxwell.

OECD (1999) 'Frequently asked data – OECD health data 97 – inputs and throughputs', <http://www.oecd.org/els/health/fad_2.htm>.

Pacolet, J. (ed.) (1996) *Social Protection and the European Economic and Monetary Union*, Aldershot/Vermont: Avebury.

Pickup, L. (1990) *Mobility and Social Cohesion in the European Community – a forward look*, Luxembourg: Office for Official Publications of the European Communities.

Pierson, C. (1992) *Beyond the Welfare State? The new political economy of welfare* (reprint), Cambridge: Polity Press.

Pieters, D. (1991) 'Will "1992" lead to the co-ordination and harmonization of social security?', in D. Pieters (ed.), *Social Security in Europe: Miscellanea of the Erasmus-programme Social Security in the E.C.*, Brussels/Antwerp: Bruylant/Maklu, pp. 177–90.

Pieters, D. (ed.) (1998) *Social Protection of the Next Generation in Europe*, London/The Hague/Boston: Kluwer Law International, EISS Yearbook 1997.

Quintin, O. (1988) 'The policies of the European Communities with special reference to the labour market', in M. Buckley and M. Anderson (eds), *Women, Equality and Europe*, London: Macmillan, pp. 71–7.

Quintin, O. (1992) 'The convergence of social protection objectives and policies: a contribution to solidarity in Europe', *Social Europe Supplement*, 5/92, pp. 9–12.

Rees, T. (1998) *Mainstreaming Equality in the European Union: education, training and labour market policies*, London/New York: Routledge.

Rex, J. (1992) 'Race and ethnicity in Europe', in J. Bailey (ed.), *Social Europe*, London/New York: Longman, pp. 106–20.

Rhodes, M. (1995) 'A regulatory conundrum: industrial relations and the social dimension', in S. Leibfried and P. Pierson (eds), *European Social Policy: between fragmentation and integration*, Washington, D.C.: The Brookings Institution, pp. 78–122.

Rhodes, M. (ed.) (1997) *Southern European Welfare States: between crisis and reform*, London/Portland, Oregon: Frank Cass.

Rhodes, M. and Mény, Y. (eds) (1998) *The Future of European Welfare: a new social contract?*, London: Macmillan/New York: St. Martin's Press.

Room, G. (1982) 'The definition and measurement of poverty', in J. Dennett, E. James, G. Room and P. Watson, *Europe against Poverty: the European Poverty Programme 1975–80*, London: Bedford Square Press/NCVO, pp. 155–62.

Room, G. (co-ordinator) (1991) *Observatory on National Policies to Combat Social Exclusion. Second annual report*, Brussels: Commission of the European Communities.

Room, G. (1994) 'European social policy: competition, conflict and integration', in R. Page and J. Baldock (eds), *Social Policy Review 6*, Canterbury: Social Policy Association, pp. 17–35.

Rowntree, B.S. (1901) *Poverty: a study of town life*, 1st edn, London: Thomas Nelson.

Rubery, J. and Smith, M. (1999) *The Future European Labour Supply*, Luxembourg: Office for Official Publications of the European Communities.

Rubery, J., Smith, M. and Fagan, C. (1999) *Women's Employment in Europe: trends and prospects*, London/New York: Routledge.

Ryan, P. (1991) 'Introduction: comparative research on vocational education and training', in P. Ryan (ed.), *International Comparisons of Vocational Education and Training for Intermediate Skills*, London/New York: The Falmer Press, pp. 1–20.

Saltman, R.B., Figueras, J. and Sakallerides, C. (1998) 'Assessing the evidence', in R.B. Saltman, J. Figueras and C. Sakallarides (eds), *Critical Challenges for Health Care Reform in Europe*, Buckingham/Philadelphia: Open University Press, pp. 400–8.

Séché, J-C. (1994) *A Guide to Working in a Europe without Frontiers*, Luxembourg: Office for Official Publications of the European Communities, 2nd edn.

Shanks, M. (1977) *European Social Policy, Today and Tomorrow*, Oxford/New York: Pergamon.

Singleton, A. (1998) 'Measuring international migration: the tools aren't up to the job', in D. Dorling and L. Simpson (eds), *Statistics in Society*, London: Arnold, pp. 148–58.

Soisson, J-P. (1990) 'Observations on the Community Charter of Basic Social Rights for Workers', *Social Europe*, 1/90, pp. 10–13.

Spicker, P. (1991) 'The principle of subsidiarity and the social policy of the European Community', *Journal of European Social Policy*, 1 (1), pp. 3–14.

Statistics Sweden (1995) *Women and Men in Sweden: facts and figures 1995*, Stockholm: Statistics Sweden.

Steindorff, C. and Heering, C. (1993) 'Familienpolitik und Recht im europäischen Integrationsprozeß', in E. Neubauer, C. Dienel and M. Lohkamp-Himmighofen (eds), *Zwölf Wege der Familienpolitik in der Europäischen Gemeinschaft. Eigenständige Systeme und vergleichbare Qualitäten?*, vol. 22.1, Stuttgart/Berlin/Köln: Kohlhammer, pp. 131–59.

Stratigaki, M. (2000) 'The European Union and the equal opportunities process', in L. Hantrais (ed.), *Gendered Policies in Europe: reconciling employment and family life*, London: Macmillan/New York: St. Martin's Press, pp. 27–48.

Sykes, R. and Alcock, P. (eds) (1998) *Developments in European Social Policy: convergence and diversity*, Bristol: The Policy Press.

Teague, P. (1989) *The European Community: the social dimension. Labour market policies for 1992*, London: Kogan Page in association with Cranfield School of Management.

Teague, P. (1998) 'Monetary union and social Europe', *Journal of European Social Policy*, 8 (2), pp. 117–37.

Teague, P. and McClelland, D. (1991) 'Towards "social Europe"? Industrial relations after 1992', *Cross-national Research Papers*, 2 (5), pp. 8–22.

Titmuss, R.M. (1974) *Social Policy: an introduction* (edited by B. Abel-Smith and K. Titmuss), London: George Allen & Unwin.

Townsend, P. (1979) *Poverty in the United Kingdom: a survey of household resources and standards of living*, Berkeley and Los Angeles: University of California Press.

United Nations Statistical Commission/Economic Commission for Europe Conference of European Statisticians (1987) 'Recommendations for the 1990 censuses of population and housing in the ECE region: regional variant of the world recommendations for the 1990 round of population and housing censuses', *Statistical Standards and Studies*, N° 40, New York: United Nations.

Vale, A. (1991) 'The European Women's Lobby', *Social Europe*, 3/91, pp. 107–9.

van Oorschot, W. and Math, A. (1996) 'La question du non-recours aux prestations sociales', *Recherches et prévisions*, N° 43, pp. 5–17.

Venturini, P. (1989) *1992: the European social dimension,* Luxembourg: Office for Official Publications of the European Communities.

Vogel, J. (1997) *Living Conditions and Inequality in the European Union 1997*, Eurostat Working Papers, Population and Social Conditions, E/1997-3.

Walker, A. (1993a) 'Introduction', in A. Walker, A-M. Guillemard and J. Alber (eds), *Older people in Europe: social and economic policies. The 1993 Report of the European Observatory*, Brussels: Commission of the European Communities, pp. 1–6.

Walker, A. (1993b) 'Living standards and way of life', in A. Walker, A-M. Guillemard and J. Alber (eds), *Older People in Europe: social and economic policies. The 1993 Report of the European Observatory*, Brussels: Commission of the European Communities, pp. 8–34.

Walker, A. (1998) *Managing an Ageing Workforce: a guide to good practice*, Luxembourg: Office for Official Publications of the European Communities.

Walker, A. and Maltby, T. (1997) *Ageing Europe*, Buckingham/Bristol, PA: Oxford University Press.

Index

Numbers in square brackets indicate box references to official documents at the end of chapters. Numbers in bold refer to whole chapters.

acquis communautaire, 13, 78, 89, 219, 242
action programme(s), 13, 20, 28, 67, 70–2, 88, 118, 121, 138, 140, 166–7, 179, 190, 202, 218
  for education [3.1], 43, 54–5, 62–4
  for equal opportunities [6.5, 6.6, 6.14], 114, 118, 121–3
  for health and safety [4.12, 4.13], 76
  for implementing the Community charter [1.11], 10, 26, 71, 143, 225
  for migrants [9.7, 9.23], 207
  for older and disabled people [7.6, 7.11], 144–7
  against poverty and social exclusion [8.3, 8.8], 167, 170–3, 176–7, 179
  see also social action programme
Adapt, 176–7
Advisory Committee on Safety, Hygiene and Health Protection at Work, 68
age, 15, 34, 57–9, 61–2, 71, 86–7, 92, 98–101, 106, 108, 114, 121, 129, 131, 134, 137, 140–3, 147–55, 157, 160–4, 165, 180, 185–7, 206, 231, 235
ageing, 14, 134, 140–1, 146–52, 159, 161, 197, 219, 236, 240, 242
  see also demographic ageing, population ageing
Agreement on Social Policy [1.6], 11–13, 18–19, 22, 28, 47, 74, 94–5, 116–17, 121, 142, 168, 219, 240
  article 1, 11, 15, 22
  articles 2–5, 12, 15, 27
  article 6, 16, 27, 117
  article 7, 16, 94
AIDS, 74–6, 87, 90
allowances, 8, 104, 153, 183
  see also family allowances,
amended treaties, 15–17, 74–7
  see also Consolidated EC Treaty
Amsterdam
  see Treaty of Amsterdam
apprenticeship(s), 58, 202
approximation, 7, 11, 21–7, 67, 70, 87, 118, 137
asylum, 16, 208–10, 212, 214, 227, 232
Austria
  ageing, 151–2
  caring, 159–60
  education and training, 55, 58–60
  equality legislation, 127, 129–30, 132–3

EU membership, 36, 231
family policy, 103–4, 108–9
family structure, 100, 102
health care, 84–5
income maintenance, 185
migration, 213
policy for older and disabled people, 153–4, 157
social exclusion, 182
social spending, 32–4, 237
welfare system, 22, 31, 36
working conditions, 79–80, 82

Belgium
ageing, 151–2
caring, 159
education and training, 55, 57–8, 60–2
EEC membership, 1
equality legislation, 116, 126–7, 130–3
family policy, 104, 106, 108–9
family structure, 102
health care, 85, 87
income maintenance, 185–6
migration, 199, 202, 204–5
non-European immigration, 209, 211–12
policy for older and disabled people, 153, 157
social exclusion, 188
social spending, 33–4, 237
welfare system, 21, 31, 35
working conditions, 79–81, 83
benefit(s), 3, 8, 12, 25, 34, 36, 85–6, 92, 108–9, 119, 131–7, 141–2, 144, 146, 150, 152–6, 159, 168, 179, 183–8, 193, 195, 200–1, 213, 222, 227–8, 237
earnings-related, 36–8, 129, 155, 157, 162, 165, 185, 188
employment-related, 97, 185, 196, 227, 243
flat-rate, 36–8, 131–2, 136, 154–5, 157, 185–7
universal, 21, 136, 243
see also child, family, invalidity, means-testing, sickness, survivor's benefit
Berghman, Jos, 10, 25
breadwinner, 103, 129, 135
Britain, 36, 61, 139, 155, 190
see also United Kingdom
burden of proof, 12, 126
Burrows, Noreen, and Mair, Jane, 79, 81, 119, 128, 234

cancer, 70, 76, 87, 89–90
care, 31, 136, 144–7, 150, 158–61, 175
see also childcare, health care, medical care
care services, 159, 175
carers, 156, 158–9
caring, 129, 133, 135–6, 141–2, 148–9, 153–4, 158–62, 227
census(es), 98–9, 101, 112
child benefit(s), 107, 109, 111, 129, 235
childcare, 109, 118–20, 122–3, 128, 132–4, 138, 161, 239
children, 4, 53, 57–8, 91–2, 95–6, 99–100, 102–3, 106–9, 119–20, 129–30, 132–4, 148, 154, 156, 159, 166, 182, 186, 204, 206, 211, 215, 227
at risk, 106, 133
protection of, 43, 71, 93, 225, 239
Church, 31, 36
citizenship, 8, 36, 38, 50, 136, 154–5, 157, 193, 198, 207, 210–13, 221, 224–8
of the Union, 193–4, 226, 232
rights, 91, 170, 210–11, 213,

citizenship rights (cont.)
226–8
civil servants, 203–4, 215
Clasen, Jochen, and Freeman, Richard, 34
cohabitation (unmarried), 98, 101, 105, 108
cohesion, 22, 48, 93, 168–9, 178, 183, 190, 228, 232, 241
economic, 5, 42, 222
economic and social, 7, 10, 16, 26, 39, 122, 145, 166, 168, 171, 174–5, 177, 222, 232
social, 6, 25–8, 224
collective bargaining, 3, 39, 68, 70, 77, 162, 241
Collins, Doreen, 1, 3, 23, 192, 196, 199
Committee of the Regions, 169, 190
common market, 5, 11, 21, 23, 42, 67, 141, 165, 191–2
communication(s)
on education and training [3.3], 43, 50, 52, 55
on equal opportunities [6.17], 124
on a Europe of knowledge [3.10], 49
on family policy(ies) [5.3], 93–4, 97
on modernizing social protection [2.3, 10.3], 28, 39, 96–7, 110, 129, 207, 223–4, 240–2
on older and disabled people [7.7, 7.14, 7.16], 141, 145, 147, 161, 242
on public health [4.9, 4.15], 76, 88
on structural assistance [8.10], 177
on subsidiarity [1.13], 12
on supplementary social security [9.13], 193
on support for employment [8.13], 177, 223
on undeclared work [4.16], 80
community care, 158–9
Community Charter of the Fundamental Social Rights of Workers (Community charter) [1.10], 7–10, 43–4, 70–4, 94, 116, 142, 168–9, 193, 217
preamble to, 7–8, 92, 177, 221, 225
§§1–6 on freedom of movement, 22, 26, 43, 45, 71, 169, 193, 225
§§7–9 on living and working conditions, 22, 26, 70–1, 225
§10 on social protection, 168, 225
§§11–14 on freedom of association, 225
§15 on vocational training, 44–5, 49, 225
§16 on equal treatment, 44, 94, 116, 225–6
§§17–18 on consultation and participation, 225
§19 on health and safety at work, 26, 44, 71, 225
§§20–3 on children and adolescents, 43–4, 58, 71, 225
§§24–6 on elderly and disabled persons, 44, 142, 144, 225
§28 on Commission initiatives, 10
competition, 2–3, 5, 9–10, 18–19, 24–5, 41–2, 66, 77, 85, 87, 113, 115, 141, 169, 197, 218, 224
competitiveness, 10–11, 15, 22,

24–6, 42, 44, 48–9, 56, 82, 96, 142, 161, 176, 196, 218, 222–3, 228–9, 235–6
compliance, 52, 77, 79, 125–6, 234
Consolidated version of the Treaty establishing the European Community (EC Treaty) [1.8]
  part 1 principles, article 2, 28
    article 3, 75, 88, 117
    article 12, 194, 232
    article 13, 15, 111, 117, 142, 194, 207, 232
  part 2 on citizenship, articles 17–22, 194, 232
  title III on free movement, articles 39–42, 16, 203, 232
  title IV on visas, asylum and immigration, articles 61–9, 16, 209, 227, 232
  title VIII on employment, articles 125–30, 16–17, 28, 49, 118, 228, 232, 239
  title XI on social policy, education, vocational training and youth,
    articles 136–45 on social provisions, 15–16, 21–2, 28, 47, 74, 94, 117–18, 143, 202, 226, 232, 237
    articles 146–8 on the European Social Fund, 16, 175, 232
    articles 149–50 on education, vocational training and youth, 16, 28, 47–9, 57, 204, 232
  title XII on culture, article 151, 28, 47, 205, 226, 232
  title XIII on public health, article 152, 16, 28, 75–7, 226, 232
  title XVII on economic and social cohesion, articles 158–62, 16, 26, 169, 175, 232
  title XIX on environment, articles 174–6, 16, 28, 75, 232
  article 251, 117
  article 310, 194
  Protocol N° 30, 12, 220
contraception, 99
Convention on Human Rights, 4, 8, 107, 194, 226
convergence, 6, 15, 22–3, 25–30, 32, 37, 39–40, 45, 57, 63, 95, 109, 136, 153, 157, 169, 212, 236–7, 243
  see also recommendation(s)
co operation, 1–6, 12, 17, 22, 27–9, 43–56, 68, 70, 72, 75, 84, 88, 173, 178, 193, 208, 236
co-operation procedure, 7–8
co-ordination, 6–7, 10, 12, 22–4, 27, 29, 46, 63, 75, 91, 111, 171, 189, 195, 226
core and periphery, 78, 181
Council of Europe, 2, 4, 8, 15, 91, 100, 103, 107, 180, 194, 212
  see also European Social Charter
Cram, Laura, 238–9
culture(s), 10, 25, 28, 47, 50, 55–6, 204–6, 226, 232
Czech Republic, 37, 86, 131, 183

De Swaan, Abram, 24, 214
Deacon, Bob, 32, 37
decision(s)
  75/458/EEC, 77/779/EEC, 88/231/EEC, 93/136/EEC on disabled people [7.11], 145

decisions (cont.)
89/457/EEC on poverty programmes [8.1], 170, 179, 182
95/593/EC on equal opportunities [6.14], 123
645/96/EC on health promotion [4.12], 76
646/96/EC on cancer [4.12], 76
647/96/EC on AIDS [4.12], 76
102/97/EC on drugs [4.13], 76
declaration on racism and xenophobia [9.10], 207
Delors, Jacques, 5–7, 18, 25, 27, 43, 69–70, 217, 239
demographic ageing, 140, 149, 151, 242
demographic trends, 14, 93–4, 98, 104, 111, 145, 198
Denmark
ageing, 149, 151–2
EC membership, 1
education and training, 57–8, 60–1
equality legislation, 126–7, 130–3
family policy, 103–4, 108–9
family structure, 101–2
health care, 84–5, 87
income maintenance, 186
migration, 200, 204, 208, 213
non-European immigration, 209, 211–12
policy for older and disabled people, 154, 162
social exclusion, 170, 182, 188
social spending, 33–4, 237
welfare system, 21, 31, 36, 38
working conditions, 77, 79–80, 82–3
dependants, 23, 84, 91–2, 110–11, 130, 135, 150, 154, 156, 165, 175, 195
dependency ratio, 148–9, 161
Diamantopoulou, Anna, 224, 243
directive(s)
68/360/EEC on freedom of movement [9.3], 195
73/403/EEC on national censuses [5.1], 98, 171, 232
75/117/EEC on equal pay [6.1], 118
76/207/EEC, 79/7/EEC on equal treatment [6.2, 6.3], 119, 143
86/378/EEC, 86/613/EEC on occupational social security schemes [6.7, 6.9], 119, 143
89/391/EEC on health and safety at work [4.1], 71, 86
89/48/EEC, 92/51/EEC, 95/43/EC, on recognition of diplomas [3.2, 3.5], 46–7, 202
91/383/EEC, 91/533/EEC on employment contracts [4.4, 4.5], 73, 80
92/85/EEC on pregnant women [4.7], 73, 96, 120, 130
93/104/EC on working time [4.10], 73, 89, 96, 120
94/45/EC on works councils [4.11], 74
96/34/EC on parental leave [6.16], 96, 121
97/81/EC on part-time work [4.14], 75, 82, 229
directorate(s)-general (DGs), 124, 229
DGV/EMPL, 95, 172, 223, 229, 239
disabled people, 44, 96, 108, **140–64**, 169, 174, 176, 185, 218, 225, 227–8, 239
discrimination, 15, 27, 43, 75,

93, 117–19, 126–7, 129, 135, 137, 139–40, 142, 146–7, 161, 175, 178, 192, 194–5, 207, 212–13, 221, 228, 232
distribution of resources, 1, 88, 221
Ditch, John, Barnes, Hilary, Bradshaw, Jonathan, and Kilkey, Majella, 103–4, 109–11
diversity, 10, **21–40**, 41, 49, 51, 55, 62, 91, 100, 184, 205, 217, 232–8
  cultural, 210, 226, 242
  linguistic, 47, 53, 206
division of (household) labour, 119, 136
divorce, 101, 107–8
doctors, 46, 85–6
drugs, 75–6, 90, 208
Dublin Convention, 208
Duff, Andrew, 17, 209, 228
Dumon, Wilfried, 95, 105

earnings, 34–5, 92, 109, 131, 136, 149, 153–4, 156, 162, 165, 170, 181, 183, 185–7
economic activity, 84, 113, 134, 152, 158, 206, 242
  see also labour force
Economic and Monetary Union (EMU), 14, 18, 22, 28, 30, 32, 36, 84, 88, 97, 157, 161, 169, 191, 198, 212, 217, 219, 226, 230, 237
Economic and Social Committee, 13, 117, 169, 190
education, 5, 15–16, 25, 28, **41–65**, 70, 75–6, 90, 93, 98, 105, 107–10, 113, 116, 120, 126, 145, 148, 176, 178–9, 181, 191, 196, 202, 204, 206, 215, 221, 223, 229, 232, 235, 239
EEC Treaty [1.2], 2–4, 67–8
  part 1 principles, article 2, 2, 68, 93, 171
    article 3, 2, 167
    article 7, 192, 194
    article 36, 68
  part 2 title III on freedom of movement, articles 48–58, 3, 23, 42, 52, 92, 192–3, 203, 207
    article 91 on dumping, 9
    articles 100–1 on approximation, 3, 23, 116
  part 3, title III on social policy, articles 117–22 on social provisions, 2–3, 6, 11–12, 15–16, 21, 23, 26, 42, 67–70, 72–3, 91, 94, 113, 115–19, 125, 128, 141, 143, 236
    articles 123–8 on the European Social Fund, 3, 42, 47–9, 68, 167
    article 235, 93, 116, 170
    article 238, 194
eligibility, 103, 107–9, 157, 179, 187, 213, 227
employment, 3–11, 14–20, 28–29, 31, 34–9, **41–65**, 68, 70–80, 82, 84, 87, 89–90, 91, 94, 96, 98, 105–8, 113–23, 127–37, 143–6, 149, 152, 154–61, 165–70, 172, 175–8, 180–1, 185, 187, 189–90, 191–8, 201–8, 211, 213, 218, 221–9, 232, 235–42
employment contract(s), 66, 71, 73–4, 77, 79
employment guidelines [1.18], 17, 19–20, 49, 118, 145, 177, 228, 239
employment law, 25, 191
Employment Observatory, 176
enlargement, 14, 18, 30, 32, 39–

enlargement (cont.)
40, 44, 49, 77, 100, 167, 169, 175, 177–8, 194, 214, 217, 219, 233, 241–2
environment, 15–16, 28, 60, 66, 69, 75, 86, 107, 232
working, 4, 6, 69, 71, 74, 76, 81, 83, 87, 141, 200
equal opportunities, 13, 16–17, 31, 43, 54, 92, 94–6, 106, 114–8, 120–4, 126–8, 137–9, 218, 223, 228, 239
equal pay, 2–3, 15, 18, 113–18, 121, 124–7, 134–7, 239
equal remuneration, 116
equal treatment, 27, 44, 113, 116–17, 119, 121, 124–5, 127, 129–30, 135, 137–8, 143, 193, 195, 206, 221, 225–6, 234
see also directive(s)
equal value, 108, 116–18, 125–6, 134–5
equality between the sexes, 11, 15, 74, 93, 113, 115–8, 121, 123–5, 127, 135, 175
Erasmus, 52–3, 55
espace social, 5
Esping-Andersen, Gøsta, 30–1, 36, 155
ethnic groups, 34, 180
Eures, 195, 203, 216
European Agency for Health and Safety at Work, 72, 240
European Agricultural Guidance and Guarantee Fund (EAGGF), 7, 168
European Atomic Energy Community (EAEC) [1.3], 2, 4, 67
European base-line of living (EBL), 181
European Centre for the Development of Vocational Training (Cedefop), 51–2, 240
European Centre of Public Enterprises (CEEP), 6, 90, 121, 138
European Coal and Steel Community (ECSC) [1.1], 2, 4, 67
European Commission Childcare Network, 120, 131–2
European Council, 17, 178, 218, 233
European Court of Justice (ECJ), 81, 114, 119, 125, 128, 173, 200, 209, 233–4, 238–9
European Foundation for the Improvement of Living and Working Conditions, 69, 80, 147, 240
European Observatory on National Family Policies, 94–5, 105, 109–10, 112, 146
European Parliament, 7, 13, 16, 20, 76, 89–90, 93–7, 107, 110, 112, 114, 142–3, 163, 169, 175, 190, 194, 207, 211, 215, 224, 231, 233, 243
European Regional Development Fund (ERDF), 7, 168
European Social Charter (Council of Europe), 2, 4, 8, 15, 91, 194
European Social Fund (ESF), 3, 5–7, 15–16, 43, 48, 68, 113, 167–8, 171, 175–6, 190
European social model, 22, 29, 37–9, 64, 67, 219–20, 223–4, 238–41, 243
European Trade Union Confederation (ETUC), 6–7, 90, 121, 138–9
European Women's Lobby, 114

Eurostat, 32–4, 40, 52, 59, 65, 86, 98–102, 110–12, 148–52, 156, 159, 168, 182, 199, 205, 212, 240
Eurydice, 51–2, 65
extramarital births, 98, 101, 108

family allowances, 36, 107–9
family benefit(s), 35, 95–6, 107–9, 119, 148
family credit, 186
family obligations, 94, 116, 120, 228
family policies, **91–112**
family responsibilities, 93, 96, 120–2, 133, 154, 228, 231
family reunion, 193, 208, 212
family size, 99–100, 102, 105, 108, 158, 166
family structure(s), 92, 95, 97–103–5, 110–11, 113, 115, 166, 241
father(s), 1–3, 132
Federal Republic of Germany, 1, 21, 58, 106
  see also Germany
Ferge, Zsuzsa, 37
fertility rate(s), 98–100, 102
Finland
  ageing, 151–2
  education and training, 55, 57–60
  equality legislation, 127, 131–33
  EU membership, 36, 231
  family policy, 104, 106, 108–9
  family structure, 100–1
  health care, 84–5, 86–7
  income maintenance, 182, 186
  migration, 205, 213
  policy for older and disabled people, 154, 156–7
  social exclusion, 175, 188
  social spending, 32–4, 237
  welfare system, 22, 31
  working conditions, 79–80, 82
flexibility, 17, 46, 73, 75, 77, 96, 121, 128–9, 132, 134–5, 234–5
Flynn, Pádraig, 95, 133, 238–9
foreign workers, 207, 210, 214
Fortress Europe, 192, 209, 213, 227
framework directive [4.1], 12, 72–3, 76, 79, 88, 120
France
  ageing, 149, 151–4, 157
  caring, 158–60
  education and training, 57–61
  EEC membership, 1
  equality legislation, 113, 116, 125, 127–8, 131–3
  family policy, 103–4, 106–9, 111
  family structure, 100–2
  health care, 85–7
  income maintenance, 185, 188
  migration, 197, 199, 203–4, 213
  non-European immigration, 209–12
  policy for older and disabled people, 162
  social exclusion, 174, 177, 183
  social spending, 33–4
  welfare system, 2, 5, 21, 31, 35, 38
  working conditions, 77, 79, 81, 83
free movement, 7, 16, 50–1, 202, 209
  of labour, 3, 5, 66, 161, 192, 225
  of workers, 10, 16, 27, 92, 144, 193–4, 198, 212, 215, 232
freedom of movement, 22, 26, 41, 44, 62, 71, 91–2, 96, 142,

freedom of movement (cont.)
147, 165, 168, 191–6, 199–200, 203–4, 207, 209, 212, 214–16, 218, 221, 225–7, 235–6
frontier workers, 193, 201, 215

gender, 17, 34, 45, 59, 110, **113–39**, 143, 146, 206, 223, 241
Germany
ageing, 150–2
caring, 159–60
education and training, 58–61
EEC membership, 1
equality legislation, 116, 125, 127–8, 130–3
family policy, 103–4, 106, 108–9
family structure, 100, 102
health care, 85–6
income maintenance, 185
migration, 199–200, 203
non-European immigration, 209–12
policy for older and disabled people, 153–4, 157
social exclusion, 177, 182–3
social spending, 33–4, 237
welfare system, 21, 26, 31, 35
working conditions, 77, 79–83
Geyer, Robert, 231
Ginn, Jay, and Arber, Sara, 153–6
Gormley, Laurence W., 8, 194, 200
Greece
ageing, 151–2,
caring, 158–9
EC membership, 9
education and training, 58–61
equality legislation, 126–7, 129–33
family policy, 103–4, 106–9
family structure, 100–2
health care, 84–7
income maintenance, 187
living conditions, 78–9
migration, 192, 199, 201–2, 204
non-European immigration, 209
policy for older and disabled people, 156–7
social exclusion, 174, 177, 182, 188
social spending, 8, 33–4, 237
welfare system, 22, 31, 36
working conditions, 80–3
green paper(s)
on education [3.7], 48
on European social policy [1.14], 13–14, 20, 72, 196
on the obstacles to transnational mobility [9.15], 56, 202

Hantrais, Linda, 97–8, 102–3, 111, 114, 133–4, 136, 151
harmonization 1–3, 11, **21–40**, 45–6, 52, 63, 66–7, 69, 71, 75, 78, 80, 83, 85, 87–8, 98, 111, 116, 153, 218, 235–6
health, 2, 4–6, 11, 35–6, 38, 44, 46, 66–9, 71–9, 83–90, 96, 98, 105, 109–10, 120, 142, 146–50, 152, 158, 179–80, 184, 186, 200–1, 219, 221, 225, 232, 235, 237, 239, 243
see also public health
health and safety at work, 4–6, 11, 66–9, 71–9, 83–4, 87–9, 96, 110, 120, 219, 221, 223
health care, 35–6, 38, 83–7, 142, 150, 179–80, 186, 201, 237
see also medical care
health services, 16, 76, 150, 184, 226, 235

national health service(s), 35–6, 84–6, 186, 225
Helios, 145, 163–4
Hervey, Tamara, 8
higher education, 43–4, 46, 50, 53, 55, 57–9, 63–4, 235
Hoskyns, Catherine, 113, 115
hospital beds, 85–6
household(s), 96–100, 104, 107, 111, 150, 156, 172, 179, 182–4, 188–9, 229
  one/single-person, 100
housing, 98, 108–9, 142, 145, 150, 179–81, 183, 186, 188, 195, 206
human resources, 11, 43, 48, 64, 79, 175, 236

immigration, 16, 148, 165, 192, 200, 206–11, 215, 227, 232
  illegal, 212
  non-European, 209–12
  see also migration
income maintenance, 36, 153, 155, 166, 184–7
income security, 153–4, 185, 243
income support, 183, 186
individualization of rights, 129–30, 137, 161
industrial accidents, injuries and diseases, 66, 68, 78
industrial relations, 6, 11
inequality(ies), 32, 35, 56, 86, 117, 120, 135, 143, 156, 162, 175, 178, 183
insurance principle, 107, 185
  see also private insurance, social insurance
integration, 11, 24, 44, 55, 92, 123, 142–3, 144–6, 167, 172, 175–6, 186–7, 202, 204, 206, 209, 214, 216, 220, 223–30, 233, 237
  economic, 1, 3, 5, 9, 18, 26, 39, 51, 57, 140–1, 144, 168–9, 196, 214, 222–3, 242
  economic and social, 38, 64, 140–1, 143–6, 163, 171–2, 175, 189, 195, 204
  European, 1, 15, 44, 242
intergenerational solidarity, 93, 133, 146, 160–4, 183
internal market, 6–10, 18, 27, 44–5, 70, 122, 168, 171–2, 197–8, 201, 206, 217, 221–3, 227, 233
  see also Single European Market
International Labour Organization (ILO), 115
invalidity, 35, 119, 152–5, 184
  pensions, 153–5
Ireland
  ageing, 149, 151–2
  caring, 159–60
  EC membership, 1
  education and training, 58–62
  equality legislation, 126–7, 131–3, 135, 139
  family policy, 103–4, 106, 108–9
  family structure, 100–2
  health care, 84–6
  income maintenance, 187
  migration, 199, 204, 208
  non-European immigration, 209, 211, 213
  policy for older and disabled people, 155
  social exclusion, 170, 174, 177, 182–3, 188, 190
  social spending, 33–4
  welfare system, 21, 31, 36
  working conditions, 79–83
Italy
  ageing, 151–2

Italy (cont.)
caring, 159
education and training, 58–62
EEC membership, 1, 21,
equality legislation, 116, 127–8, 130–2
family policy, 104, 106–9
family structure, 100–2
health care, 35, 84–7
income maintenance, 185–6
migration, 192, 199–200, 204, 208
non-European immigration, 209–13
policy for older and disabled people, 153, 156–7, 162
social exclusion, 174, 177, 188
social spending, 33–4, 237
welfare system, 2, 31, 35
working conditions, 78–81

job aspirations, 93, 121
job creation, 17, 123, 177, 228
job vacancies, 195, 203, 239
job-seekers, 185, 202–3
Jones Finer, Catherine, 29–30

Kalanke v Freie Hansestadt Bremen (C–450/93) [6.18], 125, 139
Kleinman, Mark, and Piachaud, David, 18, 41, 223

labour costs, 9, 24–5, 77, 80, 113, 128, 130, 137, 142, 157, 197, 222
see also social costs
labour force, 38, 42, 63, 73, 97, 134, 140, 148, 150, 152, 158, 161, 165, 189, 206, 218, 228–9, 240
see also economic activity, workforce
Labour Force Survey (LFS), 62, 65, 198–9
labour law, 3, 41, 68, 77, 79–80
labour market(s), 10–11, 13, 17, 36, 45, 48, 58, 60, 62, 73–4, 87, 95–6, 115, 118, 120–1, 129, 133–4, 143, 146, 152, 154, 157, 161, 163, 168, 172, 174–5, 178, 186, 192, 197–8, 200, 202–3, 224–6, 228, 235, 237, 239, 242–3
labour market policy(ies), 38, 42, 48, 167, 176, 189
labour permits, 199
labour shortage, 42, 192, 196, 207
language(s), 43, 47, 49, 50–1, 53, 56, 194, 204–5, 211, 215, 222
leave, 71, 74, 119, 137, 235
maternity, 120, 127, 130–1
paid, 26, 70, 82, 130–2
parental, 118–22, 127–8, 131–3, 137–9
see also paid holiday
Leibfried, Stephan, and Pierson, Paul, 9, 220, 233
Leonardo, 54–5
level playing field, 9, 234
Lewis, Jane, 159
life expectancy, 99, 141, 148, 150–1, 165
Lindley, Robert, 61, 197
Lingua, 53–5, 204–5
living and working conditions, 2, 4, 11, 21, 24, **66–90**, 98, 156, 161, 179, 193, 196, 203, 215, 221, 225–6, 228, 234–7, 239, 243
living standards, 93, 110, 146, 162, 170, 172, 183
Lødemel, Ivar, 183, 187
lone parent(s), 93, 96, 98, 101–2,

105, 108–9, 131, 166–7, 182
Luxembourg
ageing, 151–2
caring, 159–60
education and training, 57–8, 61
EEC membership, 1
equality legislation, 126–7, 130–2
family policy, 103, 106–9
health care, 85–6
income maintenance, 185
migration, 199, 204–5
non-European immigration, 209, 211, 213
policy for older and disabled people, 157
social exclusion, 182, 188
social spending, 33–4
welfare system, 21, 35
working conditions, 78–81
Luxembourg summit, 10, 17

Maastricht
see Treaty on European Union
Majone, Giandomenico, 231–2, 238
marginalization, 56, 179–81
marital status, 92, 103
Marks, Gary, Hooghe, Liesbet, and Blank, Kermit, 220, 232, 234
marriage, 98–103, 111
Marschall v Land Nordrhein-Westfalen (C–409/95) [6.18], 125, 139
maternity, 35, 120, 201
see also maternity leave
means-testing, 36–7, 135, 160, 183, 185–7
medical care, 16, 75–6, 86, 160, 226, 235
see also health care
Merger Treaty [1.4], 218
Meulders-Klein, Marie-Thérèse, 103, 107
migrant(s), 3, 18, 23–4, 43, 53, 68, 87, 92–3, 110–11, 141, 167, 171, 174, 181, 193, 195–9, 204–15, 227, 231
see also immigration
Millar, Jane, and Warman, Andrea, 159
minimum income, 35, 166, 181, 186–8, 213
Misep, 176, 190
Mishra, Ramesh, 29, 39, 220–1
Mitchell, Mark, and Russell, David, 210, 213
mobility, 3, 9, 42–7, 49–53, 55–7, 66, 70, 92, 134, 141–6, 163, 167, **191–216**, 222, 225, 229
barriers to, 21, 200–6, 212
intra-European, 56, 111, 191, 196, 198–206, 211–12
of labour, 9, 191, 229
of students, 47, 50–2, 55
of workers, 3, 63, 92, 141, 143–4, 163, 222
model(s) of welfare, 21, 29–32
Bismarckian, 34–5, 38, 84, 92, 184
continental, 21–2, 31, 34–6, 84, 153, 156, 165, 184–6
institutional redistributive, 30–1
residual, 30, 37, 155–6
rudimentary, 156, 187
see also welfare regimes
Moravcsik, Andrew, and Nicolaïdas, Kalypso, 230
mortality rates, 87, 148, 151
Mossialos, Elias, 86–7
mother(s), 4, 91, 103, 108, 115, 128–34, 226, 235
lone, 109, 131

mother(s) (cont.)
  working, 68, 94, 128–9, 133
mutual recognition of qualifications, 41–2, 45–8, 57, 63, 200, 202, 213, 235

nationality, 43, 185–7, 192, 194–5, 198, 204, 207, 210–11, 213, 227
naturalization, 210–11, 213
Netherlands
  ageing, 151–2
  caring, 158
  education and training, 57–61
  EEC membership, 1
  equality legislation, 126–7, 130–2, 134
  family policy, 103–4, 108–9
  family structure, 100, 102
  health care, 85–7
  income maintenance, 185, 188
  migration, 199–200, 204–5
  non-European immigration, 209, 211–13
  policy for older and disabled people, 153, 155, 157
  social spending, 33–4, 237
  welfare system, 21, 31, 35
  working conditions, 79–83
New Opportunities for Women (Now), 54, 123
new technologies, 49, 51, 53–6
night work, 71, 73, 81–2
Nordic states, 21, 34, 82, 101–3, 127, 157, 159–60, 183, 186–7, 209, 225
Nugent, Nigel, 230, 238

Objective 1 regions, 174, 177
older people, 25, 35, 38, 86, 91, 119, **140–64**, 165–7, 171–2, 181, 201, 228–9, 231, 234–5
opinion(s), 6, 13, 17, 23

paid holidays, 73, 82
  see also leave
parent(s), 95–96, 99, 103, 106, 109, 114, 119, 129–33, 159, 182, 185–6, 211
participation of workers, 66, 70–1, 225
part-time work, 70, 73–5, 79, 82–3, 88, 90, 118–20, 134–5, 137, 154–6, 207, 227–9
paternity, 103
pension(s), 35–6, 38, 129–30, 140–4, 147–58, 161–2, 164, 165, 172, 183–4, 195, 200–1, 215, 227–9, 235, 237, 243
pensionable age, 119, 144
pensioner(s), 84, 149, 151, 154, 162, 197, 201
Pieters, Danny, 25, 30, 231
Poland, 37, 100, 104, 131
polarization, 38, 166, 181
policy-making process, 1, 6, 21, 92, 111
political union, 18, 44
population ageing, 14, 18, 84, 88, 147–53, 157, 160–1, 163, 207, 241
Portugal
  ageing, 151–2
  caring, 158–9
  EC membership, 9
  education and training, 55, 58–9
  equality legislation, 126, 130–2
  family policy, 104, 106–9
  family structure, 100
  health care, 84–7
  income maintenance, 187
  migration, 192, 199–200, 204
  non-European immigration, 209–10, 212–13
  policy for older and disabled people, 156–7
  social exclusion, 170, 174,

177, 182, 188
social spending, 8, 33–4, 237
welfare system, 22, 31–2, 36
working conditions, 78–82
positive action, 53, 117, 122, 124–5, 136
positive discrimination, 139
poverty, 5, 155, 165–73, 178–84, 186–90, 218, 224, 229, 231, 233, 236, 239, 242
see also social exclusion
poverty line, 179, 181–2, 188
poverty trap, 186
private health care, 38
private insurance, 84
private sector, 105, 126, 135, 157–8, 173, 206
proportionality, 1, 12, 18, 219–20, 230, 241
public health, 16, 28, 66–7, 70, 74–7, 83–4, 88–90, 223, 226, 232
public sector, 35, 38, 85, 127, 131, 135, 203–4
public service(s), 136, 192, 206

qualifications, 3, 34, 41–3, 45–8, 50–3, 57–9, 61–3, 66, 176, 189, 191, 193, 196–7, 200, 202, 229
see also mutual recognition
qualified majority voting, 6–7, 11, 69, 72, 74, 76, 88, 120, 193–4, 208, 219, 232, 234, 242
quality of life, 4, 14–15, 39, 110, 144, 228, 241, 243
race, 207, 212, 221
racism [9.10], 207, 209, 215, 223
recommendation(s)
on convergence [2.1], 27–8, 95, 97, 144, 236
on dignity at work [6.12], 120
on retirement age [7.3], 143
on sufficient resources [8.6], 172, 184, 188
reconciliation of paid work and family life, 94, 115, 120–1, 132, 134, 161, 175
recruitment, 133, 202
redistribution, 35, 106, 221
redundancies, 11, 66
Rees, Teresa, 54
refugees, 171, 181, 208, 212, 214, 216
regions, 25–6, 167–8, 170–1, 174, 176–8, 192–3, 198, 200, 215, 222, 232
regulation(s)
3–4 [9.1], 1408/71 [9.4], 574/72 [9.5] on social security for migrants, 195
1612/68 [9.2] on freedom of movement, 92, 96, 111, 195
311/76 [9.6] on statistics on migrants, 207
2052/88 [8.2], 2081/93 [8.7], 1260/1999 [8.14] on the structural funds, 168, 174–5
118/97 [9.16] on special schemes for civil servants, 195, 204, 215
1262/1999 [8.15] on the European social fund, 175
religion, 15, 142, 207
research (R&D), 51, 56
resettlement allowance, 3, 167
residence, 26, 45, 71, 84, 154, 157, 185, 187, 193, 195, 201, 208, 211, 213–14, 216
retirement, 35, 119, 129–30, 142–4, 147–9, 151–4, 157, 161–4, 165, 175, 184, 225, 229, 237
Rex, John, 208, 210
Rhodes, Martin, 22, 230

right(s)
of children, 4–5, 92
of citizens, 4, 14
of establishment, 3, 42
social security, 92, 120, 129, 195, 215, 234
of workers, 4–5, 7, 66, 94, 193, 224–5
Room, Graham, 5, 180, 183
Rowntree, B. Seebohm, 181
Rubery, Jill, 134–5, 149, 207

safety net, 35, 37, 155, 167, 224
Saltman, Richard, B., Figueras, Josep, and Sakallerides, Constantino, 85
Schengen Agreement, 208–9
school-leaving age, 43, 58
Sedoc, 195, 203
segregation, 38, 135
self-employed workers, 42, 72, 79, 119, 138, 143–4, 165, 174, 203, 214–15
service sector, 79
sexual harassment, 120, 127
Shanks, Michael, 1, 170, 217, 238
sickness, 35, 84, 201, 227
Single European Act (SEA) [1.5], 6–7
article 3b, 12, 236
article 100a, 7, 69
article 118a, 69
article 130a–d, 7, 168–9
Single European Market (SEM), 7, 9–10, 20, 25, 71, 76, 166, 191, 221–2, 226
see also internal market
single-parent families, 171, 181
single-parent households, 166
see also lone parents
skilled workers, 198, 204
skill shortages, 44, 61, 197
smoking, 70, 150
social action programme [1.9, 1.16, 1.19], 1, 4–5, 14–15, 19, 42, 68–9, 93–4, 96, 113, 121, 144, 170, 217–18, 222–3, 237, 240
social assistance, 35–6, 84, 142, 159, 165–6, 168, 172, 181–90, 201
social chapter
see Agreement on Social Policy
social citizenship, 36, 226, 235
social costs, 2, 8–9, 35, 97, 148, 223
see also labour costs
social dialogue, 1, 5–7, 10, 13–-14, 26–7, 69–70, 236, 239
social dumping, 1, 8–9, 24, 142, 222
social exclusion, 144, 147, **165–90**, 222, 238–9
see also poverty
social inclusion, **165–90**, 243
social insurance, 11, 21, 31, 34, 35–8, 84, 92, 107, 129, 136–7, 142, 153–8, 160, 181, 184, 201, 228, 231–2, 237
social partners, 6, 13, 17, 48, 60, 64, 70, 75, 123, 175, 239
social plinth, 1, 7–8
social protection systems
see models of welfare, welfare regimes
social security, 8, 10–11, 23–5, 27, 34, 36, 38, 41, 66, 68, 74, 83, 92, 107, 113, 119, 127, 129–30, 137–8, 143–5, 153–4, 156, 165, 171, 179, 181, 185, 187, 193, 196, 200–3, 214–15, 232, 234
entitlements, 3, 103, 135, 143, 196, 231

social services, 8, 107, 140, 183
social space, 1, 5–7, 24, 43, 217, 224
social spending, 9, 223
social state, 231
social union, 19, 243
Socrates, 53, 55, 124
solidarity, 18, 31, 39, 50, 77, 85, 106, 172–3, 177–8, 184, 190, 219, 222, 241
  see also intergenerational solidarity
southern European countries, 22, 31, 78, 101, 107, 159, 182–3, 187, 192, 199, 212, 218
sovereignty, 9, 13, 24, 39, 57, 208, 219–20, 230, 233–8
Spain
  ageing, 151
  caring, 158–9
  EC membership, 9
  education and training, 58–9, 61
  equality legislation, 130–3
  family policy, 106–9
  family structure, 100–1
  health care, 36, 84–7
  income maintenance, 184, 187
  migration, 192, 199–200
  non-European immigration, 209–11
  policy for older and disabled people, 156–7
  social exclusion, 170–1, 174, 182–3, 188
  social spending, 33–4, 237
  welfare system, 22, 31, 36
  working conditions, 78–80, 82
Spec, 176
Spicker, Paul, 12
step-children, 99
structural funds, 7, 26, 38, 55, 123, 145, 167–70, 174–8, 188–90, 232–3
subsidiarity [1.10], 1, 4, 10, 12–13, 18, 20, 23, 27–8, 31, 41, 52, 55, 62–3, 71, 84, 109, 122, 136, 161, 184, 219–20, 230, 234, 241
subsistence, 36, 144, 168–9, 238
survivor's benefit(s), 35, 119, 129–30, 152, 196
Sweden
  ageing, 149, 151–2
  education and training, 57–60
  equality legislation, 127–8, 130–5, 137
  EU membership, 32, 231
  family policy, 104, 108–9
  family structure, 100–1
  health care, 84–7
  income maintenance, 186
  migration, 205
  non-European immigration, 212–13
  policy for older and disabled people, 153–4, 157
  social exclusion, 175, 182, 188
  social spending, 33–4, 237
  welfare system, 22, 31, 36, 38
  working conditions, 79–82
Sysdem, 176, 190

take-up, 132, 183, 205
targeting, 30, 53, 95, 105–6, 124, 171, 176
tax (taxation), 17, 22, 24, 34–6, 38, 84, 96, 103–4, 108–9, 129, 136–7, 154, 160, 179, 187, 191, 228, 243
tax relief, 103, 109
teachers, 47, 55, 204
Teague, Paul, 6–7, 70, 87, 230
technological change, 16, 54, 62, 79, 176
temporary work, 70, 80, 82
Tempus, 53

third-country nationals, 11, 74, 209, 227–8, 232
Titmuss, Richard, 30, 41, 153, 155, 220
Townsend, Peter, 179, 181
training, 3, 5, 13, 16–17, 25, 38, **41–65**, 69–72, 76, 80, 90, 108, 113, 123–4, 133–4, 145, 174, 176, 178, 191, 196, 202, 205, 215, 218, 221, 223, 225, 228, 235, 239
transferability of rights, 191, 195–6, 201–2, 213
Treaty of Amsterdam [1.7], 15, 18–21, 74–5, 117, 121, 124, 140, 142, 176–7, 189, 191, 194, 208–9, 212, 219, 228, 230–1, 233, 239–40
  see also Consolidated EC Treaty
Treaty of Paris [1.1], 2
Treaty of Rome [1.2], 11
  see also EEC Treaty
Treaty on European Union [1.6]
  article 2, 14–15, 27
  article 3b, 12, 236
  article 8, 193–4
  article B, 222, 226
  article F, 226
  article K.1, 208, 227
  title II, 27, 193
  title VIII, 47

unemployment, 15, 18–19, 32, 35, 42–3, 48, 79, 81, 83, 96, 118, 129, 137, 147, 152, 165–6, 171, 174, 176, 184–8, 192, 195–6, 200–2, 207, 217, 219, 223, 231, 236, 239–40, 242
United Kingdom
  ageing, 151–2
  caring, 159–60
  EC membership, 1
  education and training, 55, 57–61
  equality legislation, 121, 126–8, 130–1, 133–5, 139
  family policy, 104, 106, 108–9
  family structure, 100–2
  health care, 84–7, 225
  income maintenance, 186–7
  living conditions, 79
  migration, 199–200, 204–5, 208
  non-European immigration, 209–13
  opt-out, 8–9, 11, 19–20, 74, 121, 219, 241
  policy for older and disabled people, 155–6
  social exclusion, 170–1, 173–4, 177, 181–3, 188, 190
  social spending, 33–4, 237
  welfare system, 21, 31, 36, 38, 225, 241
  working conditions, 77, 79–83
unskilled workers, 192, 197, 211

Val Duchesse, 6–7, 239
visas, 16, 195, 208–9, 227, 232
vocational (re)training, 3, 15–16, 28, 42–5, 47–8, 50–2, 54–5, 58–63, 68, 76, 116, 119, 121, 123, 127, 137, 142, 148, 167, 172, 202, 225, 232, 239
Vogel, Joachim, 100, 150, 156, 182–3
voluntary sector, 146, 160, 172

wage discrimination, 127
wages, 34, 162, 169, 179, 195, 225
Walker, Alan, 146–7, 157, 162
welfare pluralism, 38–9, 136, 221

welfare regime(s), 30, 37–8, 106, 154–5, 165, 184
corporatist, 21, 31–2, 34, 37, 63, 92, 153, 184
liberal, 30, 37, 155, 209–11, 214
social democratic, 31, 36, 154–5
see also models of welfare
welfare state(s), 24, 29–31, 37, 39, 98, 110, 140, 184, 186–7, 220
welfare tourism, 25, 142
white paper(s)
on European social policy [1.15], 13–14, 39, 48, 95, 120, 123, 128–9, 146, 176, 223, 229, 238, 240–1
on growth, competitiveness and employment [3.8], 42, 48
women's rights, 113–14, 118–24, 128–34
workforce, 2, 14, 44, 49, 54, 79, 82, 147, 165, 197
see also labour force
working age, 43, 88, 149, 151–2, 161, 166, 175, 227
working hours, 44, 66, 71–3, 80–2, 88
working population, 38, 96, 167, 207, 225
working time, 70, 72–3, 77, 79, 81–3, 89, 120, 122, 128, 234
work-time organization, 75, 79, 83

young people, 42–5, 47, 50–5, 57, 60–1, 63, 68, 71–2, 106, 145, 148, 176, 187, 189, 197, 202, 229, 235
young workers, 42, 52, 68, 193, 225
youth, 15–16, 28, 47, 54, 171, 202, 232
Youth for Europe, 53, 55